The Female Ego

THE
Female
Ego

Susan Price

RAWSON ASSOCIATES : NEW YORK

Library of Congress Cataloging in Publication Data

Price, Susan———.
  The female ego.

  Bibliography: p.
  Includes index.
  1. Women—Psychology. 2. Ego (Psychology)
I. Title.
HQ1206.P74   1984   155.6'33   83-43113
ISBN 0-89256-264-1

Published simultaneously in Canada by McClelland and Stewart Ltd.
Composition by
Westchester Book Composition, Inc.,
Yorktown Heights, New York
Printed and bound by Fairfield Graphics,
Fairfield, Pennsylvania
Designed by Jacques Chazaud
First Edition

For Stephen M. Price,
my husband, colleague, and best friend

The greatest thing in the world is to know
how to belong to oneself.

MONTAIGNE

❧ Contents ❧

✎ Acknowledgments ✎

I wish to express loving thanks to my family, Stephen, Angela, and Michael, for supporting the growth of my ego. I appreciate the women who have influenced me, Lois Johnson, my mother, Violet Fitch, my aunt, Mabel Vaughn, Rena Johnson, and Lucile Vaughn, my grandmothers, and Madame Marinka Gurewich and Elva Kelsall, my music teachers.

The most important people influencing this work were my clients, whose therapeutic gains are described on these pages as a grapevine of shared solutions to women's ego problems. I appreciate the mothers of the Head Start students at Educational Alliance in New York City, who taught me about the female ego in motherhood.

I am grateful to my teachers and colleagues, especially Mary Boulton, Ph.D., Dorthea Dawson, A.B., Richard Erskine, Ph.D., Linda Fitch, M.A., Patricia Hill, M.S., Virginia Price, Ph.D., Rebecca Trautmann, M.S.W., and the wonderful therapists at the Counseling and Human Development Center in New York City.

Many thanks go to Patricia Berens, my agent, for believing in this book, to Toni Sciarra for valuable editorial suggestions, and to Eleanor Rawson, my editor, for her great expertise and her enthusiasm.

Love to Dr. Frank Vaughn, my grandfather, whose commitment to human healing continues to inspire me.

✍ Before You Begin ✍ This Book

When my editor told a successful businesswoman about *The Female Ego*, her response was, "I didn't know we were supposed to have one." She responded spontaneously to the issue addressed in this book—women's increasing awareness that they need to develop strong egos. Some of the ideas in this book apply to both men and women because ego strength is a human capacity, and indeed men are sometimes good role models for the growth of the female ego. But powerful cultural conditioning has caused the female ego to develop particular strengths and weaknesses, which render women's ego needs fundamentally different from those of men.

Many authorities on human growth and development focus on the mothering figure as the primary ingredient in the healthy growth of the child. She lends her ego to her child, nurturing healthy dependence and, later, applauding independence. Whether or not a woman decides to be a mother, she usually has been given cultural conditioning to be a supporter of other people. But what about support of herself and her own ego? Too often a woman takes better care of others than she does of herself. Supporting others gives a woman very special skills, and yet it also can diminish her ability to make her *own* life work and cause her to underrate her own valuable contributions.

The Female Ego is for women who know how to be the ego

builders of others but in the process neglect their own egos. It is for the woman who wants to construct a solid base of strength and self-confidence on which to build a life that expresses her fullest potential.

1

Women
Need Ego Strength

It is a very hard undertaking to seek to
please everybody.

Publilius Syrus
First century B.C.

This is the age of the female ego, and it is a very positive and
hopeful time. The world needs the feminine, and females
need the world—both for their own fulfillment. The age of the
female ego can make great contributions to humankind—for peace,
for ecology, for nurturance, for wholeness. The seeds have been
sown by the pioneer feminists, and they are now starting to shoot
forth and flower. There has been a tragic imbalance, which we
now have the possibility of correcting—a correction that will result
in equal power, cooperation, and the actualization of great human
potential. The qualities a woman has are good. She needs only
the power of the female ego to manifest them. This book offers
advice and guidance for the growth and maturation of the female
ego.

During the last ten years of working as a therapist, I have witnessed some amazing transformations in women. Women have
taken to heart the permission to grow, and they have the determination and courage to want to become their best selves. They
come to therapy because they do not find it acceptable to be depressed, and they are not satisfied with merely coping either. *Women*

want to claim joy as a way of life: they want to find themselves and express themselves with authenticity.

I am seeing women become much more active—searching out answers and finding creative solutions for their problems. Being a therapist is exciting, even exhilarating, because I see firsthand the energy with which my women clients are working on their lives. I see no self-involved navel-gazing but an outgoing search for meaning and a commitment to making a worthwhile contribution to life.

The true frontier for today's woman is in the psychological realm. She is fighting a battle within herself to achieve self-esteem and is questioning forces in the environment that do not support her quest for a complete and healthy ego. The real transformation in a woman occurs when she is completely on her own side, discovers her true needs, and uses her ego to get her needs met. This woman, who has developed herself, is ready to tackle some of the major problems in our world.

Beneath the Surface

"I don't understand why I feel so depressed," Stephanie confided, "because I don't have any good reason to be unhappy." It was her first therapy session, and from a superficial look at her life it appeared that she had every reason to be happy. Unlike many people who come to therapy because of a specific crisis in their lives, Stephanie came to see me because a friend had urged her to seek help. "We were sitting at lunch, and my friend looked at me closely. She told me that she could see that I was depressed. At that moment I started to cry, and I have been on the verge of tears for days," she said.

The facts of Stephanie's life indicated that she had achieved the "dream" of fulfilled womanhood. She was married to an attractive and successful businessman. Her two children were healthy and bright. She was working part-time in a media field. She had the household help and the vacations that most women dream of. Her perfectionism was obvious in her impeccable dress and cultivated good looks. But Stephanie was losing ground emotionally: internally she was not well pulled together. She felt profound relief when her friend saw the truth and, in effect, gave her permission to ask for help. Behind a polished exterior was a woman who was feeling depressed and insecure.

How can a woman have what Stephanie had and yet not possess a strong ego? "Everyone tells me I am so lucky, and my friends usually turn to me to help them with their problems," she said, "and yet I feel very weak inside." Like many women, Stephanie could be very helpful to other people, but she did not take care of her own needs. She was so out of touch with herself that she did not even know what her needs were or that she was not meeting them.

In time, the reasons for Stephanie's emotional problems became clear. Stephanie's lack of ego strength was largely the result of lack of support, both internally and externally. Her husband was away much of the time, and Stephanie had little opportunity to receive the loving encouragement that she needed from him. In her job environment she had to fight hard for recognition. Caring for her children drained her energies, and most of her friends saw her as the woman who had everything.

Internally, Stephanie had limited resources as well. Her parents had never understood why she had come to the East Coast, and they grudgingly admitted that she was due some credit only when she gave them grandchildren. A spirited woman, Stephanie had made a life for herself in spite of little caring from her family. But the lack of a foundation of loving encouragement was catching up with her. It seemed that no one cared about Stephanie's ego. No one devoted any energy to bolstering her self-esteem. She proudly played the role of a successful woman, but the fundamental lack of support was undermining her confidence.

Stephanie worked dutifully to please everyone around her. She was a companion and hostess for her husband, a devoted daughter in spite of her parents' lack of support, a dedicated worker, and a conscientious mother. Her intimates thought that she was wonderful. But all that did not give her what she needed. She was on a one-way street in which she gave, but rarely did anyone give directly to her.

Stephanie had become guilty about her unmet needs, and for weeks she would apologize whenever she cried in therapy. Her lack of self-esteem was apparent in her disparagement of her needy state of mind.

Many Women Are Struggling

As I listen to my clients I find myself searching for the main stumbling blocks women face. It is true that the ideal of what a woman should be has expanded, and this new goal can be an exacting taskmaster. Pioneers have opened the way for us to enter most professions and have extended the parameters of our strivings. As a result, many women are attempting to do too much in too little time and are longing for a break. From listening to my women clients I know that the workplace is not particularly satisfying for a great many young women. They find themselves with the careers they have trained for, yet they yearn for a mate or a baby or a long afternoon in which to bake bread.

Sometimes I feel like a therapist who has been assigned to a regiment in the military. My office is an aid station where my clients come for a dose of healing in the middle of a day in battle. Women, especially, come with badly bruised egos from the front lines: the business world. Operating in a macho world, fighting for respect, and lacking in collegial support, they press ahead in spite of their collection of battle scars. On the home front the challenges to the female ego are no less risky as women work to express the generous, nurturant parts of their personalities without being masochistic. They are struggling with courage and determination to make their busy, difficult lives work.

The female ego's struggle for self-confidence in these two theaters is further complicated because each theater requires different, even oppositional, sets of skills. It is very stressful to be aggressive and assertive at work and then have to become gentle, empathetic, and full of love at home. Many women expect themselves to deliver perfect performances in both arenas.

This struggle to succeed in two worlds does not satisfy me as a solid answer, however, to explain a certain rigid character structure that I continue to observe in women, including myself. Somewhere in a woman's programming is a single operative principle, which at once holds back her ego from growing but keeps her pouring her energies into other people, into routines that bore her, into relationships that are not working, and into dead-end jobs. In contrast to the male ego, the female ego often is undeveloped in the area of being self-serving and ambitious. But most of the women I know are not lazy. The women I see in therapy often are living very busy lives, even though they feel out of touch with their inner wants, needs, and talents. The question to ask is, What part of a woman's programming gets her stuck and yet keeps her so busy playing roles that make her miserable?

People-Pleasing

My work and personal experience have led me to believe that the main thought pattern that gets a women's ego in trouble is the desire to please other people. Because a woman's entire identity can be rooted in her ability to be pleasing, she can be emotionally victimized by those who withhold their approval. This is rarely the case for men, who have internal permission to be self-directed and even to be antisocial when they are focused on their work. A simple example is the male doctor or businessman who can walk past colleagues and not even speak to them if he is deep in thought. This behavior is acceptable *in a man*. In contrast, a woman is expected to have a pleasing smile on her face and to be responsive at all times.

Technically, your ego is your internal psychological system that meets your needs and solves your problems. When we say that a woman has a good ego, we mean that the inner system for meeting her needs is doing a good job. She is able to know what her needs

are and to find satisfying ways to meet her needs in the environment. Because a woman is often more concerned with pleasing
others than with pleasing herself, she can find herself in a trap in
which she hardly uses her ego to meet her needs.

Superficial manifestations of the mandate to please others can
be seen in a woman's obsession with her looks. The superwoman
not only must have a beautiful home and a fat paycheck, but she
must look as if she just stepped out of a beauty spa. Neurotic people-
pleasing also has psychological manifestations, and the main one
is profound fear of loss of love. Love or approval from others is
more important than self-esteem to a people-pleaser. Approval from
others *is* her self-esteem. *Being a people-pleaser means that a woman
lacks an ego that functions on behalf of the self.* She surrenders her
potential for happiness to others and is motivated not by her needs
but by her fear of losing love. When and if she becomes more self-
serving, her fears will seem to be justified. Those who enjoy having
her be a doormat will be quick to accuse her of selfishness.

When a woman faces her adaptations to others, she is on the
path to claiming her own ego. By understanding the dynamics of
people-pleasing, overcoming her fear of selfishness, and understanding how she really would like to be spending her time, a
woman learns the true meaning of self-esteem. In shedding such
adaptations she will discover hidden talents and untapped energies.

In my work with women I have observed the following people-
pleasing conditions which lead to ego impairment:
- lack of family support for a woman's *independent* growth
- getting her primary positive strokes for *pleasing others*, instead
  of for mastering skills
- accepting negative criticism for not pleasing others
- abandoning herself to support others, instead of being firmly on
  her own side when there is a conflict

A woman must deal with the traditional expectation that she be
a nurturer and supporter of others. This role can cause a woman
to have a diminished sense of self, compared to the male ego,
because the results of these strivings are not quantifiable. She can

feel deep pleasure in her happy family and attractive home, but those gains are not rewarded in ways that deeply satisfy the ego, such as recognition, money, and concrete work products. A woman's work often is noticed only when it is not done. Functioning in this way, a woman may have hardly any ego. In addition to providing human connectedness and nurturing of others, the female in our culture often finds herself providing support services in her job. There is nothing wrong with these traditional female characteristics, which, at their best, embody a sensitivity to other people and a commitment to being supportive of others. Without ego strength, however, this orientation can cause a woman to feel insecure and unimportant because she is too easily taken advantage of or taken for granted.

Women Need Encouragement

The need for an ego boost is not neurotic: *it is a legitimate human need to have someone in your corner rooting for you.* We learn to be on our own sides when we learn to give ourselves the support we once craved from others. Many a woman uses this knowledge when she bolsters the ego of the man in her life. She knows the power of an internalized voice of praise, support, and love, and she helps her man think well of himself when he falters. *Women must now seek this bolstering for themselves.*

Developing Your Ego

Don't be timid about developing your ego because of a fear of being overbearing. Most women have a long way to go before egotism is a problem. In fact, the essence of ego strength is that you have *more to give* to life. A healthy ego is outgoing, not self-absorbed.

In our culture we accept the existence of the male ego: proud, self-assertive, and self-seeking. A man learns to look out for himself in order to get what he wants and needs. A man with a healthy ego creates for himself a life in which he has both an arena for independence and ambition and an oasis of support at home. Men with strong egos understand that a sense of self-worth is derived from the mastery of skills, and they understand the importance of politics in getting where they want to go professionally. A healthy man also knows that he deserves an understanding companion who encourages his ego.

When a woman learns to combine ego strength with the traditional female qualities of nurturance and concern for others, she discovers the unique power of the female ego. If you lack ego strength, being sensitive to others can make you vulnerable, but when such sensitivity is combined with ego strength you can open any doors, whether to success in business or politics, volunteer work, mothering, or creating a home. As the female ego grows, it fulfills its function of meeting a woman's needs as a *first priority*. This is a radical shift in the way many women have been functioning.

Why Settle for Less?

By not using your ego, you are settling for a life that is unnecessarily difficult and even painful. You will suffer with problems instead of solving them. Without an ego you have a tendency to wallow unnecessarily in negative feelings. But when you use your ego, you will seek support and ways to maintain good feelings. Without an ego you have no boundaries, and you express a personality that is vague and wishy-washy. You will live under the control of the parents and the culture that programmed you, *and you will give too much power to the people with whom you live and work*. The anger and resentment you feel at being so controlled will escape inappropriately—at yourself, your boss, your loved ones. Using your ego, you are protected by your own boundaries; you will command respect and express clear opinions.

Without an ego you tend to feel either like a victim of misfortune or a recipient of occasional luck. If you have a healthy ego, you are in charge of your life and make good things happen for yourself.

The choice is between impotence and mastery. Is it time for you to work on your own ego?

To assess your needs for ego growth, consider the following questions:

- Do you feel that your time and energy belong to you?
- Do you have pride in work that you do well?
- Do you feel that your love relationships are growing in the right direction?
- Are you free to function independently and willfully?
- Do you believe that you are entitled to get your needs met?
- Are you confident in expressing your opinions, both negative and positive?
- Is it OK for you to limit relationships or projects that are not working?
- Are you glad to be who you are, with the looks, intellect, and personality that you possess?
- Do you see yourself as a contributor in life?
- Do you thrive on new challenges?
- Are you objective about criticism of yourself and able to reject what is inaccurate and use what is accurate for growth?
- Are you free of hurt feelings and resentments and flowing with positive energy?
- Do you feel that you have good insights into what is happening inside and outside of other people?
- When you have an argument or difference of opinion with someone, can you stay on your own side?
- Do you believe that your future is going to be happy and exciting?

Every yes answer is an indication of ego strength. Of course, no one has a perfectly healthy ego, but a woman with a good ego will be able to answer yes to a majority of these questions. The no answers indicate areas in which ego building is needed.

Achieving a healthy ego will make you feel vitally connected to the real world through work, interests, and relationships. You will no longer feel overly sensitive. Instead of personalizing everything, you will experience detachment. You will find yourself welcoming constructive criticism and easily rejecting boorish put-downs. You will claim greater freedom and will make your own decisions. You will learn the art of taking good care of yourself. The female with a healthy ego lives her life well. Why settle for less?

What to Expect from This Book

The Female Ego is your guide to ego growth. Your ego is able to grow when it is free from inhibitions, fears, and unproductive defenses. By gaining insight into the way your female ego was influenced in childhood, and an awareness of stumbling blocks and inhibitions of the female ego in general, you will find direction for the growth of your own ego. I will share with you the results of my work in conducting therapy with women whose egos have grown through such a process. These insights into how the female ego grows are also a result of the work I have done on my own ego, and I will share these discoveries with you. For you to be able to profit from these guidelines, you must commit yourself to the following principles of female ego building:

- You need to *open your mind* to the adaptations you have made to others that led you to become less than your best self. I will show you how many women have compromised themselves and therefore do not use their own ego strength. You must be honest about your own compromises.
- You must be willing to understand the dynamics between people for what they really are without sentimental blindness or wishful thinking. You cannot grapple with the issues of your life unless you are committed to the reality principle: seeing people and situations for what they really are.
- You have to become a strategist. *Instead of being a victim of life, a woman with an ego looks for solutions.* Much of good therapy involves devising strategies that work for change. You must become a master strategist, scheming and planning ways to solve each of life's problems.
- You have to be honest about your particular needs. These include your dependency needs as well as your needs for independence, nurturance, appreciation, love, and sex.

- You must become comfortable about directly seeking ways to get your needs met once you have acknowledged them. Staying needy keeps your ego weak.
- You must risk feeling strong. For many women feelings of confidence, power, and potency are unknown. To build your ego you must be willing to relinquish any familiar feelings of weakness, passivity, or insecurity. You must choose instead the solid experience of mental health and power.

The following are some of the main issues we will explore together in *The Female Ego*:

- How can the female ego become stronger in a crisis situation?
- What aspects of childhood programming keep an adult woman from having a strong ego?
- Why does motherhood often lead to female masochism, and how can a woman change this pattern?
- Can the female ego be effective in a male-oriented business world?
- How do successful women tackle the psychological barriers to success and enjoy their achievements?
- How can a woman maintain a vital ego in maturity?

Women who have strong egos are committed to living the best lives they can. If you work at developing your ego, you will soon possess your own set of psychological tools. The outlook for the female ego is very promising if you believe as I do that problems are for solving, that good results take work, and that growing is life's greatest joy.

2

The Female Ego
in Crisis

Life is full of suffering, and it is also full
of the overcoming of it.
                              Helen Keller

A day may come in the life of a woman when she realizes that
she is not living her life as she wants to. She feels a deep
inner longing that is not for attachment to someone else but is a
longing for herself. She may experience a longing for life as she
thinks it is supposed to be and clearly is not. This is a time of
discouragement as well as intense hope. If she can face the challenge of learning to live as her authentic self and move beyond
the place where she is stuck, she can use her discomfort and pain
as a catalyst for change. Crisis is often what makes us grow. When
the female ego is in crisis, new strengths must be learned to meet
the challenge.

An Unwelcome Visitor

No one wants to experience a crisis, even if it does provide an
excellent situation for profound ego growth. There is no adequate
consolation for the woman who discovers that she cannot conceive
a child and experiences the shattering of the myth that fertility is
a given capacity. The death of a beloved friend does not belong
in the script of a person who intends a happy life, nor do divorce,

illness, identity crises, painful relocations, or accidents.

You do not want to have a crisis of confidence when you realize that your life is not working. You are bored with a self whose activities have become a thousand meaningless rituals, and you feel shut down and vaguely know that you are depressed. A crisis is a negative challenge, an unwanted visitor who crashed the party. It ushers in a period of disequilibrium: the status quo is no longer viable, familiar behaviors get no results, and the mind is in a state of unmitigated dis-ease.

A Precipitating Crisis

People usually come to therapy because of what we call a "precipitating crisis." Sometimes just coping with this crisis solves the problem. In other cases, the precipitating crisis is a symptom or a trigger to a necessary process of profound change within a person. Instead of needing its battery recharged, the car needs to have the transmission rebuilt or the motor overhauled. When a woman is in crisis, she will discover basic ego weaknesses that need to be resolved or life issues that need to be examined and approached in a new way. Some women decide at the time of crisis to take on the courageous task of entering a process of genuine change.

One example of a precipitating crisis for a woman is being fired from a job. After dealing with the pain of this experience, a woman can examine what she really wants to do with her life. She might find that she is floundering because her sense of her own identity is not solidly based on her talents. She might become deeply in touch with what she always dreamed of doing. She then uses the therapy experience to determine how she is holding herself back from doing what she really wants to do.

Another precipitating crisis can be the death of a parent. After accomplishing the mourning process, a woman can go further and look at other deep issues. She looks at her own aging; she gets in touch with the teachings of her parents and how they have influenced her: what they wanted her to be and how she either followed the program or resisted it. In looking deeply at the lives of your parents, you begin to recognize a particular trail that they blazed, and you see the ways in which you are following the same path. Such deep observations can open up many options for a woman and can release sources of energy that have been locked up in those early relationships. In both of these cases, the therapy goes far beyond dealing with the precipitating crises.

I see crisis management as essentially an exercise in how to change. In this chapter I will share with you the approaches to healing and change that I have found helpful to women who undertake such a growth process.

Isolating the Problem

Crisis takes many forms. Sometimes there is a sense of futility and despair: a feeling of being in a trap with no way out. Here the crisis must be given a name, and you should let yourself feel what is happening to you. You must let yourself know if someone who is important to you is emotionally neglecting you or abusing you. Your job might be boring or demeaning, and it will not get better by pretending that it is not. You may be living in the wrong community given your own particular interests. Perhaps you are chronically depressed or angry. Your ego is your mechanism for solving problems. As much as you might like to avoid the negative truths in your life, the only way that your ego can solve your problems is for you to admit them. Defining the problem clearly gives a name to your angst and points you in the direction of making changes.

Often the issues uncovered in therapy point out that something that once worked for a woman no longer works for her. I have met many women who feel that they have outgrown their present lives, and although they have mastered their job or their role in the family, it is a source of boredom. Boredom soon turns to depression and even despair.

In isolating your problems, you will feel worse before you feel better. Expressing your honest feelings about your life must precede finding solutions. Otherwise the solutions will be inadequate or will repress the real problem. Crisis throws down the gauntlet, and only when you pick it up and struggle to change will you be at peace once again. To become conscious and aware may highlight your misery, yet it also illuminates the direction toward solutions.

Conscious and Aware

Fairy tales and myths have been studied by many psychological theorists in an effort to uncover a variety of truths about ourselves. Each story contains a drama of both tragedy and change to better circumstances. Rather than seeing these stories chiefly as tales about women being rescued by men, I prefer to focus on a different angle.

What is the most important moment in those scriptures of our childhood? Is it when the prince rescued Sleeping Beauty? Is it when Rapunzel finally married the prince, or when Snow White rode off into the sunset? Those were important moments, but they were not the pivotal ones. I think that the most significant moment in each tale is the moment when the heroine wakes up. At a certain moment, not always narrated in each of these stories, *the heroine becomes conscious of her imprisoned state and decides how to escape.* Her ego goes to work on her own behalf.

Snow White woke up twice, first to protect herself—"I've got to hide here in the forest"—and later—"I'll be safe and happy with this man, so I can wake up now." Rapunzel finally realizes, "I've got to get out of this tower," and Sleeping Beauty becomes sexually awakened and says, "This is worth waking up for." Our heroines wake up and become conscious and aware. The prince in each story offers a promise of something better, but it is the responsibility of the princess to come alive, get with it, and make a choice.

Becoming conscious and aware is a process many of us fight, and as a result we stay in a life pattern that is banal or painfully demeaning. What we struggle with is usually the very difficult task of seeing the *truth* of our unhappy situation and yet not feeling hopeless. In the stories, our fairy-tale heroines became conscious when they were aware of a hopeful alternative. If you are to awaken yourself to a full life you have a twofold task ahead of you. You must become conscious of your entrapment and misery, *and* you must become aware of your hopeful options.

Consciousness Raising

To discover whether your ego needs to deal with crises or impediments to your growth process, ask yourself the following questions about your life:

- Are you living in a family that consumes most of your energy but does not give you back what *you* need?
- Do your friends hold you back from attempts you make to grow and be different?
- Is your life dull and unexciting?
- Are you exhausted and weary most of the time?
- Do you sometimes feel that you are suffocating, that your responsibilities are closing in on you, and that you have no room to be yourself?
- Do you feel that you do not know which direction to go in your life?
- Do you have a strong but unfulfilled urge to make something of your life—to do something that has meaning and is absorbing?
- Do you feel that the clock is ticking and it may be too late to do the things you want to do?
- Are you angry at your mate most of the time and yet cannot conceive of being without him?
- Are you paralyzed by conflict between various things that you want to do?
- Do you feel that you are like a robot who performs adequately on the surface but lacks real meaning in life?
- Do you feel that your energy is being used up in draining pursuits?

These questions all express symptoms of the female ego in crisis. Have the courage to feel your discomfort and to find the words that best describe your specific situation.

Yes, But I'm Stuck

How can one get out of a stuck place? Therapists go around and around the mulberry bush seeking options for their clients who find themselves living a life that is a miserable trap. Often, if I offer an option my client will say, "Yes, but..." one more time.

THERAPIST: It sounds as though you hate your job.

CLIENT: Yes, but it is the best job for a woman in our company.

THERAPIST: Have you tried complaining?

CLIENT: Yes, but they are all insensitive, macho businessmen.

THERAPIST: Have you thought about applying elsewhere?

CLIENT: Yes, but I would lose seniority and be at a lower level.

THERAPIST: Is relocation a possibility?

CLIENT: Yes, but I would probably be just as miserable somewhere else.

As Eric Berne showed in *Games People Play*, a good round of "Why don't you, yes but" does not lead anywhere. Be aware of your own tendency to "yes, but" the notion of hopeful options. This response is a symptom of how stuck you are with your problems and how immobilized your ego is in helping you solve them.

Hitting Bottom

I have never agreed with the "hitting bottom" theory, which is often used in talking about problems of addiction and of which many therapists have their own version. According to this theory, a person needs to hit bottom because at that point, the only way to go is up. If the person does not want to change, she is not miserable enough; she has to hurt badly. If this were true, it would be one way of rationalizing why upbeat suggestions do not help a woman who is stuck; she needs more pain in order to hit bottom.

I feel compelled to "yes, but" the hit-bottom theory. I have found that people learn how to numb themselves to pain. A woman develops a high tolerance for misery so that she can be suffering but barely knows it. Pain loses its potency to ignite change in deeply miserable people. Unfortunately, this gets everyone who contributes to that woman's misery off the hook. It is easy to overlook a stuck person.

The Power of Pleasure

I have a different theory, and I know that it can work. This is the Garden of Eden theory. A miserable, stuck person needs to visit the Garden of Eden so as to find out what it is like to feel good. Once you have visited the Garden and partaken of pleasure, you realize how miserable you are in your regular life. This creates a double-whammy effect. You now know from experience that (1) it is possible to feel good and (2) your misery feels miserable in comparison. At once you can experience hope and a sense of your excruciating situation. *It is a combination of discomfort and hope that creates a climate for change.*

The ego needs contrast in order to have clear perception. When you are in a rut, your ego is out of touch with the options that are available to fulfill your needs. We need contrast in order to see clearly who we are and how we are living. To be effective, that contrasting experience should be one that shows us something better than our normal living patterns. Here are some examples of visiting the Garden of Eden. Invent one for yourself.

- An overfed, overstimulated executive goes camping, to experience natural living close to the earth.
- An isolated housewife puts together a glamorous outfit and takes a weekly class in the city.
- A businesswoman puts her briefcase in the closet, puts on her apron, and bakes cookies without worrying about time.

When you give yourself a gift that you need, even a small token, you will begin to develop consciousness and awareness. When you begin to give yourself positive nurturing, you will also begin the process of creative discontent, which is what waking up is all about.

Wallowing Your Life Away

In normal living, our egos help us balance the good with the bad. No matter how tragic or disappointing a situation might be, a healthy ego seeks comfort, the assuaging of tears, and the resumption of courage and hope. Looking for the proverbial silver lining is the smart way to live.

Sometimes women who are wallowing in misery are people-pleasers who feel betrayed. Adapting themselves to others did not bring them the life or the quality of relationships they want. Upset by their disappointments, they do not grow toward a healthy resolution, but their bad feelings become a chronic habit. When I am listening to a complainer I sometimes have an urge to tell her bluntly to shape up. Problems are to be *solved*. Get with it! I bite my tongue and work on hearing what's going on with her ego. The machine is malfunctioning; the record got stuck on misery, misery, misery, misery.

If your record is stuck on this theme, let's figure out why. Let's resolve it once and for all so you can play more varied tunes with the emotional highs and lows of normal living.

Overreacting

To get a handle on your problems, you must realize that the content of the problem is often not as significant as *your way of reacting* to it. All of us need to be honest about our tendencies toward hysteria. Unfortunately, hysteria has come to mean "much ado about nothing." This could not be farther from the truth. If you tell a woman she is being hysterical, she probably will scream louder and start throwing things. She may be giving an exaggerated performance, but it must be understood that hysteria in either sex is much ado about *something*. A woman with a hysterical modus operandi makes loud noises because she believes that no one is listening to her. It is likely that she is not getting the attention that she deserves, or that her reactions are carried over from a childhood in which, at crucial times, nobody listened to her.

Hysteria needs to be translated. "It's a tragic disaster; my life is falling apart" can mean "I'm shaken by the raise in my rent." "I'm on the brink of total collapse" can mean "I'm very tired and should be sleeping." A hysterical woman feels insignificant, almost as though she does not exist. As colorful as she is, she fears she is nothing. As she desperately blasts forth, she obliterates her chances of receiving needed affirmation and reassurance.

You must tone down tendencies toward hysteria. If you need to, share your feelings with good folks and experience their listening. Then stop expressing yourself and *respond* to your needs. One of the major problems for most of us females is that we have not internalized enough support. You cannot make any changes or solve any of your problems without support, and it is the lack of support that makes the hysterical woman feel empty and desperate. Learn to find help and to resist a hysterical response that does not allow you to ask effectively for support and then internalize it. Learn to take in what others offer and to realize that you are a resourceful person who can use your energies on your own behalf.

At the heart of hysteria, or exaggeration of one's responses, is the problem of *feeling* to the point of excluding *thinking*. If you want to conquer this problem you must go through the following process:

1. Be aware of what you are doing. You must admit to your own primitive way of reacting to problems. Hear yourself thinking, Nobody's listening so I'll yell louder, and understand that behaving in this way is ineffective.

2. Learn to think instead of feel. To do this, you need to decide which people are good listeners. Then, as you express yourself, have your thinking capacity turned on and perceive the signs of their listening. Notice as the listener nods a head in agreement or winces with empathy. Hysterical people do not usually pick up these important cues. Then think to yourself, Someone is listening to me now, and let the pleasure of this fact fill you.

3. Monitor the way you express yourself. Again, the key is to

think. Think of how to transmit what you have to say in a way that is compatible with the receiver. Work hard to communicate in a way that is likely to be understood. Remember that the point is *communication, not catharsis*.

4. The ultimate goal in all problem solving is self-support. When you have received the support you need from others, work your problems out for yourself. Hysteria causes a person to remain stuck in her Child ego state, wallowing in extreme emotions. You must stop discounting your own resourcefulness. This is the reason why you feel anxious and overwhelmed. Instead, know that you have been given the intelligence to solve problems and to maintain an accurate perspective. You have the capacity to think instead of feel when that is appropriate.

Narcissism

Some women who experience a chronic series of emotional crises are involved in a form of narcissism: they are excessively preoccupied with themselves. When such a woman is unhappy she becomes exclusively interested in her own feelings of misery and martyrdom. She lacks the ability or the interest to identify with anyone outside herself. With narcissism comes a grandiosity or exaggeration of her own experienced feelings. She might say, "This *always* happens to me," "What have *I* done to deserve this," or "I *never* get what I want." Such a self-centered orientation indicates a deep lack of confidence together with an unwillingness to let others be close.

As in many disorders, this attitude can often be traced to a history of neglect or even the experience of abandonment. In normal, healthy development there is a time when the child needs to see herself as the center of the universe and have that concept validated by her parents. She needs this grounded, centered sense of her own identity, and she gets it from the adoration of her parents. She may say, "Look at me, Mommy," as she dances, shows off her new dress, or does a somersault. When her hunger for this special attention is satisfied, she runs outside and plays with the other kids. The key here is to swing back and forth from *one's own needs* to an *involvement with others*, in which one focuses on group needs and others' needs.

There are two ways in which a woman can get stuck in a narcissistic orientation. Sometimes she didn't get enough of that special attention that makes a person feel a basic inner pride in being herself. Such a woman will compulsively seek admiration from others and will very likely become obsessed with giving herself the attention no one else gave her. Her attachment to herself can be expressed as an obsession with how she looks, how she feels, and how she appears to others. The second way to get stuck in narcissism is caused by the opposite condition. Here the child is given great attention from adoring parents but does not go on to forget herself and become involved with others. She, like the deprived narcissist, is locked into wanting parental adoration, which is not usually forthcoming in peer relationships in the real adult world. She substitutes self-adoration.

As a way of life, narcissism is lonely and empty, however much the narcissist aggrandizes herself. When trouble comes, as it does to us all, she looks only to inner space to find answers, not knowing how to let others in. If she is unhappy, her world is a prison. Narcissists wallow in unhappiness because their windows are closed to the people and relationships that would help restore contentment. They do not readily allow the sunshine and fresh air of others to fill them.

I have worked with several women who talk *only* about themselves in their therapy sessions. They are stuck in their own skin and are unable to get out. When you wallow in yourself you experience both inflated self-importance and deep need. To catch this tendency in yourself be honest about your own self-absorption and decide whether it is excessive. Symptoms of narcissism are hypochondria (imagined illness), obsession about how your body looks, overconcern about your clothes, and an excess of attention to the nuances of your emotions. After awhile, other people stop caring about a narcissistic person because they realize that they are not very important to her.

If you are exclusively involved with yourself, your ego must reach out and put you in touch with other people. If you are wallowing in unhappy feelings, consider the possibility that you live in a world that is too narrow. When you are involved with others you have the privilege of living in their worlds for awhile and bringing fresh energy to yourself. Love others and save yourself from a boring and sad existence.

Emotional Liberation

Many women remain stuck in a particular destructive emotion because that is the only song they have in their repertoires. A chronically fearful woman will sustain her state of mind with impressive memories of being terrified and with paranoid fantasies of the dangers that lurk around the corner. A chronically silent, angry woman dredges up memories of insults in the past, as well as a catalog of the faults of significant people in her present life. A chronically sad woman combs through her tragic memories and resonates with helplessness when she contemplates the future. Each woman—whether primarily frightened, angry, or sad—can muster up a lawyer's brief of evidence from the past, the present, and even the future to support her need to wallow in a particular feeling state. How can she free herself?

The process of freeing yourself from chronic fear involves allowing yourself to experience the emotional state which is a close cousin to fear: *excitement.* An excited person experiences quick breathing, butterflies in the stomach, and weak knees. If this feeling is labeled as fear, the tendency is to shy away from the experience. But reaching out into uncharted territories can also be called excitement, and this positive definition predisposes you to reach for it. Women who have worked with the energy shift from fear to excitement report a slight panic reaction, a surge of adrenaline, and then a euphoric high, if they do not retreat. One woman who was afraid of airplane travel told me that she consciously said *yes* to the experience instead of *no* and that she felt great joy at transcending her fear. Women who conquer the fear of public speaking have a heightened sense of power when their panic energy is mustered and turned to the positive dimension of excitement. And the greatest reward of all is the pleasure of not missing opportunities because of fear and, instead, reaping the rewards of becoming more powerful and confident.

Liberating yourself from chronic, silent anger is also accomplished through an energy shift. It is important to be ruthless and see that a silently angry or excessively critical frame of reference serves to maintain your life in a self-protective rut. Being secretly angry is a cowardly way to live because it forces you constantly to make excuses. Being angry is both easy and depressing. If you have this bad psychological habit, you must learn to move beyond it into an expansive, positive way of seeing yourself and your fellow human beings. If you look for problems, you will find problems. If your ego seeks solutions, you will find solutions. The key to moving beyond hidden anger is to look for joy instead of problems. The joyful approach does not deny that problems exist but uses energy to solve them. If, for example, your problem is chronic tension, you would seek a way to relieve it through exercise or a more humane schedule. If your problem is a difficult friend, you might need to lower your expectations if your friend will not change. If it rains on the day of a picnic, you will have a ball staying at home and having the picnic in the living room. You must use your ego to seek joy instead of getting stuck with your anger at life's problems.

The last frontier of emotional liberation is dealing with chronic sadness. It is natural to feel sad when we have been disappointed. Males often express the extreme of the philosophy, "Big boys don't cry." Women do not subscribe to this unhealthy point of view, but many of them have a problem in the other direction. Women can feel that chronic sadness is part of the female role. In some ways a sad woman is attractive to an insecure man, who wants to feel like a strong rescuer. A woman might find herself falling into the role that says, "I am weak, and I will submit," feeling that she is performing as a desirable female. The primary emotional state of women who act out the "yielding" role is sadness. A man with confidence finds such posturing boring. A healthy man wants a relationship with a vital, energetic, spunky individual, who presents him with a challenge to grow. Examine yourself to see if you have a romantic agenda that puts you in the role of being sad and helpless, in need of a rescuer/lover.

The habit of sadness presents an example of how chronic feelings are self-reinforcing. A sad woman has a low energy level. She is mopey and wistful. When she observes herself, she sees a second-class person. "Of course I am inferior," she says. "Look at how weak and ineffective I am in my life. I can't even make myself exercise." As she makes this observation, her body feels even weaker, and she is even more likely to hang back. The answer to chronic sadness and hopelessness is willfully to break into the self-reinforcing system at any point, whether it be the *beliefs* about oneself, the apathetic *behavior,* or the *emotions,* because they reinforce one another. The sad woman must experience the opposite of helpless sadness, which is power. Vigorous physical exercise can break the sadness cycle as can evidences of power in work and relationships. I work with sadness in my clients on the following four levels:

- Believe that you are powerful and take actions that support the belief that you are powerful. Count those activities, making a case against your helpless belief system.
- Modify your sad behavior. Do things on your own that make you feel strong instead of weak. Resist hanging back. Work on being assertive such as speaking up to people instead of silently nursing a hurt feeling or a resentment.
- Stop moping with your body. Be physically active and tackle physical challenges such as walking instead of riding and undertaking a fitness program.
- Control chronic emotional memories. Don't dwell on the past times when you were depressed. Do not create a fantasy world in which you imagine future defeats and cry about them.

To stay on a positive track in which your ego can function at its best, you must break your emotional bad habits. If you cannot defeat a self-reinforcing system by yourself, seek input from someone who can help you—a friend or a therapist.

Once you begin to examine feelings of sadness, you may discover that they have been masking anger. Just as men have a taboo against sadness, women have a taboo against open anger. Getting angry is not nice because it makes another person feel uncomfortable. The people-pleaser will tend to release feelings through emotions that are acceptable to others and will therefore choose sadness. I have observed that many women cry in therapy sessions when they describe someone at whom they are angry, and they define anger as "being upset." When I sense that they are really angry, I suggest that they stop crying and express themselves without tears. Then the unrevealed anger comes out, and the woman is free of the feelings that have been dragging her down. We all need to clean up our emotional acts from time to time. That means giving each feeling its due and then moving on to something else. If you are scared, protect yourself, and then move on. If you are angry, get mad, and then move on. If you are sad, express it, and then muster your strength to move on. And if you are happy, support that feeling by celebrating. Increasing your joy can inoculate you against wallowing. An honest emotional expression is elegant: true, timely, short, and satisfying.

Overprotection

Wallowing in negative emotions can be a way of remaining a coward. We are tempted to numb ourselves with false misery to avoid experiencing the humiliation of being human and possibly making mistakes when we actively pursue what we want. Pessimism is cowardice. In playing it safe, you sit on the sidelines waiting for a perfect opening in the rough-and-tumble game of life. When you are afraid to live your life fully, you can get used to receiving attention for having problems. And if you are a chicken, you will never develop your ego. A woman with a healthy ego confronts herself when she is being a coward.

If there are things you need to do that you are not doing, consider the possibility that you are giving yourself too many *relief strokes*. All of our behaviors are maintained through some form of positive reinforcement—even negative behaviors such as not doing something. When a woman complains to me that she has been procrastinating about filling out an application or writing her resumé, I know that she is trapped in a passive-aggressive system that is supported by relief strokes. Here is how this system works.

Margie wants to interview for a job, but she is anxious about it. She must bring her updated resumé to the interview. She plans to write the resumé on Saturday night. When Saturday comes she does not want to write it and says to herself, "I'll wait and do it on Sunday." At that moment she is flooded with blissful relief: the anxiety about the interview is gone, and the struggle over the task of writing the resumé is gone. She feels good in contrast to how she had felt when she was planning to tackle those tough challenges. She has given herself powerful positive reinforcement for *not doing* her tasks. For many women this behavior echoes a childhood in which their parents made things easy by telling them not to "overdo" or by giving them too much support in times of sickness and incapacitation. By giving herself relief strokes, a woman avoids the very activities that make her ego strong and teaches her ego to be out of commission.

The reason this behavior is called passive-aggressive is because a woman is channeling her *aggressive* energies into being *passive*. This pattern is common among women and explains how and why many women prevent themselves from being actualized as people. The key to breaking this pattern is to become aware of the power of the relief stroke: "Whew, I didn't have to do it!" A very common relief stroke that women give themselves is saying, "I'm glad I'm not a man," meaning, "I'm glad I don't have to do all of the hard things a man has to do." Taking the easy way ultimately leads to being in a prison in which you are stuck with unfulfilled dreams, undeveloped talents, and a deficit of strokes that can be obtained only through *what you do*. You must learn not to pamper yourself by taking the easy way. Successful men, by and large, have learned to look down the corridors of power and control the immediate desire for ease and comfort in order to commit themselves to long-term goals. You can incorporate this attitude into *your* behavior.

One of the hallmarks of a strong ego is the capacity for delayed gratification. This is not the same as no gratification, which is a trap for the female ego. Delayed gratification means that you can work hard at a task that may not be pleasant in order to have a gain in the future. A woman must look at *the long picture, not the short one*. It might feel cozy to lie on the sofa watching TV, and your mother might have encouraged such self-nurturing, but a fabulous resumé that you had to stay up late to complete will give you the ultimate large rewards. A woman with an ego knows this and will not settle for less.

Am I Blue?

People don't talk or sing much about being blue anymore. Maybe the language of the clinician has taken over that of the ballad singer, because you certainly hear a lot about people being depressed. Therapists talk about endogenous depression (it shows up in the blood chemistry), masked depression (it's there but is covered up), manic depression (pathologically extreme highs and lows), and low-grade depression. Most of us simply say, "I'm feeling depressed." Depression is often the symptom of emotional crisis which brings a woman into therapy.

I know what it means for a woman to be in that low and shut-down state. She feels dull, empty, and hopeless. The world appears to be a bleak place, and people are potential sources of disappointment. Being in the depressed state is the opposite of being a psychological winner. A healthy woman is not depressed—her ego is working for her, sustaining her with a sense of inner well-being. She is full of joie de vivre and is getting on with life, energetically. You have neither the time nor the inclination for depression when your ego is managing well.

Being Depressed Is Not the Same as Wallowing

The woman who wallows is *actively* miserable. The depressed woman is simply shut down. Sometimes a depressed woman is so distanced from feeling her pain that she cannot even say, "I'm depressed." She might say, "I'm lazy," "I can't seem to get going," "Nothing seems to grab me," or "What's it all about, anyway?" A woman in a severe depression feels alternating numbness and pain. To an outsider she seems lacking in emotional color. Of the four primary emotions, mad, sad, glad, and scared, the obvious feeling tone is sadness. The eyes look sad, without hope. She has a dreary case of the blues.

Depression and Expression

What most fascinates me about depression is that the symptoms are about the same for all of us, but what is going on beneath the surface varies tremendously. The most elementary guidebook for therapists would suggest that a depressed person needs to get angry. My experience has not shown this to be the only answer. I have discovered that depression is a lid that is placed on the emotional pot. Instead of the normal bubbling and steaming of emotional expression, a person clamps on this lid, and the feelings stay inside. And by staying inside they do damage to a woman, almost like an attack from within.

There is a simple principle at work in the case of depression. Depression is a process which is the opposite of expression. An expressive person does not get depressed. That is why Zorba the Greek danced at the funeral of his beloved son. For him it was a question of dance or die from an inner attack of depression. In our culture, most of us are timid about intense emotional expression, which holds us back from the healthy solution to depression.

When does a woman get depressed? Often it is when she has an important emotion to express and cannot do so. I once worked with a woman who was depressed after getting a great promotion at work. The repressive style of her family taught her that women do not have permission to win and celebrate victories. Consequently, she repressed her joy about her triumph and became depressed because of her refusal to face the pleasure it gave her. I remember Simone finally crying for her father, who died too young, and Jill reliving the panic of her car accident. I think of the women I have taught how to have temper tantrums by pounding and kicking pillows. Even more powerful are the women who shakily let love into their lives when they express loving feeling toward their work, another person, or even a flower.

What is fascinating about these cases is their essential similarity: powerful emotions were hidden in the dull exterior of a depressed person. Yet what unique expressive tasks each had to perform to throw off that blanket of depression! *Our unexpressed feelings can poison us and rule our lives.* Once they are expressed, we become alive and available for the normal emotional experiences in life.

The Release Button

You can master a technique that can help you deal with times when you get depressed. This technique is not for dealing with deep grief or with trauma from childhood as much as it is for dealing with depression caused by everyday happenings in a relatively normal life, although the principle is the same as that used in therapy for healing profound depression. If you are depressed, think back and mark down the date when your depression started. Depression is a reaction to an emotional occurrence. It is easy to forget what the trigger was, both because it probably was something unpleasant and because it may have been something small. For example, your depression might have been triggered by a moment in which you experienced hurt feelings. The hurt was then swallowed, and a depression set in. You may have believed that you deserved to feel bad, or that it was impossible to work things out with the person who hurt you, or that it was a matter of pride not to admit that you were sensitive to what occurred.

As soon as you let yourself remember the moment your depression started, you have your finger on the release button. You must now express that feeling and let it go. The best way to do this is to tell the person whose remark may have hurt you, "It bothers me when you tease me about being fat, and I don't want you to do that again." Or perhaps you had a victory that you forgot to celebrate. You must find a way to rekindle that joyful feeling and share it with someone. If you were angry, you must find a way to express that anger directly. By being on your own side, and not swallowing your feelings, you will release yourself from depression.

The final way to press the release button is for you to express the feeling adequately to yourself. If someone criticized you, for example, don't get hung up on whether or not the person who upset you was telling you the truth. Say to yourself or write on paper, "It bothered me when Allison criticized my work. I do not want to hear criticism from her, and I was not prepared for what she said. She chose the wrong time and did not help me by saying what she did, even though there is some validity to what she said."

Pressing the release button has to do with being your own advocate. By claiming this position you will not swallow your feelings and become depressed, no matter how silly you may think them to be at times. A depressed person feels she has no right to deal with feelings when they occur and holds onto the belief that nobody can be trusted to care. This is a terrible habit, which leads to shutting yourself down—sometimes for weeks. By venting the feeling and giving it its due, you will not let it color your whole life. Keep your finger on the release button, so that you can get on with living.

Female Repression

I am convinced that a woman can be generally depressed when her talents are not being fulfilled. I once worked with a woman whose energies were consumed in working with her young family. She loved them dearly but was plagued by depression. One summer all of the children went to camp, and she went to summer school and studied math. She had been an excellent student as a child. Her depression lifted, and she continued her graduate studies after her children came back from camp. The depressions never returned, and she felt anchored in her own intellectual growth process and in her plan to be a teacher in the future.

In therapy I encourage women to develop their best talents and be specialists in something, not just generalists. There is a tremendous personal release and fulfillment in doing something with true expertise. And if these powers are bottled up, a woman is very likely to be depressed. One of my outlets always has been music, and I continue to study. The professional musicians I have known during my life are among the happiest people I know, and I believe that it is because they have developed their powers of expression. Perhaps it is full expressiveness that sustains the life and artistry of many musicians into their eighties and nineties. To avoid depression, a woman must gear herself toward a life that expresses the fullness of her talents.

The Expressive Mode

You can evaluate the health of your lifestyle by the amount of excitement you feel. We humans are built for challenge, anticipation, and rewards. In addition, our psyches thrive on human contact—intellectually stimulating contact, blissful contact, humorous contact. Check your emotional barometer. Have you laughed from your guts this week? Tenderly cried? Had a nondestructive outburst of temper? If you have, you probably are living in vital contact with others.

The British call it a "stiff upper lip," an educated person calls it "being reasonable," a parent calls it "behaving yourself," a teenager "plays it cool," and a businessperson is "playing the game." The politician warns, "Don't make waves." If we take these messages deeply to heart, we will cut down on our expressiveness. There are times when we have some very important irrational— even disturbing—things to say. The irony is that expressing these feelings usually means airing the truth. Not expressing our truth is to lie by default. And those lies make us sick inside.

Often a woman is afraid to express the pressing feelings under her depression because she is afraid the feelings will engulf her or another person. "If I get angry I might never be loved again," or "If I start having fun, I won't ever want to go to work again." The truth is that feelings are *dissipated* through honest, clear expression.

Then a person can get on with living. Our general expectation of men is that they have the right to talk straight and be confrontational when necessary. Such behavior is part of our image of the courageous male. A female who has inhibitions about emotional honesty can learn something from the direct approach of many men. One of the reasons that men can be less "emotional" than women is because their feelings are dissipated through honest, clear expression. When you say what you have to say, and then come to closure, you can drop it and get on with living. By staying in an expressive mode you will be active and creative—not stuck in "being emotional."

A woman must be aware that her habits of repression are supported by our culture. We receive more acclaim for how we look than for what we think. Our deep feelings and convictions are not of consequence in our roles as people-pleasers, where the focus is on the feelings of others. Overbearing male egos can lead us not to trust our own reactions. Our repressed state has even been made out to be romantic, as the mysterious female connects her fragile and subtle self in a romantic encounter with a confident, worldly male. We must get over the notion that there is special merit to being withdrawn and realize that it is *socially induced* repression, not her female nature, that puts a woman out of touch with the gut reactions that make her a whole person.

The Taming of the Shrew

There are some women who are out and out shrews, angry, discontented, and negative. Think about a shrew you know. She may be superficially attractive, but her sour disposition gets the best of her. She may inspire pity, but her negativity drives helpers away. Her angry orientation may give her some semblance of strength, but she gets her power from hurting or intimidating other people. According to her, the men in her life are wimps whom she does not respect. She has difficulty finding associates whom she enjoys.

Only Shakespeare could invent a powerful man who would

undertake the task of taming a shrew. In real life, self-respecting men won't do it. A shrew must tame herself. Almost every woman has a bit of shrew inside. I am going to draw a vivid picture of this behavior, and if the description fits, change is in order.

Basically a shrew is a high-spirited, rebellious woman with a chronic case of sour grapes. Even as a healthy person, she would be a powerful force to deal with. Convention bores her; routine is a trap, and she has little respect for authority, unless it has earned her respect. She resents mistreatment with a passion and is a poor loser. Being nice costs her a painful amount of energy.

A shrew is often very discriminating, loving what is aesthetically pleasing to her. She may be highly literate, a queen of charisma, or an accomplished artist. Yet she struggles with the converse, her repulsion at ugliness and banality. She is an elitist and a snob.

This woman becomes a shrew when the balance tips and she cannot live as the spirited filly that she is. Her life circumstances have not given her the support that she needs to be her full self. She has acquiesced, and she is miserable and furious about it. As strong as she is, she still needs the guidance and support that will lead her to develop her substantial gifts. Without this support, her energy is not flowing in the right channel, and she finds herself conforming to authority figures whom she hates, absorbing mistreatment in the form of not being respected for who she really is, and feeling that her work is demeaning because it does not reflect her taste or her talents. She sees the positive affirmation that she receives as a token for her willingness to compromise herself. Love is therefore out of the question, and manipulation and adaptation become the name of the game. A shrew is soured on life, and the people who are close to her feel her hostility.

> My tongue will tell the anger of my heart
> Or else my heart, concealing it will break.
>
> Katherine, act 4, scene 3
> Shakespeare, *The Taming of the Shrew*

The ego of a shrew is in crisis. Since the function of the ego is to solve problems and to lead you toward sources of fulfillment, the ego cannot work if you believe that you never will be able to have what you want. Most shrews are in life patterns in which they feel compromised, and they believe there is no way out. The shrew in Shakespeare's play was subjected to the stilted, formal rituals of upper-class life, a sister who outshone her, and an arranged marriage. A shrew feels that there should be a way out of this pattern but believes that there is not. Her life script is a prison.

> You mean to make a puppet out of me.
>
> Katherine, act 4, scene 3
> Shakespeare, *The Taming of the Shrew*

Within this prison, she adapts begrudgingly. But if she has been a good girl for too long, she has to do something to get rid of her anger. She may have affairs, do something to hurt or embarrass another, abuse her children emotionally or physically, or abuse herself with alcohol, drugs, or reckless behavior.

> I see, a woman may be made a fool,
> If she had not a spirit to resist.
>
> Katherine, act 3, scene 3
> Shakespeare, *The Taming of the Shrew*

I once worked with a woman who was married and occasionally wanted to go out with her women friends. Two or three times a year she would go bar hopping and stay out all night. This pattern, which she could not explain to herself, nearly destroyed her marriage. Another woman would occasionally get embarrassingly drunk at parties, feeling that she needed to prove her freedom in this way. And another woman enjoyed affairs with married men in which there was intrigue and the danger of being found out.

Some other shrewish behaviors are complaining about something upon greeting an intimate, raining on others' parades, fault-finding, missing the point and blemishing a detail, heaving miserable sighs, looking awful, dragging around, being gloomily distracted, subtly comparing your companion with a "better" someone else, topping another person's story, correcting grammar, and getting on the other person's case. Even acting shy or withdrawn can be a hostile act of accusing a nice person of being a monster. If you have adopted any of these habits, you must see them as unproductive and rebellious. Instead of going after what you need, and inspiring love and support, you are keeping yourself stuck by rebelling.

Often a shrew is completely unaware of her effect on others. In fact, she most likely gave up on others a long time ago. Other people don't love her, she reasons; they only want her to adapt to their wishes. She is angry, and she is stroke-starved. She may get a little emotional relief from dumping on a victim, but this yields a sense of disappointing contact which affirms her life view.

Getting Shaped Up

If I had been discussing the male counterpart of a shrew, I might have described a high-spirited and rebellious troublemaker who hasn't got his act together yet. We might say that he needs to go into the army and get himself straightened out because he seems to need discipline. Shakespeare had the same notion about his shrew. Her tamer made her walk through mud and rain after her horse gave out. Whenever she complained she was presented with a tougher situation to deal with. He put her through the paces and ultimately "shaped her up."

A modern shrew must shape herself up. Her goal must be to find a channel for her high energy and powerful gifts. This filly needs to harness a magnificent libido. This is very different from adapting to others, which is anathema to a shrew. Discipline is not compliance; it is the organization and education of one's energies so that they can be fully expressed. True discipline can only be administered to oneself; otherwise it is obedience. A shrew is too rebellious ever to obey another person anyway. This is her gift and her curse. And she certainly curses herself and others when she pretends to be obedient.

The anger of a shrew stems from a hidden, immature dependency on others: "I'm miserable and it's your fault." Instead, she needs to turn her feelings around and say, "My life is now my fault—and my responsibility." She must have the courage to forgive the people who let her down in the past and invite loyalty and support from friends. A shrew must channel her impotent rage into potent behavior. The task of her ego is to find an arena that is equal to her gifts and do whatever is necessary to hone her talents.

The Freeing of a Woman

Judith possesses brilliant musical gifts—possibly the talent to be a fine composer. She is magnificent to look at as well, with flaming red hair and flashing dark eyes. Incongruously, she is a household drudge who never plays the piano. She complains incessantly, which drives her husband nuts. On occasion, she has a screaming fit and berates a family member. Then she cries with clenched jaws, certain that she is justified. She hates the neighborhood, her husband's job, her mother-in-law, and the lot of women.

The day comes when Judith begins to understand herself. She realizes that her deep frustration stems from her failure to express her brilliant gifts. She then must face her trek through the mud: the humiliation of beginning as a beginner, the tedium of learning to be a sight reader, and the frustration of spending vast amounts of time practicing and going very slowly. She struggles through a maze of teachers and techniques, some helpful, some not. She plays pieces that do not begin to resonate her power. She works through mental blocks, memory slips, and tension. There is not enough time, and the going is slow.

Through it all, an amazing change comes over her personality: she is easier to be with. She enjoys the comfort of others. She is less demanding; others don't have to be perfect. She draws on the emotional support that she needs and learns to give it as well.

Judith's work as an artist begins to take shape. She finally plays the advanced piano repertoire, and she starts to branch out. Among her new ventures are conducting a choir and composing her own music. Finally, one of her compositions is performed by the local chamber orchestra. Her work receives a positive critical review in the newspaper.

The personality transformation continues. Judith's dark eyes still flash, but with an intensity that is not anger. She is innovative but not rebellious. By using her ego to discipline and channel her energies, she has tamed the shrew—but not the woman. A female does not need to be tame; she can set the world on fire. And if she doesn't, she might turn out to be a shrew.

Born-Again Woman

Both personally and in my work I come across many women who started out all right in their lives but got off the track. This happened to a woman who was well-adjusted and happy in Texas but could not make it in New York and a woman who unwittingly married an abusive alcoholic who is a fine man when he is not drinking. A good example is a woman who was a crackerjack in languages in college but is now exhausted by having to negotiate the supermarket because that is her only challenge today.

A woman can feel that her life was going fine for a long time and then the bottom started to fall out. Unequipped to cope with a crisis or with a particular way of life, she loses the self she once possessed. The word demoralized is hardly strong enough to describe the way she feels. These are the women who spend time in their therapy sessions remembering how it used to be: "I used to be captain of the cheerleaders, but now I stay at home every night." "I was so slender and beautiful that I considered becoming a model. Now look at me, weighing in at 165." "We were so much in love, but now our relationship is a horror."

Sometimes bringing back something from your past will help you in your present situation. I grew up in Nebraska and spent my childhood riding horses and climbing haystacks. I did not know how important nature is to me until I found that it was difficult for me to unwind after work. I finally discovered that I could become relaxed and restored when I took weekend camping trips with my family. The outdoors is part of my childhood, and I still need that environment to refresh me.

To become a born-again woman, you must make basic changes in your present life situation. You may need to remove yourself from a debilitating relationship, get a divorce, change jobs or careers, recover from an illness or depression, restructure how you spend your time, or cure an addiction. You may need to add people to your life who will help you to make these changes. You must find the time and the place that supports your growth. When you do what you need to do for yourself, you will experience a rebirth of your former healthy self.

Sometimes the solutions are fairly simple. Many women let themselves lose parts of themselves through neglect. The press of responsibilities to family or a career can lead a woman to neglect her interests and her own personal growth. She forgets that it is very important to her to be slender or to play the violin. My therapy office walls echo with the words: "I used to love to play tennis... play the piano... sing in the choir... go to parties... tell jokes... I used to, I used to." The case becomes clear. I know that when these women resume playing tennis or the piano they are on the way to rebirth.

I will never forget a weekend therapy marathon that I led several years ago. There was one woman in the group who made everyone in the room feel uptight. She was a thin, graying woman in her fifties who said very little and had a disapproving air about her. Members of the group shared deep feelings, but she remained bitter and unmoved. Having her there was like having your most dreaded schoolteacher peering over your shoulder.

In one of our exercises we shared with one another our favorite activities from childhood. With a bit of prying she confessed that she had enjoyed tumbling. After further interrogation she admitted to having been an accomplished gymnast on a competitive level. She was beginning to make a little sense to me. It sounded as though she was a jock, and like many jocks, she was not at her best verbally.

One of the men in the group seized the opportunity to challenge her. "I don't believe you, Hannah. Give me a somersault to prove it." Her eyes gleamed, and one corner of her mouth twitched a little. She stood up and did a graceful double somersault, then to the cheers of the group did a backward one and landed on her feet. She was grinning, and her eyes glistened with tears. During the weekend Hannah practiced on the lawn during our breaks. At our final session she demonstrated cartwheels, which she had not done for years. We witnessed her transformation from being sternly withdrawn to being fun-loving. She was a born-again woman.

Activating Your Inner Child

Here is an exercise that has been very helpful in many group sessions that I have directed. With pencil and paper prepare to take a trip back into childhood. First, choose an age before you were twelve years old. Let your unconscious mind come up with an age that it would be fun to be again, and write the age at the top of the paper. Then take a fantasy trip into your past. Where were you living at that time? What was your life like? Enter that world all over again, allowing memories to be rekindled. What year was it? What did your home look like? Picture the details: the clothes, the cars, the food. Then let your family come to mind, remembering your parents at that time and your siblings. What was school like? Who were your friends? As you open up these moments in your life, remember what was fun. Recall a particular time when you had great fun. What were you doing? How did you behave when you were enjoying yourself? As you answer these questions and follow your fantasies, take notes so that this experience can be recalled.

The next task is to look over your notes and compare those

feelings with the ones you have now. How can you pull out what was meaningful then and apply it to now? If possible, share your memories with someone else, and let that person help you see that you are still the same person. There are many ways that we can keep the child within well stroked, but that means doing what children like to do. Riding bicycles, playing at sports, being outdoors, savoring the sunlight or the fresh air, enjoying a snack, cracking jokes, getting a warm hug, and feeling that a day is endlessly long—these are the experiences my clients recall when they do this exercise. Discovering this source of inner energy and joy helps you to live as your natural and beautiful self.

The Abandoned Woman

The painful crisis caused by abandonment in the life of a woman has become all too familiar. Every street in every community has someone who once bought the myth of happily ever after and now finds herself without her husband or lover. Even when the desire for parting is mutual, the scenario generally is one in which the man moves out and goes somewhere else. In every woman's consciousness is the uneasy question: "I wonder if this could happen to me?"

Most poignant is the story of the woman who has been a devoted wife and homemaker for twenty-plus years. Once her children are in college, her husband leaves her for the young woman assistant in his office who is the age of his daughters. The pain and bitterness of being discarded after a life of devotion to her husband and family is an experience that is indescribable in its torment and defies ordinary words of comfort. In another version of this story a man leaves a younger traditional housewife in the midst of the chaos of raising their young children and cleaves himself to a female who is living a more glamorous single lifestyle, or perhaps to a woman who is more exciting to him from a professional perspective. Colleagueship can be very sexy, and not a few men have been lured from the domestic scene by the heady world of work.

An abandoned woman is a living example of what a woman most does not want for herself. Because she embodies our worst fears of rejection, we may avoid and blame her.

Jealous Obsessions

As if the pain of rejection and grief over the death of a marriage were not enough, the abandoned woman has to struggle with the anguish of jealous feelings. Jealousy, intensely felt, seems to reflect badly on the person who is feeling it. We tend to believe that strong and resourceful people do not get caught in the emotional trap of jealousy, not admitting that given the right circumstances, everyone is vulnerable to this response. Jealousy is a normal reaction to realizing that someone else has something which you feel entitled to have yourself. When a woman knows that "her" man is with another woman, she experiences the angry pain of jealousy. More than once I have heard a woman admit, "It would be easier if he had died than to mourn his being with someone else."

A woman who feels abandoned can be endlessly obsessed about the circumstances of her separation and her fantasies of what is happening between the man and his new love. Her feelings are normal and understandable, although they can become a trap of unnecessary pain. The trouble is that she can find no way out unless she radically changes her perspective on life. Her happily married friends are not able to help her very much if they have not questioned the dynamics of traditional marriage—and why should they if the old patterns still seem to be working for them? Other bitter women are no help either, if all they want to do is play endless rounds of, "Aren't men terrible yet painfully desirable?"

Understanding the Power of Her Feelings

If a woman is dealing with abandonment or with abandonment anxiety, she needs to accept her feelings and understand why they are so strong. It is part of the woman's psyche to mate and procreate. There is a strong biological pull inherent in her capacity to have a baby, and for a large portion of her life she is reminded of this aspect of herself every month. Women's fantasy lives reveal erotic scenarios of being carried away, loved, and sexually penetrated by a man, and these can be understood partly as primal images coming from her biological proclivity to reproduce. To the extent that a woman has powerful urges to mate, she is dependent on the other sex, and she may tend to obsess about her mate: *who will he be?* and when he comes into her life: *what is he like?* and when he goes: *why is he gone?* or *what did I do to drive him away?*

Men do not obsess as much as women do about mating because of the complementary roles of men and women in our culture. A man does not have to obsess about emotional relating and mating. He learns that this is a woman's issue and a woman's function. Of course, men experience painful reactions to breakups of relationships, but many of them tend to take a more macho approach by withdrawing from the hurt and finding a new woman as soon as possible. The bravado of "I can replace her" can mask the pain they feel. The mating urge for a woman is somewhat different, based on her ability to produce a child in her body. This is part of her sexual process. I have heard women somewhat jokingly refer to an intense desire to bear a child as "baby lust." A man has the urge to copulate, but his urge to mate does not seem to be as strong as a woman's. These tendencies are both biological and culturally supported, but that does not mean that a woman needs to be enslaved by them. Let's give biology its due so that we are not victims of it. Because a man can do his part to produce a child for at least twenty more years than a woman can, she is bound to feel the urgency of time in ways that he does not. I experience a strong sense of urgency in my female clients when they are in their mid-thirties and have not yet borne a child. Much older women sometimes experience the same sense of urgency because of the habit of living in the female mating time frame.

An abandoned woman may be able to free herself from her obsessions about her lost mate if she understands that she is playing a broken record based on her sexuality. If she is not aware of the powerful inner force behind what she is doing, she will not generate the necessary energy to meet and cope with the needs that are causing her misery. Her ego must focus on solutions—which means finding another mate *or some other endeavor for her life*. Without such a new focus her ego will not function well, and she will engage the powerful energies given her for mating in the activity of obsessing about her losses. Just because the cultural myths of happily ever after have failed her does not mean that her libido cannot find expression and that she is condemned to a loveless life.

We must also not underestimate the power of female programming to please men. With this as her basic identity, in a culture that still evaluates women according to whom they have married, it is difficult to live as your own person—or to believe that it is possible to do so. The abandoned woman struggles with the loss of her social identity, which can be a bigger blow to the ego than the loss of a relationship that was no longer working. A woman needs to have the courage to question the very premise of a couple-based society, as well as to evaluate the importance of her own mating instincts and developed habits. She must realistically ask herself how important her urge to mate is in her life. There are three relevant questions to ask:

- Have I already done it? Perhaps being alone is an opportunity to spring free and do things that were difficult to do when you were involved in a mating bond. A woman with a healthy ego learns to let the past go and move on to the future by saying, "I've done that. It's time for something else now."
- Who's left? The obsession of abandonment often leads one to forget that there are many people in the world. A healthy ego looks for the positive and counts gains instead of losses. A woman must build on her relationships with friends and children and move beyond the "one and only" myth.
- How do I reorganize? When the ego digs into concrete solutions a woman claims mental health for herself. Knowing that her urge to mate is causing her pain, a woman must learn how to channel her energies toward goals and people other than the

person who has left her. This is the way for her to stop spinning her wheels and conquer her feelings of hopelessness.

Working through Her Feelings

A woman who is suffering with the feelings of being abandoned needs to go through an effective and healing grief process. She has experienced a death—the death of a relationship. Relationships are usually very important to a woman, and she grieves their loss. In that grief process she must express all of her gut-level emotional responses. This is very different from obsessing about the problem. Obsessions are a means of avoiding working a problem through and reaching a new plateau of growth.

When a woman summons the courage to work through her problem, she may need a helper, either a therapist or a sensitive friend. In this process she will deal with the unfinished issues between her and her former mate. She will express, if only to herself, the very specific emotions that are keeping her stuck. These issues are unique for each woman. They may involve her hurt at betrayal over a long period of time or at a much earlier time. Perhaps he was very annoying to live with, and she never was able to confront him with her anger. Perhaps he was never really there, or he was wonderful and she loved him very much. Working through is a process of intimate, specific, and vulnerable truth telling. In working through your feelings you must express the great variety of your emotions: the laughter, the tears, the hurt, the anger, and even the gratitude. *As each feeling is expressed for no more and no less than it is, you will let it go.* You will unburden yourself of the emotional baggage of being abandoned and will stop holding onto the individual who is giving you nothing.

The Theme of Abandonment

It is natural to want to avoid this subject and pretend that abandonment will never happen to you. When Hester Prynne wore the scarlet letter of adultery, she became the scapegoat for the repressed sexuality in her community. Today, the woman who has been abandoned by her husband is the scapegoat of other women who do not want to admit their own fear of abandonment. It is painful to admit that we are not well loved or that we live in a society in which women are not given the respect, appreciation, or ego support they deserve. Perhaps the case of the abandoned woman is simply the extreme on a continuum of neglect that women experience in society. There are many degrees on the abandonment continuum, and a woman should use her ego to be aware of this unfortunate reality. Many adults were abandoned by their fathers when they were children because of a divorce, and this experience is imprinted in their consciousness as *male* behavior—fathers leave and mothers stay. Our welfare structure encourages abandonment by offering better payments to fatherless families than to those with two parents.

Men abandon women all the time without physically leaving them. Men have the capacity to shut down and turn off. Most women have to deal with a man's prerogative not to speak of emotional matters, to be silent, or to leave the room or even the house when he is displeased. The cartoon cliché of a man using a newspaper to separate himself from a woman represents the way men shut out women as a matter of course. From the six-year-old's "no-girls-allowed" clubhouse to the men's social clubs, men screen out women as a way of claiming and maintaining their separate identity. A woman unwittingly gives a man's proclivity to abandon her tremendous support by her own behavior. As he becomes withdrawn, she becomes a people-pleaser: she woos him and cajoles him into wanting to be with her, and a man soon discovers that the silent treatment can get spectacular results. Man-pleasing can take so much energy that a woman does not develop other aspects of herself.

On a psychological level women fall prey to the abandonment/man-pleasing dynamic because of their separation anxieties. Realize that you may be expecting a man to "complete" you or to be an object for your skills as a people-pleaser. This situation is a setup for you and your man to play out the drama of the abandoner and the abandoned, whether it be the withdrawn husband and the solicitous wife or the heavy, painful drama of the housewife and the philandering or abandoning husband. As women learn to feel good, separate, and complete in themselves, an adjustment will occur that will help men and women to live with more mutuality. The resourceful and independent woman does not give a man power over her which he might be tempted to abuse.

Springing the Abandonment Trap

The task for the female ego is to rise up and *take responsibility for herself*. The following guidelines will help whether you are trapped in the role of people-pleaser because of abandonment anxiety or actually have experienced a painful abandonment.

- Decide how to sustain yourself right now—for the short haul. An abandoned woman is desperately in need of strokes, and she is looking to a source that will not provide them. A man cannot give you all the strokes you need anyway, in spite of the power and the promise inherent in romantic fantasies. Your main task is to express and fulfill yourself as a whole person. Begin by getting emotionally filled up by a diversity of strokes—adventure, friendships, a pleasant environment, inspiring reading, physical activities, learning something new, polishing a skill, a fitness regime, meeting new people. Add new sources of strokes to your life *immediately*.

- Remind yourself that you don't need to borrow the ego of a man in order to be a whole person. Become aware of all the ways that you are fulfilled that do not require a man. These include work, artistic pursuits, sports, friendships, family relationships, and the enjoyment of children. Women can give themselves sexual pleasure without a man. Women are discovering that they can own a home without a man and that they can buy their own fur coats if that is what they really want. Personal pride does not come from having a devoted man. You especially do not need a man to get rid of an abandonment script, that is, the man who will never abandon you in any way. Clinging to such a script is just another way to feed abandonment anxiety. You must get yourself out of this trap by knowing that your wholeness as a person is *your own responsibility*.

- Gather together all of your tools and assets. You must know what you have going for yourself: money, a job, and skills. Do a skills inventory in which you list what you do well, and keep this knowledge in the foreground of your mind. A woman with a good ego knows her assets and then capitalizes on them.
- Decide what you want. What have you always wanted to do? What activities gave you the most pleasure in the past? What parts of your life are over and don't bear repeating? Have fantasies, and observe other people whose lives appeal to you.
- Go and get it! If what you want is a job, a degree, a skill, money, travel, or even a man, use your ego to go after it aggressively.

Becoming Whole

Gretchen was numb with depression when her husband left her two months before the marriage of their oldest daughter. Gretchen had a son in college and another daughter in high school, so her nest was not yet empty, and her energies were consumed with the elaborate wedding plans. Months later, however, she was immobilized by the contained rage not only at what her husband had done but at his timing. Her body was weak from her feelings of humiliation and anger.

In therapy Gretchen undertook a working-through process in which she poured out many angry words and tears. Finally, a picture emerged of tremendous delayed gratification by both Gretchen and her husband. All of their energies had been poured into their children, and they had deferred doing what they wanted to do. In recent years, Gretchen had become even more involved in her relationships with the children, and her husband had detached himself. His two affairs were unknown to Gretchen, probably because she was preoccupied. She finally admitted that her marriage relationship had become boring and that she resented having lost sight of her own needs. Whenever she asked for something she wanted, her husband had said no, using money as the reason. Gretchen resented having her needs always come last in the family system.

The day came when Gretchen finally let her husband go, relinquishing a presence that had kept her shut down and out of touch with herself. "You know, if he had died instead of divorcing me I would feel free," she said. I asked her what she would do if he were *really* gone. "I would put a sunroom on the back of the house," she said, with tears in her eyes. "I always wanted a sunroom for my plants, and he always said no." The next day Gretchen called a contractor. As she let her husband go, and let her pain go, energy filled her body. His silences of recent years had shut her down. By completely letting him go she became filled with her own self and with her defined needs, aspirations, and ambitions.

Two years later Gretchen experimented with living with a man she had been dating, and it did not work out well. She found herself doing too much homemaking, and his constant presence was an annoyance to her. But she did care for him a great deal. He, too, was divorced, and they both decided that they had "done that already." He kept his apartment, and they spent weekends and vacations together. Gretchen was at a point in her development when her home and her man were not the total meaning of her life. In fact, her most exciting venture was her work as a professional fund-raiser, a career carved out of her extensive experience as a volunteer. "We've decided to get married and hire a housekeeper when we are in our eighties," she laughingly told me.

Escape from Hopelessness

At a time of crisis a woman must fight the impulse to disengage. Disengagement is a process in which you become cynical and disappointed in the world. Often, disengagement is the response of a people-pleaser, who has been programmed not to have personal needs. You may believe that friends will not love you when you are not pulled together, that your needs are insignificant, or that there is great virtue in bearing your pain alone.

When a woman is in crisis, she may believe that her neediness is a weakness—that she should be able to manage alone as she has always done. So accustomed is she to living without sufficient help and investment from the outside that she does not reach out for what she needs. This response can create serious trouble for her ego.

Disengagement is dangerous because a person in crisis needs to find a way out. Disengagement is based on the belief that oneself is not worth any effort and that other people are impossible and disappointing. If one rejects the support and skills of others, the mind searches for other solutions. One way out of an emotional crisis is self-destruction. This response can take the form of unhealthy behaviors or addictions and can be as extreme as suicide, the ultimate self-destructive way out of a crisis. Another way out is for the disengaged person to get rid of someone else; here, negativity and hatred are mild forms and murder is the most extreme.

The escape from hopelessness is not to be found in suicide, revenge, or any milder destructive impulses. The answer is to be found in engagement with others who will provide a loving context for the struggle to cope and to change. The answer is to get help.

A client of mine went through an extremely difficult experience two years ago when her husband was stabbed on a street corner in New York. My client's husband was wounded, but with heroic help from two bystanders and an outstanding paramedic team he reached the hospital in time to get the necessary blood transfusions.

By the end of the day he had stabilized and his punctured lung was again functioning normally. The knife had not injured any other vital organs. In describing the experience later, he told her how he had fought for consciousness during the entire ordeal. The two of them cried tears of relief and were comforted by their many friends and relatives.

In the ensuing days, Amy felt a bitterness that she had a hard time shaking off. She felt betrayed by the world and even by her husband, who had reminded her that he was mortal. Up to this time Amy had felt anchored in her good marriage, but she now found herself grimly retreating and becoming detached. The part of her that had once been soft was like steel, braced for the next tragedy and the next.

She had to deal with family, friends, and business associates and the difficult adjustment of her children. In the midst of this turmoil, Amy was pouring her spirit into her husband during his days in the hospital. Although she was working hard to orchestrate these complicated events, she was clenching her jaws behind the scenes and no longer trusting in the sweetness of life. She had yielded to the temptation of disengagement, and in her heart of hearts she felt bitter.

One day during her husband's convalescence they both saw a program on television in which Fred Rogers talked about how to discuss with children the issue of violence in our world. His simple message was the turning point for Amy in this crisis. "Look to the helpers," he said. The act of one violent person will also lead you to witness the positive acts of police, doctors, and medical staff and the concern of friends. This message shed light on a bitter, dark place inside of Amy. She slowly let herself take in its meaning for her. In the days that followed she thought about the ambulance corps, the blood bank, the devoted nurses, her loving friends and family, the prayers, the gifts, and her courageous children. She finally let herself think of her beloved husband, who willed himself not to go into shock.

When she looked at the helpers, she found their support for life overwhelming. She could relinquish her rigidity when she let herself experience deeply the helpfulness of others. Whenever the female ego finds itself in a crisis, it is time for help. If a woman is going through an experience of grief, it is very important for her to do a lot of talking with close friends. A parent who has a severely ill child needs the support of other parents who have gone through a similar experience. A woman who is experiencing the crisis of relinquishing an addiction needs the supportive network to be found in organizations such as Alcoholics Anonymous. When a woman experiences a serious crisis for the first time in her life, she will often feel that she can now identify with the suffering in the world, that a part of universal human experience has been opened to her. Making contact with other people gives a comforting sense that we are all human together. Life is fragile, and life can be painful, but it does not help to shroud our lives in the veil of denial. The woman in crisis needs to become transparent so that other people will know her feelings and her needs. Crisis is a time to welcome the ego strength of others. Growth is accomplished by those whose egos reach out and connect them to sources of life.

⚜ 3 ⚜

Ego Building
for Women

Women are growing... braver, stronger,
more healthful, skillful and able and free.
More human in all ways.
            Charlotte Perkins Gillman

A few years ago I made a change from working as a therapist
in a counseling agency to opening my own private practice.
This change meant new freedom for me. My husband was the
president of the organization in which I had been practicing as a
therapist. By going off on my own, I was severing one of the
professional ties in our colleague marriage. It was important to me
to say to everyone, "I am not a coat-tail wife whose career follows
an easy path carved out by her husband." It was now my responsibility to maintain an office and generate my own business. The
rent bill would come to me, and there would no longer be someone
else to feed me clients, keep the books, or fill out the insurance
forms. I thought, It's all up to me!

Making that commitment was the beginning of my liberation
as a person. Personal energy was unleashed from within, energy
that I never knew was there. I began discovering my own intellectual potency, a capacity for empathy and insight, and a developing skill in emotional healing.

I am describing this process in hindsight, realizing that at the
time, even though I was growing in competence, I lacked self-
confidence. I was overly critical of myself, and I worked too hard,

53

as if I were compensating for a fear of failure. I was struggling with the belief that being a woman meant that I was inadequate. My talents were blossoming, and my ego was stumbling along, trying to keep up.

I was getting good at my work, but my progress was not reflected in my private sense of myself. My self-esteem suffered because of a fear that I was selfish. My culture had taught me that if you are born female, it's not nice to think you are terrific, even if other people seem to think so. Even when more clients than I could see were calling me for appointments, I wondered, Why are they calling me?

The roots of my lack of confidence had a lot to do with being a woman. My own analyst had been a man; my closest colleague and life partner is my husband; my mentors were men; even my singing teacher was a man. I am the granddaughter of a country doctor who was somewhat of a legend in northwestern Nebraska, and he was probably the human being I admired most in the world. No wonder I felt that anyone who came to see me was being cheated, being deprived by having to work with a woman, rather than with some wonderful male therapist. I hate to admit this, but I believed that men were better.

I held this view in spite of my indebtedness to feminist writers whose books were extremely helpful to me during the most painful years of my life—my twenties—when I did not know who I was or what I wanted. Through reading, I found support for my instinctive sense of what I clearly did not want for myself. Betty Friedan's *The Feminine Mystique* helped keep me on my search for a career path, and Simone de Beauvoir's *The Second Sex* nourished my spirit during two years when my life seemed to be at a dead end before it had really begun. I guess I had to grow into what these women were pointing toward before I could believe that a woman could be a complete person. I had to go beyond longing for my own ego. I had to possess and use my ego before I could relinquish the belief that men are better.

My shift into claiming my own ego as a woman, into loving myself and embracing self-confidence, has not been simply a result of feeling professionally competent, although that has helped. Nor is it a result of any simplistic "buck-up" therapy tools. In its depths, it is a matter of the heart.

Getting to know the women I have worked with over the years has been a profound experience for me. I have learned my lesson of ego building well, because again and again I have seen women who have been programmed to put themselves second (which often means last) begin to develop and grow. I offer my support as they face a world that is full of cultural challenges and often meager rewards for doing what they need to do. I watch as they deprecate their accomplishments because they fear that ego strength will mean loss of love. I witness growing self-esteem carrying these women through situations that are short on love. Then they begin to raise the consciousness of those around them. I see their self-respect winning the day, inspiring the respect of those they care about.

Three years ago my client Carol thought she would never survive the breakup of her unhappy marriage, on which she felt deeply dependent. Ill-prepared for earning an income, she entered a training program in a bank. Because she has used misfortunes as challenges, her ego has grown. Carol is advancing in her job, has a solid network of friends, and possesses self-respect. She is not a martyr but a strong woman who grew from a position of feeling like an unhappy victim to one of being proudly in charge of her life.

My client Jill was fired from a job in which she had invested many years of laying the groundwork for professional advancement. She had begun as a secretary and had become a public relations representative for her firm. She was working toward her goal of a supervisory position. A corporate reshuffling destroyed her plans. When she completed her mourning and let go of bitterness, she seized the opportunity to do something new. She and a friend are now running a successful catering business, and her life is working better than it ever has.

When I first met Denise, she believed that a woman's life should be created for her by someone else. In spite of the financial support of her wealthy family, her life was not working. Essentially passive, she had no deep relationships, nor could she find engaging work for herself. Underlying a beautiful facade was a woman who felt insignificant. For her, ego building consisted of learning to trust her instincts and follow her true interests, instead of dismissing them as inconsequential. She has found great joy in her work with a small repertory theater. Having once been overwhelmed by her powerful family, she has learned to claim her own power and use her ego to make her life work.

Witnessing the psychological growth of many women's egos has transformed my own perceptions of what being a female means. I learned to appreciate myself through appreciating other women. You, too, can learn deep self-confidence by realizing that you are one of many talented women working to be their best selves who want to be part of the action and show the world that females have egos, too.

How Is the Male Ego Different?

The male ego is basically healthy in its orientation toward meeting needs directly. When a man's behavior is confident and self-seeking, we know that his ego is alive and well. Pride and self-esteem emanate from a strong male ego whether he is forthrightly expressing himself or quietly planning his next move. Men in today's world are expanding the capacities of their egos to become more nurturing of others, yet most of them reach out to others from an established base of self-interest. Men are often criticized by women for being too self-centered, and sometimes this criticism is justified. But don't get sidetracked by believing that overbearing male egos are responsible for your ego weaknesses.

Ego Envy

When you feel angry at a man for his self-centered ways, it is helpful to take a step back and observe the dynamics of the situation.

Marriages—in fact, all relationships—tend to be lopsided in various ways. In a traditional marriage in which a man goes to work and a woman stays home and works with her children, there are built-in imbalances. If your own needs are not being met, you will think your husband is inordinately selfish if he decides to spend all day Saturday going fishing or playing golf. Just like a man, you say to yourself, always thinking about himself. If you are really upset about this state of affairs, you might blow up or talk him out of going. The psychological point to be made here is that your reactions have much more to do with yourself than with him. You are framing his quest for recreation within the context of your own starvation for recreation. You blame him for doing what you won't admit that you want to do.

You can be so out of touch with meeting your needs that you see the man in your life as overly self-seeking. Maybe he is being normal, and you are being self-depriving. When a woman is angry at a man it is often because he is doing what she wants to do. She is a victim of ego envy.

My client Maryanne came into therapy in a rage. "I am so angry at my boy friend George because he just committed two evenings a week to playing tennis." Her face was red, and her eyes spouted bitter tears. "And I am angry at myself for being ridiculous and unreasonable. But I resent him for being so selfish." "When are you going to take tennis lessons?" I asked her. A simple truth, but a blind spot for most of us when we are embroiled in jealous anger, is that when you are angry at a man for his "selfishness" you must ask yourself about your own lack of self-seeking. Instead of criticizing men for having overdeveloped egos it might be smart to learn a few tips from them.

House Husband

During our family's vacation in the Adirondacks last summer, my husband agreed to assume the role of house husband, an experiment many couples are trying when the wife's work requires her primary attention. At this point in my life my ego needed to focus on my writing and not be distracted by household logistics and meeting everyone else's needs. My ego needed support.

I was fascinated to learn how Steve would manage. My husband is not one of those new age guys who loves gourmet cooking—he only likes gourmet eating. When he and the kids left, I could not imagine what they would eat for the next few days. Driving from the airport in Saranac three days later, they regaled me with the most unbelievable menus: fried chicken with mashed potatoes, Salisbury steak with stewed tomatoes, cherry pie, apple cobbler. I thought I was in a dream. My husband had hidden talents—a man for all seasons, he was responding to the season of my career. After I had unpacked, Angela asked me if I wanted chicken or roast beef for dinner, and a giggling Michael added the words TV dinner.

Steve's ego is intolerant of trivia. His first instinct is, You gotta eat, so get a TV dinner. My self-worth is so wrapped up in being a nurturer that I want everyone to have a special experience eating food I have prepared. These feelings are largely in the trivia category. My kids were just as happy with Daddy's quickie chicken as they would have been with my all-day spaghetti sauce with fresh basil.

As I relinquished my duties to Steve, I saw that he did things the easy way so that he could play tennis, read a book, or fish in the lake. Frankly, his orientation is selfish: let's get these annoying tasks out of the way so I can do what I want to do and have some fun. I want to improve my tennis game, be intellectually stimulated, and get high on scenery. Would you as a woman give top priority to those three activities when you are with your family?

I was interested to observe where the kids fit into Steve's scenario. His idea was that the kids could come along and practice their tennis, read their books, and accompany him on the fishing jaunts. They fished for hours in remote parts of the lake, and I know they felt very close. His nurturance, however, was structured around doing what he wanted to do. When he had his fill of the kids, he clearly said so, and I took my turn. The pleasure and fulfillment of the individual self is the name of the game for the male ego.

A Picture of Health

To get an overview of female ego strength, let's look at the manifestations of a healthy female ego. What is a woman like when her ego is alive and well?

A woman with a healthy ego possesses a foundation of high self-esteem. This is not the same as narcissism or selfishness. It is the liking of self that enables a woman to receive life as a gift to be lived and expressed. She believes in the inherent goodness of her life and gives herself permission to follow its course with enthusiasm. She works to express her genuine self: her talents, her interests, and her unique personality. She does not function as an adapted person following a script written by someone else, being compulsively nice, or primarily waiting for and on other people. She responds to her environment, of course, but not as a slave. She searches out ways to express her true self.

Ego Means Problem Solving

A healthy woman is not burdened by layers of pain and guilt, and she has found her way out of female masochism and passivity. Indications of female ego strength are the seeking of joy and the deeply felt conviction that she deserves to live an expressive life. When trouble comes, as it does for everyone, she is committed to finding thoughtful solutions. Petty negativity is dismissed. Problems are not for suffering; they must be solved.

Ego Means Energy

A woman whose ego is really working for her does not spend her days in fantasy or dreams. She knows that life is at hand, and she seizes the moment to live with fullness. When a woman comes into therapy complaining of depression, I will ask her to describe the way she spends a typical day. It often becomes clear that she is living in a depressive lifestyle that would make almost anyone feel depressed. Seeking excitement and rejecting dull routines is a characteristic of women with healthy egos. I recently visited a friend whose enthusiasm I have always admired. She was cutting and pasting the layout for a newsletter she publishes herself. "Do you like doing that part of the process?" I asked her. She answered, "I rarely do anything that I do not enjoy." No wonder she seems so happy, I said to myself. Of course, there are times when tedious responsibilities need to be met, but a woman with a healthy ego arranges her life so that she has as little boredom as possible. When a woman is excited about life, she has energy.

Ego Means Confidence

A woman with a good ego has made peace with herself and is comfortable with her many facets, her contradictions, her endowments, and her history, and she feels free to get on with living. To test your ego in this area, ask yourself the following questions:
- Is there someone in your life who needs to change in order for you to be happy?
- Do you long for the childhood you never had?
- Are you angry or disappointed about flaws in your looks or your intellect?
- Is there something about your basic nature that you fruitlessly try to change?

If your ego is functioning well, you know yourself—what works for you and what doesn't. You do not try to change things that cannot be changed, and you do not torture yourself with criticism. At the same time, you work earnestly to be your best self.

Ego Means Individualism

A woman with a healthy ego has a clear identity. Her style is authentic. Although she may be complex, there is a wholeness, an integrity to her being. The key to this process lies in self-development and self-assertion. Women have a deep psychological fear about being separate and feeling alone. As a woman becomes more expressive, this fear often surfaces. One woman finally began to share her unusually clever sense of humor at social gatherings. Even though she became more popular, she had to get over the feeling of being unsafe and overexposed. Another woman began to dress in the bright colors that she loved, and another began to express her strong political views. Both shared with me moments of heightened insecurity over being different, which I translate to mean *separate*. Women who assert their genuine selves have character. You become a whole person when you stop hiding important parts of yourself. It takes ego strength to risk exposure and individualism, but it is ultimately very satisfying.

A healthy woman has a direct channel between what is felt and what is communicated. Such a woman is candid and spontaneous because she is not in hiding but is living in an expressive mode. She seems to be making an unspoken statement, "This is who I am."

One of the healthiest women I know grew up in a very large family with financial hardships. She is not a classic beauty, and she is small in stature. Jane's outstanding quality is that she really likes people, and as a result she has an unusual network of friends. Jane works in sales in a corporation. In spite of her less than impressive education and lack of business background, she has been tremendously successful. The reason is that she has a friendly and outgoing personality. She has such skill in dealing with people that her warmth and her confidence are contagious and people naturally gravitate toward her. There are many women who because of their beauty, background, or education approximate our stereotype of the ideal female. But when I think of Jane, who does not look like our culture's images of perfection, I know that ego strength is what creates a winning personality.

A woman with a healthy ego is unselfconscious. Her squeaky voice or her thick waist are part of a whole and acceptable package. To claim your ego, you must relinquish grandiose claims to being perfect or perfectly miserable and be happy with your human life. This acceptance can give you the freedom to soar in a professional or personal arena. Women with healthy egos are truly winners on the outside as well as the inside. Paradoxically, this healthy self-acceptance will not make you egotistical or obsessed with yourself but will lead you to *engagement in the activities in your life*.

Finding Your Inner Strength

There is a simple exercise that I often use in my work to help clients tune in to the meaning of mental health. Think of someone whose life you admire, and imagine having that person become your mentor and show you how to live a healthy life. It does not matter if you do not know the person you select. It can be someone famous, someone from history, or a favorite teacher, relative, or friend. The main idea is to select a hero or heroine or someone who particularly appeals to you.

When you select an individual, close your eyes and mentally picture that person in vivid detail, getting a sense of the essence of the person. Then ask the following questions one at a time and slowly probe your mind for the answer.

- What is this person's motivation?
- How does this person operate in life?
- How are her or his problems handled?
- How do you imagine she or he spends time?

By using your intuition you can get a firm grasp on the essential character of the person you want to learn from. Going through this process can give you a personal experience of the meaning of mental health.

The person your unconscious mind selects often is someone who is very much like yourself in some way. There is an old saying, "It takes one to know one." When you become aware of the women and men you admire, you are resonating with basic strengths inside of yourself. In therapy I help my clients figure out how their favorite people represent expressed or unexpressed parts of themselves. Try this exercise yourself. List five characteristics of the person you chose. Take the qualities one at a time, and look for ways in which you are the same. This is a way to discover your strengths.

I have found that many women admire Katherine Hepburn. She is a wonderful model for a woman in both her life and art, possessing unconventional good looks, exuding femininity and sexuality in every season of her life, wonderfully strong in her forthright, take-charge manner, tender and loving of men—matching their energy and not afraid of surpassing them in intelligence or conviction. She has honed her craft and achieved dazzling career success for several decades. She is a superb model for us to observe and identify with.

We should never be embarrassed to have heroines and heroes. This is an important way in which we learn how to be healthy people.

The Invisible Woman

The professor looked around the room at the new group of students. "Good morning and welcome," he said. "I'm Professor McCleary, and this is Social Welfare, Policy and Services 101, better known as SWAPS. To begin, I would like to go around the room and have each of you introduce yourself. Tell us about yourself and any agency experience you have had prior to being in the M.S.W. program." He started with a man to his left, who appeared to be just out of college.

Carolyn was the fifth person in the row. She was entering graduate school, now that her children were all in school. As the young man completed a single sentence and number two was off and running, Carolyn's heart began to pound so hard that she was certain that others could hear it. Her turn was coming soon. Number three had little to say, and number four launched into an opinionated speech about the policies of the agency from which she had taken a leave of absence. Carolyn could hear none of the words, only miscellaneous syllables. Her palms began to sweat. She did not realize that number four had stopped. "You, in the gray sweater," said Professor McCleary. "Who, me?" asked Carolyn.

Carolyn was struggling with a life script in which she functioned as an invisible woman. She was full of opinions, even passions and convictions. But to claim center stage for only a brief moment filled her with enormous anxiety. She clearly had contributions to make, even in that brief moment in SWAPS 101. She had been active in fresh air programs and had designed a successful senior citizens' program. Years of volunteer experience had given her good preparation for training as a social work administrator. But she shunned the limelight, afraid of the flaws that might show. She was most secure in the role of supporting and promoting others.

Many Women Are Repressed

Many talented women feel that it is not nice to seek attention and that they have little to say anyway. In working with successful career women, I have seen many of them struggle to outgrow their timidity. I have seen professional women who are afraid to ask their colleagues for client referrals, secretaries who suffer over the prospect of requesting a much deserved raise, managers who wait to be asked instead of presenting their solutions to problems. I recently worked with a female lawyer who was shy about asking for money that was owed to her by a delinquent client. When a woman has been trained to be a facilitator of others, she often does not learn to take risks on behalf of herself. She limits her growth by not putting herself on the line.

Speak Up!

It is time for women to come out of hiding. Instead of asking, "Who, me?" it is time to say, "Here I am!" We need more female egos running our world. I do not want to take a simplistic view that implies that women could solve all the problems that men are struggling with in their positions of power. At the same time, I believe that the long history of women functioning primarily as nurturers has given them skills and perspectives that are very much needed in this world. The female ego has a strong and accurate sense of how things should be done for the human good. As civilizing and socializing forces, as accomplished nurturers and seekers of values, females have unique and valuable contributions to make. But the female ego must resist being pigeonholed into menial or dead-end jobs with little true authority or responsibility. Women should not let themselves be ignored.

Ask yourself the following questions:

- Am I comfortable asking for support from an authority figure? It is important for you to be in charge of seeing that your own needs are met, whether the need is a salary increase or help around the house. If you expect to be rescued by those whom you view as authorities, your ego is not taking charge of meeting your needs.

- Do I express my honest opinions during meetings? If your pattern is to act pleasant and blend into a group, you may be fooling yourself into believing that you are a participant. If you want to be part of the action of your life, your voice must be part of every event in which you participate.

- If I disagree with someone, do I say what I think? You may have the female habit of expressing yourself only when you have something pleasant to say. The truth is that solid critical suggestions are the ones that lead to constructive growth and change. If you are forever positive you are not very powerful.

- Am I comfortable making a speech before a group of people? Your answer indicates how at home you are in the world. If you are full of fears, you have not learned to see other people as colleagues with whom you can share as an equal. You can conquer your fears by taking a course in public speaking, which will give your ego a great boost.

- Do I hide behind small talk most of the time? This is a way to diminish yourself. When you do not let others hear your ideas and your deeper concerns, you convince yourself as well as them that you are a lightweight. Dig deeper and express what really interests and concerns you, rather than being superficial in your communications.

- Do I take charge or change the subject when I am bored? One way to hide is to go along with whatever is happening. A woman with an ego shapes the situations in which she finds herself by offering direction. You must practice asking questions, changing the subject, and offering your agenda if you want to be part of what is going on.

Victims Are Autistic

The feeling of being a victim is very often what holds an invisible woman back. In certain jobs, or in relationships with certain men, she feels as if the whole world is against her. The perpetual neediness of her children grinds her down to the point that she not only has no ego strength but little physical strength as well. She becomes another of the silent women of the world. Internally she subsists on martyr strokes, congratulating herself for biting her tongue, smiling instead of crying, and being endlessly patient with boredom. She is a victim and has found a way to cope.

Merely coping is not a solution. It causes miseries to go psychologically underground, where deep mental and physical damage ferments. The role of victim is not acceptable, especially when we need the talents of women in our world.

There is an alternative to being a victim, no matter what your circumstances might be. Victims help to cause their limited situations by being silent and withdrawn or by talking about trivia, which is another way of hiding. A realized woman *must start talking*: asking, criticizing, complaining, discussing, analyzing. When she lets her voice be heard about the things that really concern her, it will become stronger.

Overcoming the Fear

Becoming visible is not an easy task. Fear of being put down is often what keeps a woman silent. An even deeper fear that can keep you shut down is *your fear of losing love*. If you are trying to become more expressive, here are some principles that I have learned from working with my clients.

• Expressiveness is learned in small steps. Practice first in less important areas, and slowly move to the more important ones.

- Big blowups are not the same as healthy self-assertion but come from people who keep the lid on their feelings and opinions most of the time.

- Effective self-expression is not accusative of others but is a statement of personal views. Practice saying, "*I* think..." and "*I* feel..." instead of the accusatory sentence that begins with "You..."

- Be understanding of those who react badly to your new behavior. Don't let their negativeness limit you. Realizing that their behavior is a manifestation of their insecurity will help you not to feel intimidated by insecure bullies.

- Be prepared for people who have enjoyed feeling superior to you and will not like you as a confident person. Give them time to get used to seeing you as one of the confident people in the world.

All I remember about a summer spent at Vacation Bible School is a verse from the book of Matthew about not keeping your light under a bushel. Do we not have a moral imperative to let our lights shine? When will your light brightly shine in the human galaxy?

Who, me? Yes, you.

How Does Your Ego Work?

It has been important to me as a therapist to understand that wonderful mechanism, the ego. The ego is the mechanism that allows you to interact with your environment and to meet your needs as fully as possible. This mental system ensures your survival and facilitates your functioning on many, many levels.

Dynamic Stability

First of all, the ego is a stabilizer, keeping you balanced between excitement and peace of mind. How wonderful it is to be excited, and what pleasure there is in being at peace.

As you know, the stresses of living tend to push us out of the normal emotional range. Instead of being excited, we feel driven, overstimulated, and exhausted. Instead of feeling peaceful, we can feel bored, empty, and lethargic. If your ego is really working for you, when you become too excited you will seek peace. When you feel a bit lethargic, you will seek pleasant stimulation. This keeps you in a dynamic stability in which you are alive (but not manic) and serene (but not bored).

What do you do for yourself when you are feeling overly stimulated? Every woman needs her own set of tools for relaxing when she needs to. One woman I know re-reads a favorite novel after a stressful day. A soothing scented bath, some yoga exercises, or a solitary walk are all tools for a woman to use for finding peace within herself.

What do you do when life is tedious and boring? Learning something new, varying your routines, or making environmental changes are important tools. One woman I know regularly moves her furniture around, and another takes many different routes on her walk to work, simply to create variety and stimulation.

A collection of these strategies will keep you in a healthy rhythm between excitement and peacefulness. Your ego alerts you when you are in trouble and need to use one of your techniques.

The Ego Meets Your Needs

Another function of the ego is to meet your specific needs. A sharp ego will direct you to the need that is most important. In the following example let us look at Sally's needs and how she met them.

Sally, who has a strong ego, just got home from work. She was almost in the living room when she went back and locked the door to her apartment (safety). She went to the bathroom (physical comfort) and then put the frozen lasagna in the microwave (hunger for food). She sat down to watch her favorite television program (rest and laughter) until John got home. She jumped up and greeted him, and they talked over a glass of wine (intimacy and love). They had dinner (food, strokes). After dinner Sally finished her report for work (finish work) and then went for a long walk alone (exercise, centering). When she got home she made love with John (sex, love, intimacy) and fell asleep (rest and peace).

Had Sally's ego been malfunctioning, she might have procrastinated on her report or not taken the walk she needed to release tension. She might have taken her walk with John and missed the chance for communion with herself. She might have denied her sexual needs, forgotten to eat, or left her door unlocked. Fortunately, because she has a solid ego, her day ended well.

If you have inhibitions about meeting your own needs, then your ego is unable to function properly. If you are not adequately meeting your own needs, you might find yourself wishing at times that someone would take care of you. The answer is for you to devote conscious attention to yourself, making certain moment by moment that you are doing what you need to do for *yourself*, until adequate self-care becomes an automatic, habitual response to your needs. Some women are so out of touch that they do not take adequate care of the basics: food and rest.

Your Ego Sets Priorities and Makes Decisions

The ego makes decisions within the process of meeting needs. Using her ego, Sally knew that she should lock her door and put on the food *before* she sat down. The ego answers the question, What shall I do next? The ego makes thousands of decisions, functioning very much like a computer—gathering information and sorting it out. It works like this: What shall I have for dinner? I don't feel like cooking so it must come from the freezer. John likes pasta. I love pasta. I want something light so I'll just have a little bit. The lasagna is good and easy. This thinking and processing is almost instantaneous for a healthy ego. When a person is suffering from mental fatigue or psychological stress, one of the first functions to burn out is the decision-making capacity.

A typical symptom of a woman on a burnout course is that she cannot decide what to wear or what to eat. If you blank out when faced by a menu or a closet full of clothes, you need a mental rest to get your decision-making faculties cooking again. If you are chronically sluggish, you may need to give your ego some challenges to sharpen decision-making skills. If your ego is not working well in this area you need to ask a basic question: Am I overloaded with responsibility (burned out) or underloaded (unchallenged)? Many women who function poorly are either burned out yet pushing themselves to do more, or underchallenged yet seeking rest from the exhaustion of boredom.

One of the areas in which many women need to grow is in setting priorities—deciding what is important and what is not. Women can stay in low-level jobs simply because they are so detail-oriented or task-oriented that they do not form long-range goals for themselves. Their inability to distinguish the large issues from the small ones makes them poor prospects for positions of authority. You need to have perspective and use judgment in deciding what is important and what is not.

Try these exercises in setting priorities:

- List the three most important things you did today in order of their importance. Next, do the same for last week, last month, and last year.
- List the five most valuable people in your life and why they are important to you.
- Describe where you would like to be in five years. Then list the steps you need to take to get there.
- List the three most satisfying activities in your life and the amount of time spent on those activities per week. Then list the three least satisfying activities and the amount of time they engage you.

This thinking develops a strong ego. It is only when you know what is important and what is not that you can focus on the large issues of your life.

I once worked with a woman who complained that she never could make decisions. I asked her for examples, and these were some she gave: Where do I want to go for the weekend? What shall I wear? Whom shall I invite? The truth was that she used these questions as ways to waste her time obsessing about details, thus avoiding making decisions. Making hairsplitting decisions will get you nowhere. You need to think about the important issues such as, What is my best talent? In what business can I make the most money? What will enhance the quality of my life? How can I plan for a good future?

The Ego Decides How to Respond

A woman with a healthy ego not only chooses what to eat for dinner with dispatch but also chooses how to respond to any given situation. A strong ego will allow you to stop, think, and respond as you want to. You are not a victim of stimuli. If a superior at work calls you in and criticizes your performance, you can choose to laugh, disagree, agree, not respond, apologize, ask questions, get angry, be quiet, request another chance, justify yourself, or cry. Your response will be based on an integration of the truth, the politics, and your feelings. You will be firmly on your own side and choosing your move well.

You may not believe this, but other people do not create your emotional responses—you do. When a woman says, "He made me cry," or "He hurt my feelings," I do not agree. If you were raised with an older brother who bullied you to tears, you have within yourself a conditioned response to cry when someone gives you a hard time. There are other emotional options, however, and the female ego must choose her responses. Otherwise she will feel like a hopeless victim of other people.

How can you gain control of your responses? One way is to be in control of the "causes." Choose the environments, the work, and the people to whom you naturally respond positively. But we cannot always control the world. If you habitually respond in a way that you do not like, practice having a delayed reaction. For a woman who cries in therapy every time she mentions her father, it is clear that these are not tears of cathartic release but an exercise in helplessness. "Stop crying," I will say. As she learns to say this to herself, she gains control over her responses and gains in ego strength. An automatic angry response needs similar controls. Learn to delay your response. Have no response. Then rationally *choose* your response. In an age of therapies that encourage cathartic release, this may seem like odd advice. I believe strongly in the value of primal release if there is work to be done on deep trauma or grief. But in the living of your life, excessive emotional reactions are a waste of energy, and they put you at the mercy of others. We need our egos to help us live down women's reputations for being hysterical.

The Ego Solves Problems

The ego helps solve problems. To do this effectively the ego must gather and assimilate information. If, for example, you are unhappy in your job, your ego needs to scan the outside world for information: What other jobs are available? Whom do I know who is happy in her job? What do the books say? What do my contacts have to say? The ego also scans one's memory bank and accesses pertinent information. What was my best job? What am I most happy doing? For women particularly it is important to ask, What did my mother always say? Was she right? Your ego puts all this information together and comes up with an answer. Sometimes there is a eureka moment, a creative leap, which puts it all together. This is the case when a frustrated dancer and animal lover finds happiness as a choreographer for dancing bears. Sometimes there is laborious trial and error, and your ego informs you, "No, that's not it yet." Your ego regulates your needs against the available supplies. The solution may be that this is the best we can do for now, and we will keep an eye out for better in the future. With an eye to reality and sensitivity to inner needs your ego gets you on your own best track.

Many of the women I work with put their energy into complaining instead of problem solving. The ego's function is to solve problems. When you expend your energy in complaining, the ego becomes overwhelmed. You are telling yourself, This problem is not solvable. Women are not afraid, as are many men, of appearing to be a wimp. They will play a good round of what Eric Berne called "Ain't it awful" with friends and mates. Instead of getting an ego boost from solving their problems, they get what are called secondary gains, in the form of attention from others and temporary relief from having to *do* something about the situation. These are rewards for neurotic behavior, in this case being a complaining victim. When you discharge your problems by sharing them in the form of complaining, stop yourself. The motto of the female ego should be: Problems Are to Be Solved.

The Ego Knows the Difference between the Inner World and the Outer World

You can evaluate the competence of your ego by testing your skills in observation. Since you need to process information in order to solve problems, how good are you at getting the facts straight? In life, you deal with two sets of facts. There is the outside world, which some people call reality, and there is the inner world of feelings, thoughts, memories, and fantasies—so you deal with facts from inner space and outer space. If I fantasize about flying saucers, that does not mean that I actually saw flying saucers. If I am afraid of men with black mustaches, that does not mean there is one in my closet. And if I imagine that my husband is angry, that does not mean that he is. The ego must clearly separate what is happening inside from what is happening outside. This is the first phase of what psychologists call reality testing.

Women with separation anxiety often try to merge mentally or emotionally with other people. Their vision of the perfect human experience is one in which two people beat with the same heartbeat, feel the same feelings, and think with the same mind. This is not possible. A woman with the urge to merge can be confused about how what she is feeling is separate from what the other person is feeling.

"I know my husband can learn to love music," says the woman whose husband is tone deaf. "Alice will enjoy ballet just as I did," says the woman whose daughter would prefer basketball. "I'm sure my boss senses I'm unhappy," says a woman who is suffering silently. The point is that your reality is *always different* from the reality outside of you. Learning to be comfortable with separation and incongruence will make your ego strong and your life more exciting. The fantasy of merging is only a fantasy and a boring one!

The Ego Knows What Is Happening in Both the Self and the Environment

Your ego must be a sharp and accurate scanner of the environment, picking up information about opportunities and politics. Provincialism won't get you very far. Your ego will grow as you see yourself as part of a larger world. Your ego must also run an internal scan, following your own emotional processes and receiving the messages that your body, feelings, dreams, and fantasies are communicating. Dig into your deepest concerns, your most vital interests, and particularly your most challenging problems so you can deal with what is happening inside yourself.

The Ego Knows What Is Happening within Other People

The next level of ego growth is the development of empathy. You first view other people as part of the outer world. Then you go beyond, listening to another person so as to know her or him from the inside out. You must not confuse your feelings with those of the other person, even though you can feel her or his inner feelings.

Empathy is a strong capacity of the egos of many women, just as it is an undeveloped capacity in many men. Women often can read people, decipher body language, and respond to what is going on inside others with great skill. There are some women, however, who have not developed this ability.

A woman who understands other people can be a strategist par excellence. She can maneuver around difficult people, knowing precisely what their needs are. She can therefore get a lot done.

The Ego Can Observe the Self

In doing therapy with women, the most exciting point is when they use the observing ego. To be in an important situation and to be able to detach and see it as an outsider gives you an indescribable sense of personal power. It is as though the moment is a play and you become a member of the audience who observes everything, even yourself. Then you become the stage director of one of the characters yourself. By maneuvering one character—yourself—you can change much of what happens.

At a business lunch, the point is to be socially involved and yet make a business contact as well. Perhaps you are trying to sell something, make a deal, or at least make a lasting impression. As you talk, your observing ego listens and reports to you. It's going okay, or You had better not say what you had planned to say, or Move in now and make the deal. This technique involves a double level of functioning in which you both plot your moves and keep the ball rolling. This is the quality of thinking well on your feet. Your eyes are scanning the audience, and you quickly respond to the demands of the moment in a clever and thoughtful manner.

One of the most important ways for the observing ego to work for you is for it to be benevolent. Sometimes a woman will report that a voice in her head says, Oh, you klutz, you shouldn't have said that, or I don't think you have a chance to succeed here. Be sure that your observing ego works on your own behalf. The observations should be positive and constructive, helping you to win. With this system working for you, you will be alert and will feel in control of social situations—even those that don't go exactly as you would like them to.

The observing ego gives you a most important human capacity: perspective. This quality will make you more truly wise and intelligent than will the possession of a high IQ. A woman who is too invested in her own point of view often is being less than smart. The observing ego allows you objectively to see what you are doing. Such clear seeing allows you to enjoy yourself when you are doing well and correct yourself when you need improvement.

The Self-Seeking Ego

If life is a play and we are the characters, each of us is cast in a particular role. In this play of life there are starring roles, supporting roles, character parts, tragic heroines, comediennes, servants, walk-ons, and understudies. How do you get the role you want? In the drama of life, the stars are the ones with the best egos. These are the people whose psychological equipment works for them. If they have talent, they pull it together and express it. If they show promise, they go on toward fulfillment. If they are precocious, they follow the path toward mature expression. Even if they are losing, they know how to change to a winning course.

Many women tend to resist this truth. When we see a woman who apparently has everything she wants, we tend to think of her as lucky. We forget that her fit body is the result of her commitment to a diet and exercise plan; her good marriage has taken work and struggle; her career is the result of grueling years of training; and her home is the result of planning and hard work.

Michelle, a client of mine, suffered painful sibling rivalry with her younger sister. After returning from a weekend visit to her sister's home, she tearfully told me that not only was her sister beautiful and had a wonderful family but that some of her pottery was displayed in the local jewelry store. I questioned Michelle. Why does your sister have it made? Was her life handed to her on a silver platter? The answers contained the truth behind all successes. She worked very hard at her life and in doing so, she developed a strong and healthy ego which continued to make things work for her.

Women with healthy egos know that they have to work at life, just as a leading lady in a play must learn her lines, must keep herself looking good, and must cultivate her own distinctive style. This is hard work, and a woman must do it for herself. It is a real challenge to organize the lives of your children, to make a sales call, to create a polished look for the office, to keep the books, or to order the supplies for a family business. The women who run their lives well have good working egos.

It's OK to Have an Ego

Sometimes the term "ego" is used in a negative context. A woman can "overassert her ego." People can have too much ego or overly sensitive egos. Egomaniacs are worse yet! So much for being overdone. What a tragedy it would be if Mozart had lacked the ego strength to conceptualize his unique works, or Rembrandt, or Shakespeare, or Sigmund Freud. Large—even grand—egos can produce great work. I have come to realize that ego does not mean the promotion of the self as much as it means the *application and expression of the self.*

Often when we criticize someone for having too much ego we mean that the person is being overbearing with others. This behavior indicates a lack of cooperation with other people and an obsessive desire to dominate. It is a form of antisocial behavior that often results from deep inner insecurity. It certainly has nothing to do with having a good ego. Ego strength simply means that you are full of life and health. If we are to explore the ways in which your ego works and how it can work better, we must start from a friendly place, believing that it is neither good nor bad to have an ego; it is a fact of life.

A Sense of Entitlement

Self-esteem is the fertile soil in which a strong and healthy ego thrives. A person with a good ego does not question her right to have the role she most wants to play. She wants the best for herself and seeks it directly, efficiently, and skillfully. She lives her life as well as she possibly can.

But isn't this selfish? asks the voice of self-doubt. Having a strong ego is being selfish in a positive sense, for women with strong egos have the most to give. *A person with a healthy ego gives from a full cup, not an empty one.* She gives lovingly but never gives all. She is at the center of her own life and belongs to herself. She prizes herself and is therefore prized by others.

The Age of the Female Ego

This is the period in history when the female ego is coming into its own. Women today laugh at Freud's notion of penis envy. A woman therapist recently said to me, "Why would I want to have anything different from my wonderful female body?" This is the time for women to think their thoughts, to express their opinions, and to become themselves. This is our time. The best thing that is happening in our society today is the growth and development of women. Women across many generations have embraced the rich and varied facets of the human potential movement, and they have used these tools for their growth and evolution.

I recently went to Minnesota to visit my mother, who has spent her life as a homemaker. In her sixties she is no more a traditional homemaker today than I am—although she used to be. Her bookcases are filled with the books that have helped her to grow. From Erich Fromm to Eric Berne, she has assimilated what works for her. Although once she was housebound, she now is deeply involved as a volunteer counselor and in an exercise program with aerobic dancing and cross-country skiing.

It has been valuable for me to be able to see my mother as a role model for myself, yet it has been only recently that I have allowed myself to take this step. Up until this time, like many other women, I thought of my male mentors as role models for acting properly in the world. Another role model is my physician grandfather, and I always thought that he was my source of training for practicing healing in an office. But if I am honest, I realize that when I am with a client I act more like my mother and my aunt than like my grandfather.

My mother has always been centered in her body and has been fascinated by nutrition and the effects of exercise. As a result of her influence I feel a healthy acceptance of my body. I never worry about my health because my mother taught good self-care. She also modeled for me the ability to have fun. She is very playful, and I realize that she programmed into me an early warning system for stress. I have complete permission to have recreation and fun in the middle of a busy life.

Perhaps the most significant quality that my mother has demonstrated to me and to everyone who knows her is generosity of spirit. She does not believe that you can spoil people by giving to them, and she does not play withholding games. Because I live in a world in which there are many levels of deprivation, and I work in a profession in which a suspicion of neurosis and bad motivation abounds, the generosity of spirit my mother modeled has been a beacon of truth in helping me resolve conflicts. At times when I feel discouraged, I tune into her philosophy of life that generosity, warmth, and giving will create healing.

It is my hope that in the future successful women will understand themselves in other ways than by identifying with their fathers or male mentors. In this age of the female ego women can respect and model themselves after other women. In doing so, women can experience new levels of peace of mind and psychological integration. Following other women makes it easier for a woman to love herself. We may feel like immigrants who have traveled to larger worlds, but we do not need to disparage our beginnings. I am especially impressed with the earnest desire to grow that I witness in women clients. At a time when there is much to lament about the state of our planet, I see women's successes in developing themselves as a powerful source of hope. Women are developing their egos with a perseverance that is impressive. This is the age of the female ego.

4

The Female Ego
in Childhood

> Attachment is the great fabrication of illusion. Reality can be attained only by someone who is detached.
>
> Simone Weil

Women Are Programmed

Your childhood is always with you, influencing you. Your early years are your foundation, and your present life has a great deal to do with how firm that foundation is. Through conditioning—a system of influences, rewards, and punishments—we are trained to follow our scripts. The first act of conditioning is often in the naming of a child.

What's in Your Name?

Understanding the meaning of your name might require some clever detective work. A few examples can help you get on the track.

- Being named after a person can indicate that you are expected to follow in that person's footsteps.
- Being given a name that was thought to be beautiful can be an expression of love, as well as an expectation that you will be beautiful and a source of pleasure.
- Women given the first names of men or family surnames often have traditional male expectations such as academic or career success.

80

• Some names require specific virtues such as Grace, Amity, Faith, and Hope.

When you understand the meaning of your name, you will understand the beginning of your script. There is nothing wrong with having a script or being conditioned. This part of the parenting process is a given fact of life. We all need to be socialized and shown how to live. There is a point, however, when a woman must use her ego to break away from the part of her conditioning that confines her. She needs to take charge of her own life as an adult, and this means writing her own script. I have known several women who have changed their names at times of personal growth and change.

Coming to Terms with Your Past

We do not have to follow our programming. In fact, many of us rebel or make alterations because what was intended for us is not in harmony with our own desires for ourselves, or even with the era in which we live. Nonetheless, the influence of the past is strong, whether you are flowing with the basic plan or rebelling against it. To know your own script you must go back and analyze your childhood closely and determine what is controlling you from that time that is not in your awareness. You need to be aware that you were assigned a script and are not as free as you would like to be.

Try to analyze what your parents' expectations for you were and possibly still are. Ask yourself: What kind of a woman did my father expect me to be? What kind of a woman did my mother expect me to be? Have I fulfilled their expectations? Are their wishes in conflict with my own desires? In our culture it is more acceptable for boys than for girls to be rebellious. Boys are allowed to choose more unexpected adventures in the process of separating from the family. One of the most important questions for a woman to ask herself is, How obedient am I to the expectations of other people? The problem with being excessively obedient is that it can cause you to live an unauthentic, robotlike life. *The task of the female ego is to be authentic.* This is the solution to the problems of childhood and is often a major concern in therapy.

The Birth of the Ego

When we are tiny embryos in the womb, we are part of the body of another person. At a certain point in physical growth, we are ready to be born, to press forward, and to do certain things for ourselves. The proverbial cutting of the cord literally puts the human creature on its own.

But psychologically there is a delay in achieving independence. In the mind of the baby, the mother still is part of itself. The baby is in what is called the symbiotic phase, which means that it cannot conceive of separateness because it does not yet have an ego. This is a period of immaturity and dependency on the part of the baby which means I am hungry = you feed me; I am not comfortable = you comfort me.

An understanding of the symbiosis and dependency of early life is extremely important to understanding female psychology for several reasons. Every person, baby boys and girls alike, goes through the experience of being helplessly dependent on the nurturing figure in her or his life. It is normal and human to have dependency needs, and the extent to which they are satisfied allows the next stage to take place, which is the development of an independent ego. Even after we outgrow the infantile experience of dependency, dependency is one theme of human life which deserves attention, and as adults we still base our independent achievement partly on the encouragement, support, and assistance of other people. Although the theme of dependency and attachment may be the same in early development for boys and girls, a striking cultural difference manifests itself later in life.

In working with women, I have found that it can be very meaningful for them to face up to and accept their dependency needs. Women need to fulfill these needs, and there is nothing wrong with doing so. From the days of infancy we need to have helpers who are devoted to making our egos feel strong, and, paradoxically, this support is what allows a woman to be truly independent. When a woman allows herself to accept that she needed nurturing when she was a baby, whether those needs were fulfilled or not, she is able to understand more fully what she expects from a lover later on. She is also able to appreciate that she may continue to provide nurturing for men and yet she may be stuck because nobody is providing devoted, loving care to her. When we accuse a woman of being too dependent, we are often describing a woman who is truly needy.

Ideally, for the ego to have the appropriate initial nurturing, the mother does for the baby everything that the baby cannot do for itself and does not let the baby experience the painful frustration of unmet needs. Psychologically, this nurturing is an experience of merging. A mother has the capacity to merge her ego with her baby. This is what we sometimes call maternal love or empathy. The mother responds to her baby as if the baby's feelings were her own. Babies cannot ask for what they want, but their mother knows. Soon all the funny cries and gurgles become familiar communications. "She's tired, that's her cranky cry." This is not an intellectual exercise. It is an urgent, even passionate empathy. A mother can be in great discomfort when her baby cries. She feels the baby's feelings as her own, and when she meets her baby's needs, she is at peace. When a mother surrenders to this symbiosis, she lends her baby her ego and her wisdom and her body to meet the baby's needs.

Gradually the baby begins to develop an ego, but it will not be well developed for about two years. The first sign that a baby is developing an ego is best observed when the baby cries to be fed. The mother gets up to prepare herself for nursing or to prepare the formula. The baby stops crying and *waits*. In that silent moment the baby's mind is somehow comforting itself by knowing what is to come. The baby can sustain a moment of true separation. For a minute or two she has an ego, separate and self-supporting. In the midst of being needy, the baby relies on her own thoughts instead of on her mother. Paradoxically, by counting on a nurturer's reliability, a baby can develop a separate self.

In normal development, the ego is born when a child is approximately two years old. This is not a very happy time for a child because it is not fun to realize that she has been deluded, that she is, in fact, a separate self—and a little one at that. A baby feels powerful and large when attached to mommy and feels little and frightened as the symbiosis with mother loosens. The birth of the ego is a time of conflict and pain. Strangers seem threatening, so the child clings to the mother. But although mother's lap is safe, it is beginning to be boring. The birth of the ego ushers in a phase of growing and separating aptly called the "terrible twos." It is push-pull time with the mother, who cannot do anything right, and a time of incredible assertion—"I do it 'self!"

The developmental issues here are the same for males and females—the need to be adequately nurtured as well as the need to detach from the nurturing object. If you are to take your ego seriously, you must take these basic needs very seriously. In helping women examine their early childhood programming we look at whether their love needs and their needs for independence were thwarted.

The first question for you to ask is, How satisfying and constant was my period of symbiosis? Did I receive enough holding, demand feeding, stroking, and playing? Most of us know whether our mothers were comfortable with these activities. It is significant if a sibling was born before you reached the age of two, causing your mother's premature detachment. Dependency needs must be fulfilled in order for independence to take place.

The second issue involves whether your mother or other caregiver really allowed you to be independent. When you finally realized that you were a separate person, and subsequently fell in love with the world, did your mother let you separate from her? Did she let you spit out your cereal, be Marco Polo exploring freely around the house, try to do everything yourself? Sometimes mothers allow their own insecurities or controlling ways to interfere with a child's efforts to grow and differentiate from her. Or a mother can be so good at the symbiosis period of the relationship that she does not know how to respond to the separate child.

And finally, was your mother able to "roll with the punches"? We certainly expect a lot—if not too much—of mothers, and I will explore this subject more fully in the chapter on motherhood. The mother's job during the "terrible twos" is to allow the child her independence and then to let her come back and pretend to be a baby again. Support of both activities is necessary. Contradictory as it might seem, dependency supports independency. The child knows when ego strength is depleted and she needs another dose of mother's magic. Some theorists call this internalizing a good object, which, translated, means carrying mother's loving face around in your head. At this age, a young child needs it both ways: delighted approval for independent behavior and large doses of tender, loving care.

Symbiosis and the Female Ego

Some of the women with whom I have worked are in a symbiotic conflict with their mothers. They feel independent and resourceful in living their lives. But when they are with their mothers they seem to lose their sense of themselves. They experience a powerful invitation from their mothers to regress, to feel little, needy, and cared for. One woman client is revolted by the sentimental cards that her mother sends her, and another is angered and upset by a weekly packet of inspirational literature and articles of advice from her mother. A woman once said to me, "It would be easier to love my mother if she did not try to kill me with kindness." These women are still fighting their way out of a symbiotic trap. The issue here is the struggle not to let oneself be infantilized by a mother who still sees in her grown daughter a dependent little child.

There is an exercise that I have used many times with women who need to complete their psychological separation from their mothers. Because a woman and her mother are of the same sex, a woman cannot grasp her separateness as easily as a boy can. Whether you feel rejecting of your mother or feel affection for her, this exercise can help you to experience separation.

Begin by naming a characteristic of your mother's, and counter that characteristic with the way in which you are different. When you do this exercise, write down each sentence. It will go like this.

My mother likes to cook.
I like to cook, but only on the weekends.

My mother likes a man who putters around the house.
I like a man who wants to play tennis.

My mother likes to visit her sister once a week.
I can't stand to be at her sister's house.

My mother enjoys concerts.
I prefer going to the movies.

Make a list that includes as many items as come to mind. When you come upon an aspect in which you both seem to be the same, find the shade of difference. People are never identical. Be sure to list the qualities that bug you about your mother. When you are still hooked on symbiosis, you tend to think that your mother has to be the way you want her to be in order for you to be happy. Here is a way to work through that problem. Read through the list slowly. End each statement by saying, "and that's OK with me." It will go like this:

My mother likes to visit her sister once a week, and that's OK with me.
I can't stand to be at her sister's house, and that's OK with me.

Work with yourself until you can let both yourself and your mother be separate people. Accept differences, and you will claim your own ego.

Attachment and Separateness

A mature adult's model of going out in the world for challenge and excitement, and then returning home for love, is not very different from the way a two-year-old functions. When I work with women who find independent pursuits difficult or painful, I often find that there is not enough love in their lives. Some of the best consciousness-raising groups for women are the ones that provide an oasis of loving support.

A Woman's Stroke Diet

In examining the development of your ego, an important question to ask is, How do I get my strokes? This is one of the most useful things you can know about yourself. A personal stroke diet, originally developed in childhood, is what shapes a woman's life. We are conditioned by what is withheld as much as by what is given. If we do not get recognition, we will soon run out of steam.

In working with their own children, women have a good understanding of the principles of behavior modification. Children, like puppies, are influenced by what behaviors their mother praises and what she scolds, and they begin to adjust themselves to their mothers' smiles and frowns.

This process continues into adulthood as we adjust ourselves to one another according to how we are being stroked. Since women often identify themselves with the process of giving strokes, they often are out of touch with what they are receiving. Because we hunger for attention, the quality of the attention a woman gets or the lack of attention largely influences how she spends her life.

Small Strokes Can Meet Our Needs

There is a secret about strokes that I have recently come to understand and have seen work miracles. Most strokes are small ones, and small strokes are often the best because they are the most easily assimilated. And you have it in your power, no matter what is going on in your life, to go out and bring them to you.

You could compare a needy, stroke-starved woman to someone lost in a desert for several days. Once she has been found, she is brought to a local hospital. Even though her hunger is great, she is not fed a six-course dinner. She could not yet tolerate it. Instead, she is fed a cup of soup, one small spoonful at a time. This may not seem adequate for the great inner need for food, but eventually small bits of nourishment, spoon by spoon, will satisfy her.

When working with a withdrawn or stroke-hungry woman, I begin her treatment by searching for small ways in which she can increase her strokes. She usually is not ready for big strokes such as falling in love, landing the perfect job, or taking a great vacation. My suggestions may seem puny, but they work. Exchange a warm greeting with the people with whom you do business—a newspaper carrier, a cashier, the dry cleaner. Call your friends regularly; enjoy the sunshine; wear a pretty scarf. Your goal is to get used to receiving easily assimilated positive strokes.

One of the best strokes I received recently was from a man who cuts the grass of the house we rented during August. After a long day of typing, I went for a walk with my husband. When we returned, there was a little basket filled with freshly picked green beans and a note: "For your dinner." That stroke made me feel wonderful.

The Problem with Insufficient Strokes

Many women simply do not get enough strokes. Sometimes a woman does not even know that she is emotionally undernourished. She is so focused on what she can *give* that she forgets that her well can run dry. Ultimately it is very demoralizing not to receive rewards that recognize, if not compensate, you for your efforts. In the traditional woman's work of nurturing others, compliments and solid feedback are often lacking. In the world of work, where many women are struggling for their places, the rewards can be insufficient both in recognition and money.

Many women possess remarkable inner strength and reward themselves with a sense of doing the right thing, but that is not enough. There is something of the martyr in this approach, which many daughters have learned from their mothers' self-deprecating ways. If a woman is to have an ego, she has to ask for and receive plenty of strokes. The female ego needs outside validation in order to grow just as the male ego does.

Negative Strokes Are a Poor Substitute

When a woman is not getting sufficient attention for herself, she sometimes seeks negative attention. Negative strokes are very potent and can be highly stimulating to the stroke-hungry woman, even if they cause her to feel bad. Human beings generally prefer to feel unhappy than to feel nothing at all.

Women with low self-esteem put themselves on a negative stroke diet. If your mother or father did not feel good about themselves, you may have learned some of their emotional bad habits. An important question to explore is, What did my parents do that made others angry at them? The tough question follows: Do I do the same things? The exchange of negative strokes—criticism, complaining, anger, and worry—can be a matter of habit. You can get into the habit of being negative and inviting negative responses and not even realize that you can use your ego to choose a better way. A woman loses only when she delivers or invites negative strokes.

A negative stroke diet is a bad psychological habit which reinforces the position of anyone who feels oppressed. In a culture that has high expectations for women to serve others and is critical of women's abilities—from mother-blaming to attacks on their professionalism—women must struggle to avoid becoming enmeshed in a negative stroke system. Here are four traps to avoid:

- **Rescuing**

    As people-pleasers women do things for other people that they could do for themselves. When a woman overdoes on the giving to others, she gets tired and out of touch with herself. Her negative strokes are fatigue, anger, jealousy, and a sense of being cheated. She easily does more than 50 percent of the work in maintaining relationships, is taken for granted, loses her identity and purpose, and can find herself floundering. Then she is blamed for not being more together as a person.

• Complaining

A woman can sacrifice on behalf of others and then ruin her chances of getting any credit for her good works because she complains about having sacrificed. Obsessive people-pleasing can make you into a persecutor of others in which you dish out negative strokes: bossing, nagging, yelling, and whining. Only by changing your involvement with others can you stop persecuting them with your complaining.

• Not Taking Charge

One terrible source of negative strokes is failure to accomplish anything. If she worries excessively about others, a woman can fail to accomplish much on her own behalf; and even if she does, her emotional energy is not focused on herself so she can enjoy her accomplishments. If you lack the sense of progress that results from taking charge of your life, your self-worth is diminished. You become a self-effacing female who lives with a sense of emptiness.

• Second-Class Syndrome

Many negative stroke systems result from a woman's second-class status in society. There are ways that a woman's own behavior perpetuates her second-class status. *Guilt* makes the second-class syndrome operate within a woman. In its depths, guilt is the way you internalize the resentments you dare not express. You turn anger against yourself in the form of guilt. Everything is *your fault*. Guilt is therefore an adaptation to others. The desire to please others makes a woman guilty instead of angry. She loses the energy and power of her genuine "not nice" feelings, which, if expressed, could lead her to make positive changes in her life. By identifying with the second-class position of the people-pleaser, she does what Freud called "identifying with the aggressor" and will feel guilty, sad, depressed, or scared instead of rightfully angry. Guilty behavior announces to the world, "I am second class."

A negative stroke diet has its roots in a childhood in which a woman learned not to be on her own side, to absorb negative attention, or to perform in ways that were not in her best interest. Many women learn a negative stroke system by observing their mother's inability to defend themselves against negative strokes. I have seen women in therapy blame their mothers for lacking self-respect and then repeat the same patterns in their relationships. When you give your mother negative strokes you are participating in a negative stroke system, and it will not help you to overcome similar tendencies in yourself. The answer for women lies in believing that women are not fair game for the negativity of others and that respect for women is to be expected and demanded when necessary.

Ask yourself the following questions to learn whether you are living on negative strokes:

• Do you often feel insulted or cheated?
• Do you blow up regularly, having adult temper tantrums?
• Do you complain frequently to those who are close to you?
• Do you carry secret grudges for days or years?
• Do you always have a major problem?
• Are you generally exhausted or unhappy?

The answers to these questions will tell you if you are in the habit of living on a negative stroke diet. A solution that sounds simplistic but is profoundly helpful is to change your diet. Your emotional calories contain no nutrition, and therefore they keep you pursuing more empty strokes. Let the insults go, let the temper go, stop complaining, forgive the grudge, and stop obsessing about problems. In the great vacuum that is created, find things in life to feel good about. Begin by looking at the people you know and focus on what you like about them.

A woman who follows a positive stroke diet can find enjoyable people, interesting activities, and challenging work. A positive approach to living gives the ego support, hope, and direction. The ego can function only in a positive direction. Even when there are problems, the ego looks for a solution.

The reason many parents have taught their daughters (who usually are more available for this conditioning than male children) a negative, passive approach to life is because some of them have felt terribly stuck in their own lives and have been blind to options. Fortunately, women today can live in larger worlds. If you discover that you are living on a negative stroke diet, it is time to make a radical change.

You Can Give Yourself Strokes

Once we have been conditioned or trained by our parents, we give ourselves inner strokes when we do what they have programmed us to do. As a child it was my job to do the dishes in the evening. Today, I often do not want to clean up the dishes, but when I complete the task I have a special sense of inner well-being. A voice in my head tells me that I am a good person who did a good job. When another family member does the dishes it is hard for me not to help. It's not that I like to do dishes; I want to have that little stroke that I automatically give myself.

You can use this principle to help your ego. Practice congratulating yourself consciously for what you do. This is what healthy egos do. Admire good work—the home you have created or the way you have tackled a tough day. Find ways to bring yourself rewards for active, positive living. Learn pride in yourself. This is a natural way to be. You need only to give yourself permission to appreciate yourself.

Getting the Right Balance

Not only are women often stroke-starved, but the way they sometimes seek to get strokes is not good for ego growth. Since separation is a key to ego development, a woman functioning primarily as a nurturer can be in trouble. If she does not receive objective praise: "Mom, you did a great job helping me with my homework tonight," she will try to get her strokes on a more dependent level. She will savor intimacy and closeness with her children, enjoying the vicarious pleasure of being happy because *they* are happy. This can be a great source of pleasure, but it does not give enough strokes to the *individual* and *separate* ego of a woman. She is left seeking nonverbal intimacy as a primary source of strokes, and at some point her family members will push her away in the quest for their own egos.

A woman trying to pursue a career can feel equally lost if she has grown up believing that emotional closeness alone gives meaning to life. Her career-seeking boy friend resists becoming domesticated, and she painfully longs for empathetic bliss. I have often counseled young career women who were their family's sweethearts during childhood. They cannot fully comprehend getting strokes in the world for hard and good work. These women are learning the tough lesson that being adorable is no longer enough to make them feel very good, and yet they have not yet learned how to get strokes for competency. They still want strokes to come their way automatically, and they resent having to earn recognition.

Other women have the opposite experience. These are often highly successful women who come to therapy because they are unable to find joy in satisfying relationships. Having been deprived of unconditional love, these women learned to get all of their recognition in the form of good grades in school and honors for accomplishments. Such a woman believes that she is only as good as what she achieves. Her ego is often undermined by a depression when her needs for such recognition are not being met. She does not feel the security of knowing she is lovable no matter what.

Are You Getting a Balanced Stroke Diet?

Here are some questions about strokes that you can use to decide whether you are getting a balanced stroke diet:

- Do you get general strokes of affection? Intimacy, personal compliments, and the magic words "I love you" give us unconditional strokes for simply being ourselves.
- Do you get strokes for accomplishments? Our egos thrive on conditional strokes—strokes for what we do. These strokes are not the same as love. Many women have not learned how to count their accomplishments. Keep your own records of what you do. Your ego needs this reinforcement.
- Do you get strokes for your efforts, even though there are no concrete results? We especially need the sustaining encouragement of people close to us to help us through situations when our efforts show little or no results. You need to have friends and intimates who support your efforts during difficult times with positive comments such as "It's a difficult job applying for graduate school," or "What a trooper you are taking care of those twins."
- Do you get strokes for your competency? We like people to notice our special way of doing something, not just what we do. "The way you handled that argument was masterful," or "What little stitches on that hem." Strokes for competency are pure gold for the female ego. Many women are good at giving this bolstering. Let the people in your life know that you have an ego that thrives on being noticed.
- Do you try to get strokes for suffering or struggling? These are negative strokes. Beware of them. Unfortunately, martyrdom can inspire resentment from your intimates just at the times when you desperately feel that you need support.
- Do you get strokes for being playful? Laughing, playing, and even being silly lighten our burdens and fill us with joy. Every woman has an inner Child ego state. Being playful opens the child within to receive emotional nourishment, which might be in the form of social activities, an organized sport, or a hobby. You will find that your capacity to give and receive strokes will grow when you connect with the playful and spontaneous child inside you.

- Do you get strokes for a talent or for being intelligent? Getting strokes for specific talents or intelligence particularly helps a woman's ego to grow because traditionally women have not been stroked for these attributes. These strokes defeat the terrible notion that she is replaceable.
- Do you get enough physical strokes? Touch is one of the most fulfilling forms of stroking, reaching us on an unconscious level. We, of course, have important sexual needs, and we also have the need for simple human affection. There is nothing like a hug from a good friend or holding hands with your mate.

Beware of Being a Stroke Snob

Some people have a very low account in their stroke bank because they are stroke snobs. They are satisfied by only the most perfect stroke—beautifully worded, subtle but deeply flattering, coming from the lips of a revered person, and then only if it is really meant. A stroke snob discounts strokes by saying, "You're only just saying that because you think I want you to." This response maintains a self-depriving system. Stroke snobs do not realize that some of the best strokes are like a satisfying, homemade, warming meal that you eat in a friendly group in the kitchen rather than as a ritual in the formal dining room.

Getting the Strokes You Need

You learned your stroking patterns in childhood, so you may need to change some of your attitudes about strokes. Here are the four main areas of confusion I have found in my work with women who are struggling to change their stroking patterns.

- **Is Love a Matter of Luck?**
  Many women believe that love cannot be planned and cultivated. This is not true. Loving is a matter of commitment. Loving

feelings accompany loving actions, and if your parents did not catch on, it is not too late for you. Actively become a loving person, a generous, helpful friend. Select friends who are willing to be committed to their relationships. This course of action will pay off in an increased exchange of strokes.

- ### Is It Polite to Ask?

Many of us learn in our families that females need to be excruciatingly polite and not ask directly for what they want. As a result, some women are utterly mute at expressing their own needs. A major part of my work with women is supporting them in the process of learning to ask for what they want. When you start asking for strokes, a terrible spell has been broken. You might disarm people at first, but you are teaching them a good lesson. Remember that most people are self-absorbed, and even empathetic people cannot read your mind and know what you need from them.

Asking is not the same as criticizing. You must not begin by saying to your friend, "You never notice how hard I work." Say something like, "I need to be reminded of what a good job I'm doing. Encouragement helps me a lot." Keep your requests specific and positive.

What if someone says no? That is absolutely all right. By asking for strokes, you are not giving an ultimatum but simply offering an opportunity. The process will work only if you are sensitive to the people you ask and allow them to refuse if they want to. This open attitude requires a strong ego, but your ego will grow as you practice this attitude. A self-centered mate might initially respond with, "Well, I need encouragement, too!" Agree with him and use *his* need as an opening for increased stroke exchanges. When you begin to ask for strokes they may not automatically follow. Give your words time to settle. It is a matter of catching on to the fact that everyone's ego grows when needs are communicated directly.

- ### Is It Hard to Give?

One of my ways of freeing the flow of strokes is through having made a commitment to myself to bring more joy into my life.

Whenever I experience a positive reaction to someone, I make a point of verbalizing it. Sometimes it is delayed: "I meant to tell you how lovely you looked last week in that blue dress." If you take this approach you will discover that it is not hard for you to give to others or for them to give to you.

• Is It Boorish to Brag?

Men brag, and women also need to tell their own exciting tales of victory and conquest, whether they occurred at the board meeting, on the tennis court, or in dealing skillfully with a child. Invite your friends in to see a newly decorated room or a new possession. Openly celebrate your successes as well as your birthday. Share your experiences, your clever solutions to problems, and your pride. Only bitter or jealous people do not enjoy such enthusiasm. This is not just male ego behavior—it is ego behavior.

Getting Enough Strokes Frees You from the Control of Other People

We are very easily controlled by other people when we are not getting enough strokes for ourselves. Here is a story about someone I know who learned how to deal with a stroke vacuum.

Rose was basically a strong and self-assured woman, confident of her skills. Her husband ran his own accounting business, and Rose had worked as secretary to the administrator of a large community hospital for nearly fourteen years. Rose was a tough woman who ran the office like a ship. Some people thought she really ran the hospital, but she brushed such claims aside. Enjoying her competency and the appreciation she received, Rose was uninterested in personal glory.

Her boss's retirement coincided with her youngest daughter's leaving home for college. Rose seized this opportunity to get a job in the city, which was a dream she had deferred for years. She easily landed an executive secretarial job, working for a vice-president of a large corporation in New York City.

When Rose came to see me, she was demoralized and angry.

She was running errands, making coffee, doing demeaning little tasks that were not in her job description, and being treated patronizingly as if she had no brains and was over the hill. Rose was losing the sense of dignity she had taken for granted for years, and she spent her days in angry obsession about her inconsiderate boss.

Rose could not understand why she was putting up with the situation. We often do not know how weak we can become without strokes. Headstrong as she had always been, Rose was losing self-confidence without the rich source of strokes that she had taken for granted for years. But she did not want to quit until she had given it one more round.

The first step for Rose was to develop awareness that she was operating in a stroke vacuum. The praise and recognition that had supported her in the past were gone. Once she realized how needy she was, however, she understood her embarrassing attempts to please her insensitive and withholding boss.

The dynamics were very different six months later. Rose realized that she had been internally relying on *remembered* strokes from her hospital pals who were no longer her co-workers. Memories of strokes do not sustain a person. Rose began a campaign to get to know as many people as she could, branching out by making contacts with people in other divisions and lunching with as many different people as she could. Within two months she had several acquaintances and two friendships that were becoming solid.

There were two strategies in Rose's campaign. First, she made herself visible. It was a real ego boost to her when people began calling her by name. She made the most of running errands, and people in other departments looked forward to having her drop by. Second, Rose focused her interests on other people. She took a great interest in what was going on in other departments, and people became impressed with her as an intelligent and interested worker.

Rose did not try to improve the impossible situation with her boss. She did not rock the boat with him but cultivated contacts elsewhere. Rose let many people know who she was and what she was like. Soon, a smart vice-president in another division of the company arranged her transfer to be his own secretary.

The All-Purpose
Dream Girl Machine

One of my early discoveries was that parents tend to have limited expectations for their daughters. We can feel sorry for the man who is born into a family that expects the sons to run the family business whether they want to or not. But more tragic may be the woman for whom the family has no real, challenging, concrete expectations. She does not carry the banner of her parents' aspirations; she has no deep hopes or dreams of others to fulfill; and she does not struggle with the terror of being considered very important. Lack of a strong role to play creates a horrible vacuum; it is performing in a play with no lines, limited action, and little direction. I have seen many women struggle with their lack of definition and the fact that no one really cared what happened to them.

I also have noticed a lack of family support for women who seek to define themselves through a commitment to hard study or work. Such a woman is commonly asked, "What do you want to do that for?" or told, "Don't overdo." When she seeks to change course she often will hear, "Can't you just stick it out where you are?" When she tries to "find herself," she appears ridiculous, the assumption being that there is nothing to find—no destiny to fulfill, no spirit to reveal itself in acts of greatness.

In such families, however, there is a place for women. Within most family systems women receive recognition and join the larger group by facilitating the smooth running of the family. Doing the work that shows only when it is not done, a woman often finds her place in domestic functioning: baby-sitting and doing chores. A woman often receives rich strokes when she pleases others *and not so many when she pleases herself.*

The operative principle for such a woman is that *she has been programmed to be programmable.* This is why her script is unspecific, her aspirations whimsical, and her work functional. The ultimate "woman" is an all-purpose machine available to do many jobs. She is a generalist in the art of pleasing others, not a specialist in the art of pleasing herself. *The modern superwoman often is a new deluxe model* of this same generalist.

When a woman is a programmable people-pleaser, her ego is not free to make choices that are in her best interest. *Some people do not deserve to be pleased*, and some situations ensure that a woman will be mistreated if she attempts to please. And yet a woman often stubbornly continues to play a nice, sweet, accommodating role, no matter what the result. Such a rigid, undiscriminating response is a result of childhood programming.

When we joke about a woman's prerogative to change her mind, we are pointing to this core issue of female conditioning. She *must* be changeable so she will be available to respond to the various needs of others. This conditioning is why a woman needs others so desperately.

The media tell us that the most desirable people-pleasers are very young and perfectly formed. As soon as lines of wisdom, wit, or pain distinguish a woman's face, she loses that all-purpose quality and is no longer a dream girl. If a woman believes what she is hearing about herself, she is prone to dislike her most interesting and unique qualities—the face and body that reflect her life experiences, her developed opinions, and her unique ways of being.

The Empathy of a People-Pleaser

To describe women as overemotional indicates their role in a dynamic family system. Often women are delegated to feel the feelings of the entire family. A woman feels her husband's weariness, her son's struggle in school, a sick child's pain, and her daughter's need to wear the same styles all the other girls are wearing. A woman takes the emotional pulse of everyone who is close to her, and her heart beats with their joys and their pain. In fact, people get angry with her when she does not feel their feelings. Traditionally women do feel very deeply, and they struggle to communicate this important dimension to others. In doing so, a woman allows them not to be as sensitive as she because *she is doing it for them.* Crazy as it sounds, this is how family systems operate.

Young girls learn this role when they model themselves after a mother who functions this way. They may observe her assuming the emotional role and resigning the role of thinking to her husband. Within this division the man has the last word in matters of planning, money, and other decisions.

This stereotypical pattern is slowly changing, but it still operates in many of the families we came from and is an important issue for young couples.

People-Pleasers Are Caretakers

Generosity is a noble attribute. It is saintly to put aside your own needs on behalf of others. In our culture we easily overlook the reality of the lives of most mothers. Children and husbands assume idealistic entitlement for themselves and ignore the neediness of the mother—that she is often expected to give from an empty cup and do a good job anyway. The truth is that someone else is always needy. Women's work as caretakers is noticed only when it is undone. A woman may receive many more strokes of disgruntlement than of appreciation from the needy people around her. Sometimes her best strokes are relief strokes when everyone is satisfied and leaves her alone for awhile. People are often embarrassed to be beholden to a caretaker, so they may consistently ignore her devotion. She may take this all in stride, seeing her own silent acquiescence as a further gift of caretaking.

The dynamics of this situation are complicated by a woman's natural inclinations and gifts as a mother. But my concern here is that she is *conditioned* to be a caregiver to others even though she receives very little in return that is meaningful to her personally. In analyzing the female ego, we must take a critical look at the functional woman in her misguided, martyred glory.

People-Pleasers Are Vulnerable

Excessive caretaking makes a woman vulnerable and unable to deal objectively with problems. This is why she seems to need not only someone to think for her but to protect her. She needs to borrow the ego defenses of a good, strong man. In doing so, however, she relinquishes her power. Personal power is not power over another person so much as it is inner power, the power to remain strong or invulnerable to a normal amount of life's bumps and bruises. A woman does not develop good ego defenses if she exhausts herself with empathy and lets someone else defend her.

The real disaster for the female ego occurs when she is in a serious conflict with her mate. If a woman looks to the man in her life to be her protector, what does she do at those times when he is her adversary? How does she fight with the person to whom she always looks for support? First, a woman should not let herself become so vulnerable that she needs a protector. Second, she must develop enough ego strength to fight her own battles.

The way to be less vulnerable is to stick to the following principle: *Stay on your own side.* If you are too tired to do something for someone else, say so. If you are not enjoying being criticized, say so. If someone is putting you down, think about your good qualities. If you are dealing with a bully, give him an ultimatum about his nasty behavior. Give yourself permission to make situations go the way you want them to go. It is all right for you to call a foul play or take your marbles and go home. You do not have to remain in situations that are not in your best interest or that undermine your self-esteem. Whenever you are feeling the least bit not OK, ask yourself this important question: Am I staying on my own side? A woman with an ego learns how to protect herself.

People-Pleasers Are Secretly Sexual

Much has been hypothesized about women's internal, hidden sexuality and their need to be "awakened" by a sexual partner. There are theories of hidden responses deep within the vagina that remain a mystery to a woman herself. I think that most of a woman's secret sexuality is a result of her conditioning. It is but one more symptom of her adaptability to others.

A woman has three prominent, accessible, pleasure-giving, erogenous zones: two nipples and one clitoris. Each contains erectile tissue and upon erection displays surfaces that yearn for continued stimulation and satisfaction. Almost every woman discovers and enjoys her erections. Unfortunately, being conditioned to be adaptable, she becomes confused when she is given advice by experts or lovers that is counter to her own genuine sexual experiences.

A woman's training to be a good girl teaches her to reserve her body for the satisfaction of another person, as is clinically documented by the epidemic of feigned orgasms. Sexually, women often face a double message that says, Do what I want, and enjoy yourself. Sometimes a woman's program for pleasing others takes the form of becoming nonsexual so as to be a good (nonsexual) girl for her parents. Later, as a woman, she tries to remain an eternal little girl—plain and androgynous—stuck in the latency period of her development. Another way to be nonsexual is to be dedicated to turning on a man without regard to her own sexual desires. This woman appears to be very sexual, but it is for others, not herself. A truly sexual woman is tuned into what turns *herself* on.

It is very difficult to experience orgasm when you are over-adapting yourself to the sexual expectations of your lover. Caught in the web of people-pleasing, your own true feelings are obscured.

Are women slow to respond sexually? Maybe men are just fast. Do women enjoy experiencing orgasm through different types of touch? Hurray for their uniqueness. Maybe the straightforward male approach is less sensual, and a woman's way is the real pathway to pleasure. She does, in fact, win the orgasmic capacity contest; but why are we counting? I guess to even the score. A woman must realize that her own sexual needs and experience are her norm, and trust her intuitions about her sensual self. What you feel is what you get.

People-Pleasers Are Nice No Matter What

It's true that most women are nice. When I want to sit and gab or share a problem, my favorite listeners are my women friends because I can count on them to be nice to me. They smile easily, have a ready compliment on their lips, are patient and accepting. These are beautiful, nurturant qualities. Nice women are supportive yet nonobtrusive, graceful, rarely offensive, companionable yet noncompetitive, cooperative, and well-meaning to a fault. Of course, some are not, but they are not admitted into the club. Good women are sweet, and good women are nice.

The problem is that women are often conditioned to be so accepting that they are undiscriminating. They are nice to everyone—charming to a lecherous bus driver, kind to a deceitful boss, supportive to a selfish child, sympathetic to a drunken husband, or graceful to a boorish date.

The trouble with being nice all the time is that it is a rigid adaptation that serves to make others comfortable at the expense of your own truth. When my husband was an assistant minister, beginning his career, we had a coffee hour after church. A veteran minister's wife came up to me one day after the coffee hour and said, "Doesn't your face hurt?" I must have looked confused. "You know," she said as she massaged her cheeks, "from smiling." I had to admit that she was right.

It is not natural to keep a smile frozen on your face. A smile is a natural expression of joy. Your own ego is not functioning when you are being nice no matter what. This is a hard habit to break because it usually was learned very early. In fact, there is a good name for a woman who is not perpetually nice. For a woman to know and express her own truth she must get rid of these adaptations. A good place to start is to wipe that phony smile off her face.

People-Pleasing Is Defensive

At the heart of people-pleasing is a defense mechanism called a reaction formation. The reaction formation involves an internal rechanneling of one's energies. In other words, if I want to do one thing, I will use my energy to do something else. To accomplish this task, I must muster up a bit of extra energy to override the initial impulse. That extra effort to adapt is what gives the people-pleaser a certain toughness, epitomized by the overbearing, over-anxious mother.

So habitual is the overriding of her true desires and instincts that serving others is the only thing this woman can do. On an unconscious level she feels anger at not being true to herself, and the anger comes out in the form of being helpful in a way that is overbearing.

My friend Cathy is a good example of someone who uses the reaction formation defense. She takes her mother shopping with her regularly. Her mother tends to manipulate others by complaining, and she believes that her devoted daughter does not do enough for her. Good old Cathy could almost be said to be wearing a sweatshirt that says, "At Your Service."

After a morning of shopping patiently with her mother, Cathy wants to go home. But her mother complains that she is hungry. Cathy does not insist that they go home, nor do they grab a quick sandwich. Instead, Cathy takes her mother for a long and lovely three-course lunch.

Later, when Cathy really wants to go home alone, she invites her mother to tea. Finally, her husband drives her mother home. Later in the evening Cathy would like to go to a movie, but instead she bakes a cake for her family. She rechannels every self-serving impulse, and that extra effort to override herself gives her personality an increasingly rigid, overbearing hardness.

I sometimes call reaction formation nurturing with a vengeance. A mother who is excessively lovey with her children or a home-maker with a compulsively spotless house is often overdoing what she would rather not be doing. A woman can be energized by her secret anger about doing what she does not want to do.

Something's Wrong with Me: The Climate for People-Pleasers

For a growing girl to become a people-pleaser she must learn that there is something wrong with her natural impulses. The idea that there is something wrong with women permeates our how-to and self-help literature. Self-improvement is great, but it has become a female obsession. Created out of one of Adam's spare parts, we keep trying to fix up a machine that is too fat, too thin, or adorned in the wrong color. A dear friend of mine faced a depression at the end of a long and successful diet in which she lost about seventy pounds. "It is not the answer to life," she said. "Weight loss is boring. I still have to face learning to love myself."

I am the first person to enjoy a pretty haircut, a new lipstick, or feasting my eyes on magazine pages of gorgeous clothes. But often our pursuit of feminine beauty is not an act of self-love but an expression of self-hate. We operate with a notion that we should fix ourselves or fix ourselves up because there is something wrong with us.

Pleasing Others/Pleasing Yourself

To turn this programming around, a woman needs to know that people who try desperately to please others do not win respect. People who *demand* respect *get* respect. *You will never win at people-pleasing*; it makes you too much like a robot. An interesting woman with passions and foibles will be much richer in love than a woman who is a helpfulness machine. What people really like are interesting people.

The first step in releasing yourself from female childhood conditioning is the radical decision to *please yourself first*.

Fathers and Daughters

It is well known to researchers that many women who are successful in the world had fathers who treated them as traditional sons—taking a great interest in the serious development of their talents. In many families fathers pay insufficient attention to all family members, including the mother. Fathers' focus on work and life outside the home drains their energies and may be more interesting to them than their families. Therefore, the daughter often is the family member most cheated of the father's attention. Most fathers have some idea that they are supposed to be masculine role models for their sons and play in the back yard or go on outings to ball games or fishing holes with them. And many devoted fathers pour all of their hopes and dreams into their sons.

The reason why the relationship between fathers and sons is satisfying is because of the perceived necessity of a male role model for boys. It is important to realize that children of both sexes need two role models: mother and father. I have become aware that women often desperately need fatherly guidance for "in-the-world" acting because the workplace is still a macho world. A few fishing trips and visits to Dad's office could have helped many women a great deal. The female ego needs to develop skills for getting along in the world in an aggressive and self-confident way. One of the reasons some aspects of the female ego can be missing is because those aspects have been identified as masculine in our culture. The fathers of daughters may not want them to imitate this behavior but prefer that their daughter be an acquiescent people-pleaser who will be a foil and support to their personal power.

Every man and woman has both masculine and feminine parts of their characters. By identifying with the various aspects of both parents, we find our human wholeness and the unique mixture of qualities that works for us. By becoming polarized in our conceptions of masculine and feminine traits, the female ego has been arrested in development, or at least has had to cover strengths with a charade of feminine "weakness"—a deception that a woman herself sometimes buys. The dichotomy between fathers and daughters is part of the abandonment continuum. A young woman needs to have her father be committed to her development as a strong person. She needs to have him let her try on his strengths and borrow his ego in the process of developing her own. She does not need to be perceived as the fulfillment of the unexpressed side of himself or to be trained by him to be a phony people-pleaser— although this is too often what happens to young women.

Sometimes a woman's intense attraction to a man is based on her own unrealized strengths. Longing for her own strong self, she sublimates her ego to vicarious living through a man. What she needed as a young girl was a father who said to her, "You can be strong, too. Someday, you will grow up to be *my equal.*"

A Foundation
for a New Life

If you want to change the patterns you learned in childhood, you must develop sources of support for those changes. It does not help to dream and long for something better or to try to change anything silently, secretly, and alone.

You must first get a picture of your life and decide what areas you want to change. When I am helping a woman in this process, I sometimes ask her to picture her life as a play. I get out paper and we draw a stage and draw in all the important characters. She decides who the leading characters are and where she herself fits into the human drama that she is part of. Using this device, you can become vividly aware of what activities form the main action of your life. How do you function in a system with others? Do you have any moment of feeling like a star? Is the play of your life a comedy or a tragedy? Is it interesting or boring? How would you like to change the plot? How would you like to change your role and activities? Get a clear picture of the areas that you would like to change.

Women have trouble using time wisely on their own behalf because they are not ruthless enough. You must learn that to develop yourself, you must not try to do everything, but rather to do one thing very well. To become a specialist, you must have intense focus. This means that you *give up* what is not in your focus—minor short-range stroking—in order to achieve your long-range goals. It is a strong ego that can hold fast to future goals and deny present comfort in order to get there.

The key to starting a growth process is to find the right support structure for yourself. You cannot write a good book at night after you have worked for others all day. You cannot teach yourself everything you need to know or develop a knowledge of the politics of your endeavor at home. You must find the place and people who can help you. Therapists who begin their practices in their homes often are released from a great struggle when they rent part-time office space. How can you focus in an environment that sends you such messages as: Clean these drawers! Vacuum these floors! Think about the kids! Artists and photographers need studio space, and even if it is humble, it is wonderfully welcome. Writing may be better done in a library. One woman I know used her husband's office on weekends as a temporary spot from which to launch a research project. Your environment must send you messages that support a sense of yourself as a woman with her own work to do.

You also must tell people—especially your intimates—what you are doing. Let them get used to your aspirations. You must get strokes for your new activities. You must wean yourself from your old image and enlist recognition for the new. Children can become excited about Mom's new venture and husbands can, too, when they are convinced that they are still loved. But whether or not you have support, you must set your sights on a goal, create a setting where you can work, and ruthlessly use some of your prime time to do what you need to do.

A final key to creating new foundations is having role models. We discover who we are by imitating other people, and we gain support by observing what someone else is doing. Modeling is a more effective tool for the female ego than introspection. If you dig into inner space, you may find your world does not provide much support for change, or you would have changed already.

Modeling connects you to the outer, real world. By trying to be like someone you admire, you grow. There has been much talk about mentors for women. Finding a personal mentor can be very helpful. There is also much to be gained from an impersonal process of studying those who are good at what they do and then trying on some of their behaviors in order to find your own best style.

Growth requires support. Use your female ego to find the support you need to break out of the deep rut caused by a lifetime habit of people-pleasing.

5

The Female Ego in Motherhood

A mother is not a person to lean on, but
a person to make leaning unnecessary.
Dorothy Canfield Fisher

The Mother with an Ego

Most women become good mothers by trusting themselves, learning from tradition, and figuring out what works in their own situations. Mothering is a very difficult job, and it requires tremendous ego strength. In looking at how women manage this complex and trying experience we need to appreciate the outstanding accomplishments of the women who rear children. Mothers have to withstand mother-blaming from some parts of the mental health sector, their own energy depletion, the uneasy experience of isolation, lack of independence, being an emotional buffer for others, and finally having their children push them away so they can grow.

The experience of being a mother can make a woman feel very insecure because she has a deep investment in doing a good job in raising her child and is not always sure that she is doing the right thing. Her need for strokes makes her an easy target for negative ones of judgment and blame. Changes need to be made to relieve some of these burdens on mothers. But first, mothers deserve a great deal of credit. Their accomplishments in spite of difficulties are often amazing and attest to the great strengths of the female ego.

There was a time when I wondered if I could cope with the experience of being a mother. When I had a baby and a toddler, I was transplanted from the city to the outskirts of Princeton, New Jersey, and did not yet know how to drive a car. My commuting husband was gone for long hours and stayed over in the city two nights a week. The help and expertise of other mothers showed me how to be a mother and how to cope. Today I think that I could assemble a panel of experts in the art of mothering. On it I would include my own mother, who is skilled at being on the same wavelength as a young child. From her I learned that it is important to share with a child a sense of life as an adventure. I would include my Aunt Violet because she is the most intelligent listener I have ever met, and listening is a crucial skill in the rearing of children. She has an acute sensitivity to the various stages children go through. Next I could include a grandmother I hired to taxi my children to school until I learned to drive. She understood the value of regular presents: trinkets, toys, lollipops, and spectacular homemade birthday cakes. I would include Mama Johnson, my grandmother, who raised a dozen children and grandchildren, grew and preserved their food, and made their clothes, and then spent her sunset years teaching her grandchildren southern cooking and how to sew from their own designs.

In this brain trust I would include my neighbor, who showed me by example how both to work and be at home when the kids need you. I would also invite the teachers at the Farm School, a nursery school on a farm in New Jersey. They know that every child needs a dog or cat to pet and that the answer for separation anxiety is to "love 'em up." These are the people who have been on my team, helping me learn how to be a mother. The books don't tell you such important things as how to crack jokes with a two-year-old or which brand of car has enough parts that open and close to be pronounced "Neato." We all have access to experts, and they are other mothers, including the mother inside ourselves. Mothers all know the single most important rule about the art of mothering: *Good mothering has a lot to do with how the mother is feeling.* A mother knows that she has to help other mothers feel good about themselves if she wants to make the process of mothering as a vocation successful.

By patronizing mothers, blaming mothers, manipulating mothers, or ignoring their input, educators, medical personnel, dentists, social workers, pediatricians, and therapists do children a great disservice. Mothers need to assert their egos on behalf of their own ideas and not be intimidated by "experts." This attitude is especially necessary in regard to the health and well-being of your children. It is important, as well, to relinquish obsessions with all of the "shoulds" that one finds in the deluge of self-help literature. The robot mother who does all of the "right things" that "they" say she should do might be so busy that she forgets to relax and play with her child and enjoy the most natural aspects of mothering.

Of course, we need help from time to time. Reading about parenting is a vital resource for the woman who is learning how to be a mother. We must not expect too much of our innate instincts, for *much of mothering comes from learned skills.* But even when you consult a professional helper, you must hold onto your own ego. The mother and the father are the most important parts of the brain trust in the raising of a child. One of the dangers of being mystified by "experts" and following their guidelines is for a woman to be too subservient to them to hear what her child is telling her.

I once attended a workshop of therapists who worked with "non-thriving" infants. These are children who refuse to eat and interact with their mothers after they go home from the hospital. These researchers found that the mothers were doing the tasks of caring for their babies, but they were not playing with them. In fact, the mothers were so out of touch that they had forgotten how to play. The therapy consisted of taking the mothers into a nursery and teaching them how to play. They learned to be in touch with the child within themselves. As a result, the babies began to respond to their more natural and spontaneous mothers. The child-to-child connection is at the heart of the mother-child relationship. The art of mothering, just like any art form, leaves rigid adaptations behind and moves toward joyful spontaneity. A mother with an ego is free to be her natural self with her child.

Ego Building for Mothers

To complete a degree at Rutgers University, when I was a mother of school-age children, I was assigned to a twelve-month internship at an agency on the lower East Side of Manhattan. We had moved back to New York City and were living in Greenwich Village. A short subway ride away from my home I found myself on another planet, where adjoining shops displayed signs in Yiddish, Chinese, and Spanish. The basketball game on the corner was played by a United Nations of blacks, Hispanics, Chinese, and whites.

I was to be the social worker for thirty mothers, primarily Hispanic and Chinese, whose children attended a Head Start preschool program at the agency. I felt very green but was eager to give it my best shot. My supervisor told me that I was to counsel the mothers and plan a program that would teach them how to be better mothers.

I immediately felt like even more of an outsider than I was. I was to assume that I was an expert in something that had not been taught in school, yet my assignment was to enter this group of mothers and somehow show them the way. Since I had taken no courses in mothering, what gave me my superior knowledge? My WASP background? My general education? Oddly, I was told that I would catch on because having young children myself would help me to achieve rapport with the mothers' group. It sounded as though I was supposed to gain their trust and then sock it to them.

My second reaction was that there must be something wrong with these mothers. I imagined them stuffing their kids with sweets and potato chips and that their children must be poor little urchins with unchanged diapers. When I got up the courage to enter the room where the mothers congregated while their kids were in school, I became even more confused. Although I was armed with my social worker helpfulness, they helped me. Although I was ready to show them how to cope, they showed me how to enjoy the lower East Side. I arrived wanting to increase their resources. Instead, I met the most resourceful women that I have ever encountered in my life. I realized that these women had remarkable ego strength and that they could teach me a great deal.

They were grateful that I was there, they were extremely respectful, and they worked hard to make me feel at home. The Chinese women were extraordinary seamstresses, and the fabric they were cutting in the morning would be modeled as a garment in the afternoon. The Puerto Rican women had a special sweetness and spunk that made my day fun. All the children were fresh and clean and lovingly treated. We played with the babies and admired the accomplishments of the toddlers who attended the school. These women spent almost all of their time with their kids, and their children were lively, bright, and delightful to know.

The circumstances of some of their lives made me cringe in disbelief. Outstanding was Ramona, who was raising seven children by herself. Her husband had been the innocent victim of an attack in which the other man was killed by his own weapon in a fight. Aware of his innocence, the court gave him a "light" sentence of three years with a chance for parole in eighteen months. Managing her family and her Saturday trips to an upstate prison was an incredible strain on her. A home visit was suggested, and I braced myself for clutter, garbage, and cockroaches. On this, my first trip to the housing project, I walked into a large apartment that had little furniture except for sufficient beds and chests for nine people. It was spotlessly clean and more organized than my house has ever been. Kids were baby-sitting other kids and riding the elevator to the laundry room with endless baskets of clean and dirty clothes. Ramona possessed wisdom in knowing that physical order could help her to get through her trials. As any good neighbor, I helped her when she could not be in two places at once—at the pediatrician's office and conferring with her son's math teacher. What her ego needed was what so many mothers need—help when there are too many jobs to be done.

What kind of a program do we need? I asked myself after I had suspended the rap group that made everyone clam up. These women exhibited a certain apathy, a dreariness that all mothers know when their days seem endlessly the same and they feel themselves losing their youthful spark. If these women had a problem, it was that they did not feel good enough about themselves. Nobody was bolstering their egos by telling them that they were doing a great job. They were not receiving enough rewards. One of the results of this understandable resignation was a withdrawal from new experiences for themselves. They also tended to band together in their ethnic groups, speaking their own languages rather than expanding their horizons. This was also understandable on many levels, but maybe they were missing some opportunities.

After a summer of getting the lay of the land, I decided that the point of my program was to help the mothers to feel good about themselves—to help strengthen their egos and increase their self-esteem. The main personal concern that I heard expressed was about being overweight. Of course, this was not an issue with the size four Chinese women, but we all were interested in fitness. Using recordings, we conducted our own exercise sessions, turning the mothers' room into a studio. The overweight women had weigh-ins and shared weight-loss tips.

The Hispanic women sometimes expressed curiosity about the Chinese grocery stores in the neighborhood. They also were fascinated that the Chinese women ate heartily yet stayed thin. Once a week we took over the school kitchen in the afternoon and had Chinese cooking lessons followed by a feast. We became close as a group by chopping vegetables together. The eureka moment of the year was when Wanda discovered why she and some of their friends were fat. When she boiled her daily rice she always added at least a cup of cooking oil to the water. In the cooking class she realized that the Chinese women cook with little fat and put none at all in their steamed rice. Sharing and good feelings abounded.

Keeping up morale is the key issue with mothers. Possessing a healthy female ego means that a woman feels good about herself.

A mother whose ego is in good shape is in a position to nurture the egos of her offspring.

Our activities were highly therapeutic and contained the basic tools for ego building: learning how to get more positive strokes, becoming more independent, and learning new skills. When a woman gets the attention and affirmation that she needs she is in a position to give love. It is impossible to give love without feeling loved yourself.

Being close to this group of mothers gave my ego a chance to grow. Their network of camaraderie and ego support was stronger than that in any group I ever have joined. I experienced how collectivity and cooperation help women to surmount difficult situations. I lost my fear and shame for being different and better off because they loved and accepted me. I became less materialistic as I saw them embrace the important human experiences in life in spite of severely limited means. At times their largesse embarrassed me, and when I was given two farewell parties in one day, it was all too clear that they were the social workers and I the client. But what else would you expect from a group of dedicated mothers?

Dying on the Vine

She is such an attractive young mother, I said to myself as Adrianne described the funk she was in. Clad in a zippy jogging suit, she was the epitome of the active, glamorous Manhattan mother, complete with penthouse, housekeeper, and an outstanding private school for her children. Despite having a lifestyle anyone would envy, she said that she felt lost. As active as she was, she felt that she did not do anything.

The people-pleaser's job might be called lady-in-waiting. She waits for her children to finish their breakfast; she waits for their naps to be over; she waits for the clothes to come out of the dryer, for the furniture to be delivered, for the cake to be done. She also waits on her family, from diaper duty to meal serving to running a myriad of little errands. The lady-in-waiting loses her center and can begin to feel that she is nothing and does nothing.

Mother love is mature love. Not based on whim or passing emotional fancy, mother love's mainstay is constancy. A mother is available to do the job that is required. This commitment to love means that of necessity she often overrides her own immediate needs. Later, later, she continually says to herself. Her ego gets used to being neglected.

In mastering the important skill of delayed gratification, she might find herself on a rigid track of no gratification at all. She struggles with her unmet needs as exercises in self-control, not with a view toward meeting them. When rigidity and boredom set in, she can become trapped in inertia. With no spark of personal needs, with no flames of self-seeking passion, she has little reason to change, to look, to search, or to find. It is hard to register for a course 'way uptown, and besides, I don't even know what I am interested in anymore; nothing grabs me. Ho hum.

It is useful to understand the mothering role in terms of ego states. The transactional analysts divide the ego into three distinct operating modes which cannot be used simultaneously. We either are operating out of our Adult, our thinking and problem-solving mode, out of our Child, our creative essential self, or out of our Parent, the rule-enforcing and nurturing part of ourselves. The theory becomes increasingly complex, but the relevant point here is that the essential self and the stroke receiver reside in the Child ego state. Functioning exclusively in the Parent—or ruling—state creates a disastrous stroke drain for a woman. The task of your ego is not to relinquish this role altogether but to give it a *break*. Take a jog, a course, a trip, or an enjoyable part-time job. A woman must revitalize her natural energies if she wants to stay alive on the vine of motherhood.

Contract for Servitude

How can a mother even hope to have an ego when her profession as mother is downgraded? What does cheerfully cleaning bathroom tiles have to do with the raising of children? Unfortunately, doing housework is lumped together with the bringing forth of human life and the nurturing of human spirits. A woman faces heavy requirements as she seeks to have a smoothly running household and also to be a mother who is gifted in empathetic responsiveness.

For centuries, a woman's job has been to create a home. That home, however, is not necessarily a real home for her. Home for a woman is work. I have made a list of some of the requirements that a woman who is a mother/homemaker assumes to be part of her unwritten job contract if she is to do an admirable job. Of course, many of these rules are changing, but to the extent that you follow them you are a people-pleaser who neglects her own ego.

The Unwritten Contract
- Make everyone happy.
- Do not disturb your husband's peace of mind. (That happens enough at his work.)
- Find indirect ways of maneuvering people.
- Cultivate a good act. Cheerfulness is the best one.
- If a job you are doing is difficult, do not let anyone know it.
- Do not be rigid; always be understanding, even if people are late or forget your birthday or what you wanted for your birthday.
- Always look fresh and pretty.
- Take pride in having self-control.
- Be obsessed with the details of other people's lives.
- Remember that doing the laundry is more important than reading a good book.
- If you are depressed, that means that you are lazy. Get going!
- Hypnotize yourself with needlework if necessary.
- Do not look too sexy.
- Remember that your time belongs to your family.
- Do not take up any room in the house for your own exclusive use. Not only are you to be shared, but your space belongs to others as well as to you.
- Do not change anything or make decisions without permission.

Even your hair style must please the family first.
- When your husband is around, drop everything: (1) what you are doing; (2) your train of thought; (3) any original plans you made in his absence.
- In a conflict, ponder the other person's point of view and understand why the other person might be right. This is particularly important if you are to be an understanding wife to your husband.
- Find clever, solitary ways to meet your own needs that will not bother anyone.
- Do not have expensive hobbies or vices.
- When you break any of the above rules, you must suffer guilt.

The principle that underlies this contract is that a mother/homemaker does what she does not want to do yet remains pleasant and cheerful. This is the psychological meaning of slavery; it is not just doing what you do not want to do, but it is pretending that you are happy. If we follow this contract, we will be hopelessly off track and confused.

The Split Ego

After serving as a group therapist for a few years, I enrolled in graduate school. I wanted to be prepared to conduct the practice of individual psychotherapy. I vividly remember the sense of forging a new personal frontier on the first evening I entered my classroom. Wearing jeans and a sweater, I found myself in the company of peers: other mothers in blue jeans who were going back to school. When the professor arrived, I thought I saw exactly who I wanted to be in the future. She was elegantly tweedy, tailored, and manicured. The way she snapped open her calfskin briefcase revealed to me her fastidious control over her life. Although her delivery style was dry, the amount of information she easily imparted gave my novice hand writer's cramp. Through the entire semester I longed to be pulled together in the way that she was.

By the end of the year we had become casual friends, lunching together occasionally. The last day of the semester we had corned beef sandwiches in the local pub. I told her about the cottage we were renting for a month on the Jersey shore. She told me how tired she was and said that I was lucky to have planned a vacation; she anticipated teaching summer school. I asked her if she and her husband might like to join us for a weekend, and to my great surprise, she eagerly accepted.

I anticipated an elegant shore weekend, perhaps some sailing, sipping iced tea on the deck, and watching her children play happily on the beach with our kids. When they arrived she looked simply awful. Her teenage daughter was sulking and miserable, and her son hung onto her skirt and constantly whispered in her ear. Her husband ignored the kids and us, sat down in front of the television, and proceeded to get drunk. She seemed to be most comfortable making carrot sticks in the kitchen and worrying about her husband and her children. Out of the professional arena, this woman was the ultimate household drudge. I could not believe or understand it, and I mourned the loss of a role model.

What happens to a woman's ego at home? Why is it that a woman can lose herself at home and yet mysteriously pull herself together outside of the home environment? The phenomenon is female masochism, and it is caused by a psychic split in the ego.

The problem of female masochism is related to the nurturing skills that a woman develops. As a people-pleaser she might already lack centeredness in her own ego. Then the task of mothering with its requirement that she operate on behalf of other people gets her further off her own track. This process can be compounded by a dominating husband or one who requires that her wifely duties encompass her being *his* mother as well.

So far, we have a picture of a woman who is off course because she is so busy waiting for and on other people. Transferring her resentments into energy, she does with vigor the tasks she does not want to do. Smiling so she will please others, she fools herself into thinking she is happy. A failure if she is not pleasing others, she gets angry at herself if her bad moods show—if she occasionally loses the will to put on a good act. Her deepest wisdom informs her that loving and nurturing other people is a high calling, so that even the spiritual universe is in cahoots against her. The moments when she is careless prove her wickedness, and she throws her efforts toward other people's needs once again.

This problem is compounded by the actions a woman's family members take to undermine her confidence. The saddest part of all is that a woman will even help them do this to her. This is what Laura and Fritz Perls, who developed the field of Gestalt psychotherapy, meant when they described the dummy complex. In this neurosis, a woman is so willing to be whatever everyone wants her to be that she will become almost like a doll or a dummy. Ignoring her own feelings, she allows herself to be a target for abuse and finds herself supporting people who are not on her side. A psychoanalyst might call this behavior identifying with the aggressor. I would say that it is a symptom of a woman obsessively offering unconditional support to others. Possessing permeable boundaries, habitually voicing affirmation and no objections, a woman will be very weak when someone gives her a hard time.

A female masochist will put no limits on her time or resources if an intimate objects. Her self-esteem rests on an ego ideal of herself as a cornucopia, and when she has failed to overflow with good works for others, she has not only failed others, she has failed herself.

One of the pathological aspects of masochism is the linking of love and pain. Beginning with an experience of receiving love and pain together, a person might reason that love is worth a little pain. This linkage of love and pain forms a dangerous chain that can bind a woman to endless cycles of suffering. After awhile pain might become the evidence of lovableness: If I am suffering, I must be a good person. Masochism does not stop here, for it also tempts sadism. Children and husbands find it difficult to respect the guilty mother of the house and will unwittingly accept her earnest conviction that she somehow owes them even more than she gives them. When the working mother struggles to approximate an old-fashioned housewife, she teaches her children to feel deprived without her slavish ways. These women are not on their own sides; they are cruelly against themselves.

Some women go off the deep end entirely by bullying other people with their masochism. They persecute others from the position of being a victim. These women would not dream of taking care of themselves or taking responsibility for their feelings; instead, they complain endlessly. Some female masochists have a flair for the dramatic. They will check into a hospital for major surgery and never tell a soul (I did not want to worry you), take a second job although the first one is demanding enough, or give birth to a few extra children. These women take sacrificial duty to its most extreme conclusions.

We need to deromanticize a woman's generosity and see what it does to her ego. This is a tricky problem because we do not want to throw out the baby with the bathwater. How do we feel about generosity? Do we want to live in a selfish world? I believe that the egoless or martyred women I am talking about have a long way to go before self-interest would be a problem to them. But to address the philosophical issue, I offer here some ideas to help overcome the fear of selfishness which is at the heart of female masochism.

Is It OK to Be Selfish?

As a psychotherapist I realize that increased self-awareness is enormously helpful to people. A good therapeutic process in which people focus intensely on themselves gives them control over making their lives more satisfying. People who criticize therapy as a self-indulgent process are usually unaware of the degree of personal pain patients in therapy are dealing with. The "selfish" exercise of therapy often teaches people to stop being cruel to themselves and gives them tools for self-acceptance. Selfishness in this sense is the pathway to healing. A woman must be "selfish" enough to accept insight, comfort, and wholeness. In this sense, selfishness might better be termed "enlightened self-interest."

My case in favor of selfishness goes a step, in fact, miles further. I believe that people need to take very good care of themselves, earnestly meet their own needs, and even pamper themselves with special treats. One of the reasons I believe this is because well-cared-for people have the most to give. They do not give to inspire a guilty response and they do not give as masochists. They have enough humility to know that human beings do not function well as martyrs, but that self-immolation might win the day. A woman who takes good care of herself is well-equipped to give.

The Single Mother

The single mothers with whom I have worked in therapy are often the most guilty mothers of all. They feel the burden of being both mother and father to their children, and they feel like failures for not having provided a sit-com-perfect family setting for their children. The single mother must have the perspective to realize that there are no perfect families and that not all married parents raise their children well. The single mother needs to know that she is doing a good job and then be able to forget parenting for at least part of the time and find a life for herself. The following guidelines are offered to help give perspective to a woman who needs to function both as a mother and as a separate person who is pulling her life together (and single mothers are not the only ones who need this balance).

• Your child needs to be treated as a separate person with a life of his or her own. Your child has a need for love, but just as great is the need to be separate, which is how a child claims power. As a mother, your caring essentially means that you help your child to grow in her own way and see yourself and your child as separate persons.

• Instead of compulsively pouring energy into your child, use your observing ego to become more efficient in the use of your nurturing time. Keep both your meals and the child's clothes simple. Material possessions mean very little and can teach a child to substitute such things for either love or experiences. A serious, planned approach takes less time and energy in the long run. Carefully buying toys that continue to open up adventures and experiences for your child will give good mileage for your investment. Establishing your child with a well-planned routine of music lessons and reading will be of benefit to the child's development and will also begin a long-term pattern of properly structuring the child's time. Sometimes a woman can use her head instead of spending all her energy on her children.

• Forget stereotypes of how you should feel and have the courage to be emotionally honest with your child. If you are emotionally trustworthy, you will accept the real feelings of your child and will be honest about your own. Keeping secrets is exhausting. You should talk freely about what it is like to be you and let your child do the same.

• Experiment to find the roles that work best with you and your children. Parenting is changing; parents are performing less in the role of authority figure and are being real people. It is nearly impossible for a single parent to hold up an image of having it all together, and such an image is not nearly as healthy as the experience of intimacy a child can have with a parent who admits to being a real person.

• Remember that in the parent-child relationship, the giving is largely from parent to child. Parenting is a *job* that requires *unselfish commitment.* Even in an honest relationship, a child should not be overburdened with a parent's problems because a child has his or her own growth issues and problems to face. Often, parenting is a one-way street, and you must therefore find other ways of meeting your needs. This means that your friendships and even love affairs must take up some of your time. If your child is jealous that others are meeting your needs, you must remember that this is a fact of life with which all children must deal. Mother is not the exclusive property of a child.

• Do not be afraid of using baby-sitters or day care centers. Children still view their mothers as their primary nurturers but can learn that their needs can be met by more than one person. Use your ego to find the best source of help that you can find and then relax, knowing that your child is in good hands. A single mother must create her own extended family, and a loving stranger is just as good as a grandmother.

- Decide how you will use your children's early years for your own development. This can be a time to learn a new skill or get a college degree. Some women are starting their own businesses from their homes. Do not let children keep you from the experience of mastering an area of interest to you. You will be a better mother if you do not invest your ego in pressuring your children to succeed on *your* behalf. Cut down on housework, simplify your life, and use their early years as a time to grow.
- Share the nurturing with the children's father as much as possible. It is important that your children love their father and spend time with him, even if you still feel emotionally at odds with him. Use your ego to detach from your needs and to understand theirs. The man who was not a suitable husband for you may well be an adequate or even a good father. In the long run, he can be an important source of support for all of you. One woman I counseled decided that her children could live with their father, at whom she had been extremely angry. "When I thought about it clearly, I realized that they would be well cared for and that they need to relate to him," she said. To help her detach from her personal bitterness, she thought of his home as a sort of boarding school in which the "headmaster" had more than enough investment in doing a good job.

Mother Grows Up

When I was approaching a writing deadline, it became clear that if I expected to continue my practice and complete my book, I would have to be relieved of the responsibility of home and family for a few weeks. I want to share with you some of my growing pains as I struggled with the fear of selfishness and with changing my role within the structure of our family. It was decided that I would be present for meals and evening walks with my family but would be off the hook for chores, meal planning, cooking, and arranging the activities of the children. It was difficult and awkward at first. A messy house beckons to me, and I have difficulty working at home. I am tempted to start brewing a pot of soup on the stove, and one project seems to lead to another. I had to learn the discipline of not doing housework, even if I saw things to be done. It was hard to unlearn something that had been difficult to learn in the first place. I also had to learn not to respond if I thought my children or husband were asking for help in an area they could handle by themselves. Making my work into first priority was much more difficult than I had imagined. To be honest, there were times when I felt resentment, but my family's overwhelming response to my need was one of support. My family quickly became very good at managing their lives without my advice and without my hands doing any of the work.

After a long working weekend out of town at my aunt's house, I came home to a new study they had put together for me. It was a small room that was tucked quietly away on the third floor. This was a stroke that meant a lot to me. They had erected bookshelves and lovingly arranged the books I most use on the shelves. My family had truly risen to the occasion and had become self-sufficient and supportive.

Once, on the third day of a long and productive weekend, I began to feel gloomy. Outside the day was sparkling with fall color and icy air. Perhaps I need to take a walk, I thought to myself. My long walks had become a tradition. No, that's not it. Bake some cookies? I thought. I do love to engage in a homey cooking project; but I was afraid that project would only continue my gloom. Michael was outside doing double wheelies on his bike, and Angie was at ice-skating practice. My husband Steve was in his workshop being a happy carpenter, and I was in a funk.

What is this feeling? I asked myself. As I let the feeling intensify, its character became unmistakable. I was experiencing a bleak and aching loneliness. Having my family become self-sufficient was not enough. Having them leave me alone and support my work was not enough. Having them cater to me was not enough. What did I expect?

I briefly tried another tack with myself—one that contradicts my basic approach to solving human problems. You are a neurotic woman, I scolded myself. Nothing pleases you. You are blocked in your work, and you want to be rescued. Your family has magnanimously risen to the occasion and you are still dissatisfied. Furthermore, you have touched base with an infantile side of yourself that cannot be alone. Shape up and grow up! This approach locked a grim tension around my heartache.

At this point Angie came bursting in downstairs, talking in the boisterous voice that comes from three hours of strenuous skating with other little toughies. I wanted to feel some of her rough-and-ready energy. "Angie, will you please come upstairs," I yelled down, "and ask Mike and Dad to come up, too." When I heard a small army of feet clumping up to the third floor the sadness in me surfaced. They entered the room with friendly curiosity about what their hermit mother had on her agenda. I wrenched out the words, "I need you guys." They knew exactly what I was saying. "You do?" they chimed with question marks floating in their eyes. A tension was broken among us all. I had gone the whole way in getting my needs met, claiming my independence, to going back to them for loving.

This experience forced us to clean up our communications. No longer was I baking brownies in the kitchen in response to my need for the love of my family. I was learning to ask directly for times of closeness—for me.

Letting Kids Go

By being honest about your own human needs for closeness and love you can help your children make a healthy separation from you. Because a mother and child are originally in symbiosis, it can be very difficult to determine whose feelings are whose. When you have a strong feeling of need, are you intuiting a need of your child, or are you projecting your own needs on her? I learned some of these lessons for myself when I trained in Gestalt psychotherapy. The Gestalt theorists have an expression that delineates the process. The direction given to the client is "Sort yourself out!" Just as one sorts the laundry, the ego must define which feelings are one's own and which feelings belong to the other person.

Little did I know when I was driving to a Gestalt training seminar one evening more than ten years ago that I was to learn the first installment of the lesson I am still learning. This was the second meeting of a class that began with a lecture, to be followed by Gestalt experiments. I felt a slight wrenching as I thought of three-year-old Angela and baby Michael being tucked in by our baby-sitter. That cozy scene with its smells of baby powder and sounds of tinkling musical toys made me feel wistful, and I wondered what kind of a mother I was to be dashing out to yet another class, following my obsession to learn as much as I could. A strong image of my little girl missing me came to mind, and I drove to class reluctantly.

At the class, there was some uneasiness when the instructor asked for guinea pigs. "Doesn't anyone have a problem?" she asked the reluctant group. So halfhearted was I about being there that I felt it was a low-risk situation. I volunteered. "It isn't much," I said, sitting in the famed Gestalt "hot seat," which is simply a chair facing an identical empty one.

The trainer was nonchalant. "No sweat," she said. "Just say whatever it is." I described the funny feeling I had about leaving home but said that I was OK, it was no big deal. That was all right with her, too. "What was the main picture in your mind?" she asked casually. "The nursery with the crib," I said, "and mainly Angela missing me." The feeling had suddenly returned, even a bit stronger. "I'm getting a lump in my throat," I reported.

"Let's try an experiment," said the pro. "Look at Angela sitting in the empty chair and talk to her."

"I see you looking very sad, Angie, and you are missing your mommy, but your mommy is gone and you can't reach her," I said.

"Switch chairs and be Angela," said a voice.

I switched chairs and picked up the thread of the child's point of view. "I am missing my mommy, and I don't know where she is."

"Say it again," said the faraway voice.

I began to blubber, and an internal little girl said, "I miss my mommy; she's gone to work, and I am afraid to get out of my bed. I don't like that funny lady, and my room is too dark."

We went on for an hour, with me being the frightened child, and in the other chair, the aloof mother, and finally, the comforting mother.

This was one of the most significant personal therapy moments in my life, during which some repair of a psychic split within myself occurred. To bring me out of my profound regression, the trainer said to me, "You must greet the people who have witnessed this." Looking around the room I saw twenty graduate students like myself, mostly women, their eyes glistening with tears. A moment of embarrassment faded when I saw that they were as open as I was. I shook hands with each one, and the words from them all were similar: "I've been there myself." After class they all seemed to be talking about what their kids were doing, and the trainer said that she had been doing her own work that night about leaving a child at home.

My sadness that night was not only for Angela and Michael. It was for little Susan in 1944, sitting in her crib in a rented room in a home in Lincoln, Nebraska. Daddy was a soldier in France, and mother had left her for a night nursing job. Susan did not want to call for the landlady who was there to look in on her; she wanted her mother.

This is what is meant by sorting yourself out. I realized that I did not need to be obsessive about Angela as a symbol of myself and that this was often the real cause of "sacrificial" mothering. By doing something for our own children, we try but do not heal the inner child in ourselves. Our own children adored our baby-sitter and welcomed time to be with her. In sorting myself out, I realized that if I had stayed home with Angela instead of going to my course, I would not have been meeting her need or getting to the root of healing myself either. We cannot meet our own needs vicariously.

I had another similar important moment of enlightenment. This experience took the form of a sharp remark from the Gestalt ranks.

In 1976 I attended a conference in Austria, and for the first time I met Laura Perls. In a seminar about the physical manifestations of conflicts, I mentioned my experience at the conference. "I am feeling strangely empty-handed," I confessed. "I am not used to walking around for days without holding the tiny hands of my children—guiding them across streets and through the crowds. I guess I feel lost without my children here." Laura Perls would hear no more of such talk. She snapped at me, "My dear, you have got to separate yourself from your children."

Laura Perls, under whom I later trained, was not talking about making my children unimportant to me. She was talking about ego boundaries, which together with self-support are the cornerstones of the Gestalt view of mental health. The third principle that brings this view of health together is excitement. There are emotional sparks of excitement when separate people meet on the boundaries of their differences.

Let me invite you to an exciting life as a mother who is also her own person.

- You are invited to experience with your child the most intimate closeness that two people can have. Your baby can live inside you, feel from you, and receive your love and support.
- You are offered the opportunity as a mother to relive and redo some of your own childhood. As your children grow, you will examine and integrate your own childhood experiences with an eye to continuing the good traditions, doing some things better, and even healing old wounds. There is great joy in searching out better ways to be a loving parent.
- You will enjoy remembering that your husband is the most important person to you and that together you can nurture and amuse each other, as well as do grown-up working and playing together.
- You are encouraged to share nurturing with your husband. Let him share the rich source of affection and the opportunities for growth that will come his way when he gives himself to the human process of nurturing.
- You are allowed to be alone and separate from your family when

you need to be. Knowing that they are there for you can help
you grow.
- You are invited to let your family love you. Everyone must learn
how to love, and you can enjoy being the lucky person on whom
they can all practice their love skills, as well as receiving the
unshakable foundation that comes from having a beloved mother.

When mother grows up she learns how to separate from her
family, taking her own needs as seriously as she takes her children's.
She also learns how to get her own needs met by her family as
well as being available to give to them. A grown-up mother estab-
lishes a family system that is cooperative and based on reciprocity.

The Myth of Superwoman

One difficult decision that faces us is knowing which of our
interests or talents to pursue. Sometimes we are so torn between
two or three possibilities that we feel hopelessly stuck. Unable to
decide, we exhaust ourselves with obsessing about the dilemma,
and in the end we do nothing. This rigidity is considered to be
neurotic. It is true that a healthy ego finds a way through an either/
or trap. If I equally love to sing, invest in real estate, and raise
beagles, there is no way I can happily choose only one of these
interests as primary. A woman with high self-esteem decides that
the smartest choice is not to choose at all. She will do all three.
We are living in the age of superwoman.

It is common to hear a woman refer to her life as a juggling
act. Not only does this term describe the shape of a woman's
average day, but it is an accurate description of her overloaded ego,
creating enormous emotional and physical stress. While she is
doing one thing with her hands, there is another ball in the air,
and she has no free hand to catch it. Knowing that ball is up there
creates anxiety. When will it fall? If a woman is ambitious she
may be juggling a dozen balls, and she has nightmares about
missing a beat and seeing her life come crashing at her feet. The
adage that a woman's work is never done has taken on a catastrophic
dimension.

The superwoman is ashamed for anyone to know how badly her schedule compromises her humanity. She tensely finishes a report in the car while waiting for Kristen to come out of the dancing school. She dreads having to talk to the teacher because she has no time. On the way home she stops at a pay phone to dictate the last two pages to her secretary. She has to pick up the veal chops before the butcher closes, and she hopes there is a cake left at the bakery to satisfy her husband's sweet tooth. (The housekeeper cooks reluctantly and refuses to bake.) Our superwoman is having cramps and longs for her bed and a heating pad. When she gets home, she finds a message that someone gave her husband exceptional theater tickets for that evening and she should meet him in the city. He forgot that it was the orientation night for parents in their son John's new Cub Scout pack. She never has enough time to do all the errands and activities, so of course she has no time to rest or to have a satisfying conversation with anyone. A woman with this dilemma once said to me, desperately, with tears streaming down her face, "Why can't I look at a tree?"

Is this hopeless state really hopeless? The ego has not taken our harried woman in a direction that is in her best interest. She has come up with a faulty solution to her either/or bind, and that is why she is a juggling clown instead of a fulfilled woman, proud of her many accomplishments.

But how can I not do it all at once? The answer lies in two areas. The first is in the way your ego works, and the second is in the way you arrange your life. Let's look to inner space for the first answer. Our needs fall into a natural hierarchy. When we forget the press of external obligations and tune into inner space, our egos will tell us what to do next. My cat knows when she needs to wash, eat, nap, and so on. We do, too. When our egos come up with priority number one, we turn our antennae out to the world and look for the way to fulfill that need. The ego is a brilliant matchmaker. If you are hungry, the ego seeks out the food you need. If you are tired, your ego leads you to your bed. Once a need has been met, an amazing thing happens. The program for meeting that need self-destructs. Poof.

Then the process begins again. The next need in one's inner hierarchy comes into consciousness. The necessary means of meeting it are discovered. Contact is made. The need is met. Poof. In this process one's mind continually goes back to neutral gear, a resting place.

For highly complex needs the method is the same. But the ego has some limitations. One is that it can do only one thing at a time. Another is that the ego works best if you implement one solution before you go on to the next need. This process takes time. You foul up the system when you force simultaneous programs upon your computer. At its extreme, juggling results in a nervous breakdown—a blowout.

How can a woman work within the limits of her own ego structure? First, she must get into a mental rhythm based on three principles:

1. First things first.
2. One thing at a time.
3. Take time to complete each task.

Our psyches need *closure*. Even if a task is externally unfinished, we need to be able to bring ourselves to an internal experience of closure. It could be called "enough for now." Each piece of psychological business is to be finished and then let go. Never obsess about all the things you have to do unless you want to blow your brains out.

Learn the technique of letting things go, so that you work on only one piece of business at a time. In your mind you need to practice a meditative ritual to keep your mental activities from overlapping. Here is the ritual:

Now I am doing X.

Now I am finished doing X. (This does not mean the job is done. It means I am stopping for now.)

Now I am doing Y.

Now I am finished doing Y.

Now I am doing Z.

Now I am finished doing Z.

The sequence for our superwoman might be as follows:

Now I am driving the car to pick up Kristen. (Focus on the process of driving, thinking no other thoughts.)

Now I am finished driving. (Pause. Mentally come to closure, letting it go.)

Now I am listening to music on the tape deck. (Listen peacefully.)

Now I am not listening. (Pause. Let the music naturally drift away.)

Now I am greeting Kristen. (I see Kristen with my eyes. Greet her. Gently hug and kiss her. Feel her presence.)

Now I am not contacting Kristen. (Let the contact come to closure.)

Now I am driving Kristen home. (I drive the car. We are in peaceful silence, or we speak if it feels good and natural.)

Doing this exercise will sort out a hassled psyche. It will put you in the correct flow of making and breaking contact. Even if each activity takes seconds, finish and begin again. Mental fatigue will diminish, sometimes miraculously.

There is a relationship, of course, between the internal process and the way that you structure your life. You will need to arrange your life so that your inner process is never that of juggling. Before you reduce your schedule, you can learn skills that will help you structure your life so as to stay in mental balance.

Have you ever cleaned your house at random, moving toward whatever you happen to see first? You end up exhausted, feeling that you did nothing. A different approach is needed. You must learn to divide and subdivide your tasks, breaking each down into small, easy-to-do components. Decide in what order to do each task, and forget about all the rest while you are doing the first. As you tackle the first component, begin your "meditation":

Now I am cleaning one drawer of my bureau.

Now I am finished cleaning one drawer. (Stop. Admire your work. Rest. Come to internal closure.)

In this case you have experienced completion after one drawer, not after the whole chest or the whole room is clean. A variation is to say: I am going to go through my papers for twenty minutes.

(Stop. Do more at another time.) You will have to make plans and set schedules for yourself. Jobs must be planned and executed with an eye to coming to proper closure at several times during the day and altogether at the end of the day. This process will keep you from becoming mentally overwhelmed and full of stress.

Another skill involves ridding oneself of the drag of unfinished business. Any small unfinished task that you are carrying in your mind, even in the back of your mind, creates an energy drain. The solution is to complete little tasks with dispatch. One way to start is to answer mail or pay bills right after you open them. Delegate your tasks to a calendar, not to the back of your mind. Don't allow yourself to be drained by an unfinished detail. There are three choices:

1. Send a birthday card now, or
2. Decide not to send a birthday card, or
3. Plan what day you will send it, write it on your calendar, and forget it until then.

Do not commit yourself to accomplishing tasks you will not follow through with. Maybe you are a person who does not write letters or lead Cub Scout dens. So what? Use caution before you make a promise. As busy as your life may be, your first priority must be to cultivate a clear mind.

Sometimes a woman is a bit of a turtle, carrying her whole life around with her. This is altogether unnecessary. Yes, you love your kids, your husband, or your boy friend. But when you are going about your daily life, forget them for awhile. Women some-times complain that men are too engrossed in their work and neglect women—that their attitude is out of sight, out of mind. It is essential that an active woman adopt the same attitude. Learn it, or don't live in the world of work. Don't worry about your kids; instead, wish them well. If there are problems, take time to solve them. Obsession and worry exhaust you and solve nothing.

Trust yourself to do what is important. The world will not pass you by if you stop juggling. On the contrary, your experiences will stop passing you by because you will be *living* them. Life is not a race, so stop trying to come in first or run the farthest. Life is living in the present moment.

From time to time it is important to be able to clear one's mind totally. We need to be able to go into neutral gear and let our motors idle. Oriental forms of meditation or yoga are excellent aids to get you into a state of deep relaxation and peace.

I use a very simple form of focused breathing several times a day to clear my mind and feel joyfully at peace. I get into a comfortable position, breathe in, and then whisper one word as I breathe out. I keep my breath long, deep, and slow. This exercise takes me from five to ten minutes. The word that I whisper varies, and I let my imagination lead me to it. Sometimes I use words like peace, joy, serene, and slow. If I need to be centered I might say my name or me. If I need to be unblocked I say give, live, go, no. If I am sick, I say relax or heal. I use only one word for one little session. If you do this exercise, do not fight the distracting thoughts that come into your mind. Simply picture them floating out of your head and leaving. This exercise is not exciting. You may think it doesn't amount to much. That's what you want: to go back to square one and rest for awhile.

With inner peace as a firm habit, you will arrange your priorities and will not do more than you can enjoy. You will organize yourself around your internal rhythms. Instead of being interferences in the obstacle course of your life, your work and loved ones will be treasures. Each part of your life will be a precious jewel to be enjoyed in its own setting. The moments of your life will sparkle and glow. Superwoman is frazzled and harried. Be a human woman instead.

Humor Is an Ego Strength

Laughter releases tension. A sense of the ridiculous provides perspective. It is a way of transcending situations that are otherwise impossible. Laughter gets you off the hook and lets you be human. You also let other people off the hook when you make good jokes on yourself—the ones they would like to make but don't dare to.

The comediennes and writers who tell us that housework is a joke do a wonderful job of healing our egos. They remind us that we are not the only person who cannot do the impossible. Phyllis Diller tells us: "I'm eighteen years behind on my ironing. There's no use doing it now, it doesn't fit anybody I know!" Taking housework too seriously is the main problem with the mother/homemaker role. But if you let yourself see the farcical aspects of homemaking and family living, your ego will be able to transcend and even enjoy some of the situations that are the most impossible.

It is possible to work at developing a good sense of humor. Encourage those around you to tell you jokes, and tell a few yourself. Kids are usually full of jokes, but you have to be ready for the X-rated ones once they get rolling. Read humorous books and seek funny entertainment. Your favorite laughs can generally be rekindled. If someone else sees the humor of the moment, get on that person's wavelength if you possibly can. This is a natural human capacity; you just need to catch on to it. Humor is an important ego strength, a very real part of health and healing, and should be an asset of every female ego.

Cooperative Living

Having a child is a great shock to many women. Suddenly a woman is anchored to the house because of a small being who must be attended to at all times. Motherhood creates a very real trap in which her ego can feel overwhelmed. At the same time, the demands of housework increase because children make enormous messes, create more dirty laundry than most adults, and require special, well-planned meals. If a woman is to continue to grow as an individual during the time when she is most involved in motherhood she must use her ego to deal with being housebound. If she and her husband identify their sense of worth in the beauty of their home, she might make her housebound position into even more of a trap than it needs to be. She must find a way to get out of the house part of the time and connect with other worlds. It is important to decide how you are going to spend your energy and to get help with the tasks that you are unwilling to do. You may think you have no options, but you must find them anyway, beginning with the people with whom you live.

I am grateful to my obstetrician, who made me agree to his suggestion: "After you have been home for one week after delivery, you must get a sitter and go out for dinner, just the two of you." When the time came, it was not easy to pull myself together to go out, but it was exactly what I needed. I went through the difficult process of finding a baby-sitter. It is worth ego investment for every mother to find a good baby-sitter whom she can afford, or to work out an exchange program with other mothers, if she is to maintain her separate, growing self.

The following methods have worked for the women I know who want more than an occasional sitter:

- Exchange baby-sitting. Take care of your own and a friend's child three afternoons per week and have three afternoons free.
- Board your child during the day in a loving home so you can work or go to school.
- Have a college student or a young person from another country live in your home and do child care in exchange for a home, plus allowance. This arrangement is very workable and possible. You might even be the first person on the block to do it, as I was.
- Find a warmhearted housekeeper who prefers to do child care. She can do chores while the children nap. She will be expensive and just as difficult to find as the other options.
- Adopt a grandmother. This means hiring a woman (possibly one whose children are grown) who can become part of the home and to whom your children can feel a loving attachment. This special person is best located by putting an ad in a newspaper and offering more money than the going rate for a baby-sitter.

Clever asking and advertising will bring results. A bold friend of mine scoured her apartment building and found an unlikely woman who spoke very little English. She soon became for that family a real Mary Poppins. By advertising on bulletin boards at colleges and art or dance schools you can find competent people who need part-time work. A neighbor who is a single parent has a South American undergraduate student living in her home. Even with three children, she is able to work at a full-time job. By using your ego, it is possible to find the help you need.

As much as you desire to mother your children, having the breaks that you need is the best way to maintain the constancy of your love for them. If you can continue to grow during their infancy and childhood, you can love them without sacrificing for them.

Fathers Can Nurture, Too

When children are born, the pattern of living is much easier for the woman who does not have to say, "It's all up to me." A woman's ego can be overwhelmed by believing that she is supposed to handle it all. The energy, support, and involvement of a father can make the difference in how her ego handles this experience. It is not unusual today for a young father to take charge of the kids for an hour or two after work, which can be a joyful diversion if he makes it one. "Georgie likes hockey but not football," said a young father of his three-month-old son with whom he plays during the ball games on television.

A couple who split the restaurant checks when they were dating will find sharing domestic duties the natural way to run their home. With a bit more struggle, older couples are growing in this direction as well. Some women want a husband's help but have difficulty giving up control over how things are done. One woman complained to me, "Why does he insist on being involved in choosing the color of the kitchen tiles?" The answer was clear: It is his kitchen, too.

Couples today have made their children portable. With disposable diapers, collapsible strollers, and tiny food grinders, they go to restaurants, visit friends, and even take extensive trips abroad with young children. But this family lifestyle is possible only when you share the chores.

When homemaking and nurturing are shared, the atmosphere

within the family changes. As burdens are lifted from the mother, her ego becomes more expansive. When her life is easier, the entire family can feel more adventuresome. New activities and family trips seem more feasible. The liberation of a woman can mean the liberation of a family.

Breaking the Old Script

I know numerous women who have heard by the grapevine that their mothers-in-law thought that their sons were doing too much of the work. One client said to me, "Here I am working at a full-time job, and she talks about me as if Jack does all the housework while I sit around combing my hair." I can easily imagine the in-laws' side. When they come to dinner, they observe their son doing what is becoming a male tradition in some households: because the wife has cooked the meal, he clears the table and does not let anyone help him. After he has cleared the table, the baby cries from upstairs, and he zips up to attend to her. Meanwhile, the daughter-in-law holds the conversation together at the table and savors her glass of wine. To a mother-in-law who is a traditional mother-housewife, this spectacle must be shocking.

Aides and Generals

It is interesting to see the self-put-down inherent in the mother-in-law's attitude. Why does a man need to be protected from domestic work? Is the work terrible, and if so, why should a woman do it either? In the army there is a theory that a general needs to be free to focus on thinking and planning. This is the reason why he is always attended by an aide who does everything for him. He is driven, his shoes are polished, his food is prepared, and doors are opened for him by a silent second pair of hands. A West Point graduate told me that he learned that an officer should never be seen carrying a package, and his wife wondered what would happen if they went to the supermarket together.

This structure—with the man as the general and his wife as

the aide—has prevailed in many homes. But women with egos are deciding that they do not want to be aides any longer. They too want to focus on thinking and planning. The tasks of human maintenance in the home are difficult only when one person gets stuck doing all of it for everyone else.

One of the most distressing evenings I ever spent occurred when my husband was in seminary during the first year of our marriage. A much admired faculty member gave a speech to the student wives on how to be a good minister's wife. He described the beauty and majesty of the great ships as they enter New York Harbor. These ships symbolized our husbands. He then told us that no one watching this spectacle would know that a large ship cannot move into the harbor by itself. Behind each ship is a very strong and cute little tugboat. The tugboats were—you guessed it! Thrilled with his metaphor, he elaborated on his tugboat theory of being a wife and mother, and I went home unhappy and angry.

One of the most important challenges to today's female ego is changing the structure of the home. Every woman needs a sense of mastery, and to acquire it she needs time for her own focused work, as well as time to feel good and get filled up with energy and inspiration. You deserve your fair share of support and encouragement. Use *mutuality* as your guide for change. The goal is not to have a henpecked husband but to learn how to be fair in supporting each other's egos. And this support often boils down to who is going to make the soup tonight.

Mary and Martha

There is one area in which the role of a woman needs to undergo a change in order for her to be happier and more resourceful in fulfilling her responsibilities in a family. She needs to separate in her mind and in her time the *role* of nurturer from the *job* of housekeeping. Cleaning is not the same as loving. Cooking is not the same as caring. Scrubbing is a job; comforting is assuming the role of nurturer.

The New Testament story of Mary and Martha delineates the

difference between loving and doing domestic chores. Jesus was visiting his friends Mary and Martha. Mary sat at his feet and listened to him intently. Martha, her sister, was "cumbered with much serving," and she complained because her sister was not helping her. Jesus said, "Martha, you are troubled about many things. But one thing is needful:... Mary has chosen the good part which shall not be taken away from her." Many women are Marthas, anxious about serving others, engrossed in the chores of running a household, and frustrated because they are not enjoying themselves. Human affection and fun are not only the most important parts of family life, they are also the parts that feel good. A day when I rush home from the office, pick up groceries, and then decide to clean the refrigerator before I put the groceries away is a day when I do not enjoy my children and I feel angry and harassed. The children's carefree spirits are irritating to me when I am overdoing the housework. Love and affection must come first. They are the good parts. The mother who can choose to be Mary instead of Martha puts loving contact ahead of housework. The Marthas of the world need to learn that housework can be delegated or postponed more easily than the needs for affection and attention. By enjoying her family, she can get her own needs met as well, thus claiming her share of the good part.

Making this distinction will free a woman from the tyranny of thinking that her love for her family must take the form of a house beautiful. She will love them more if she puts nurturing before housework, and this applies to nurturing herself as well.

Breaking the Stereotypes of Who Does What

In a modern home with a working mother, it is necessary for the family members to share the chores and perhaps to hire outside help as well. I am in favor of a family learning as much self-care as possible, and I am acutely aware of the benefits to the ego for people who achieve self-support. It may be unconventional to have a nine-year-old boy be the short-order cook at breakfast, for a twelve-year-old girl to do the family's clothes washing, or for the father to change the sheets and plan the menus, but the benefits of such family cooperation enhance the egos of all the participants.

When we were first married, Steve and I lived in an apartment building for the married students at the seminary he was attending. Across the hall from us lived a couple with three children. The father was a young retired marine, and his wife was supporting the family by working at a full-time job. I was amazed because the husband organized their household so that it functioned like a military ship. Each child had chores that were vital to the functioning of this busy and unusually happy family. One evening when we were visiting them, they let us watch Karen prepare the family's breakfast for the following morning. Karen was three years old. Like a monkey she climbed up and down, walking on counter tops and assembling bowls, spoons, and mugs. "What kind of cereal do you want, Daddy?" she asked as she surveyed the shelf of Wheaties and Cheerios. I will never forget those happy children whose home was shipshape because of cooperative efforts. Mastery of tasks along with being needed and appreciated enhances the egos of all family members.

You can organize your family, too. First, make a list of all the regular chores that need to be done. Show this list to all family members, one at a time, and ask them to think about which chores they would be willing to do. This is a time of consciousness raising. Seeing the list will give them a picture of the work that you have been doing. Then have a family meeting in which you make a plan together. By this time, they have had time to give the idea some thought. You can then negotiate about who does what. Rotating jobs can be a good idea, so that nobody is stuck permanently with a job he or she would prefer not to do. I believe that knowledge of a job well done and increased morale in the family rewards such a plan and will keep it going. Children need an allowance, but family maintenance is a given, like homework, and does not need to be paid for in money. One option, of course, which is very helpful for a working woman, is to hire occasional help for the heavy housework.

Encountering Resistance

An assertive female ego holds the key to making these changes. Pussyfooting around because of other members' resistance will not work. The female ego must assert her truth, in spite of the resistance. Saying, "I'm tired and am no longer buying the groceries or doing the laundry" might be a good way to introduce this idea. Your family will change only if forced to change. One overworked woman hung a sign in her kitchen which read, "The kitchen is closed for the summer." Did her family like it? No. Did it work? Yes. At first, everyone thought it was a joke. But Mary really had come to the end of her rope. Her husband came home from work very late, her son had to eat early before basketball practice, and her daughter was experimenting with being a vegetarian. They did not have real family dinners, and yet Mary found herself in the kitchen for two or three hours each day. When they realized she meant it, the teenagers got together and made a meal late in the afternoon, and Mary joined them for a salad and a cup of tea. If Bill, her husband, got home after 8:00, he would have already eaten something that he ordered at the office. He decided it was better for his health to eat early. Together they discovered a way of having dinners when he got home early—they had frozen items from a gourmet caterer or went out for a simple dinner at one of their two favorite casual restaurants. They also have weight-watching evenings when supper is an omelet or yogurt and fruit. It had become absurd for Mary to be on kitchen duty, and when she found the courage to relinquish this job, the family worked out a successful, cooperative solution.

The following guidelines can help you teach your family to cooperate:

- Present the jobs to be done in an *objective* fashion. Use lists, charts, calendars, and written proposals.
- Be clear and objective about what jobs you are willing to do and what ones you are not willing to do.
- Let your family members struggle with the problem. Do not

rescue them with a solution that puts you back where you started.
- Get moral support from a friend outside of the family. Your family might initially withhold strokes, causing you to back down.
- Let your family know how it makes you feel to be overburdened. Tell them how you want to spend your time instead.
- Be confident in what you are doing. That means that you do not budge from your main points, even if you sound like a broken record.
- Be prepared for emotional blackmail and genuine temporary feelings of disappointment. Your family might wonder, Doesn't she love us anymore? Remember that love is not housework, and be prepared to teach them the difference.
- Get them on your side. Tell them how much their help would mean to you. Let them know that you love them and that you want your good feelings to be flowing all the time. Tell them about how much you need time for your own development as a person. Be as persuasive as you possibly can be.

Sharing the Time

In considering cooperative living in a family, we must carefully examine the quality of the time that we spend in nurturing. The love relationship between husband and wife is a first priority. When couples in counseling ask me what is important, I always say time. Love takes time. There are no shortcuts.

More time is better than less time. But the quality of that time is even more important. Couples need a combination of problem-solving time and time to have fun together. Relationships are continually growing, so there must be time for stimulating talks, heart-to-heart intimacies, and rich sexuality.

Spending Time with the Kids

What is quality time? First, your child, or each child, needs to have a date with you, alone. Ideally such a date is a daily occurrence. The highest quality of relating is intimacy, and that means one to one, just you and me. My kids call this having "times" and each counts on a scheduled half hour dose daily. If a child knows when she will have your undivided attention, she will be less likely to ask for it at the wrong time for you or to seek it by behaving badly.

What do you do during your time alone with your child? The real psychological task to be accomplished is to meet your child's need to be loved unconditionally. This means I love you no matter what and just because you are you. The best structure for this life-sustaining process is no structure. Your child will let you know how she or he needs to borrow your ego and tap into your love. Many children will complain, gripe, and tell you their fears. Your job is to listen, accept, and not talk them out of their feelings. They are getting over them by giving them to you. Subtly you might suggest a different outlook, but back off if it isn't gratefully accepted. During this process the child is letting you be her protector. By simply being there you are meeting the needs of the child to feel safe, protected, and accepted.

The second important part of "times" (after the gripe session) is the exchange of love and strokes. You may need to initiate this process at first. Remember that both mother and child need the experience of their loving connection. The best stroking is playful. Give each other back or foot massages. Touching comforts and affirms us deeply. Crack jokes or exchange funny experiences. When your child tells you an idea or a fantasy, admire his or her thoughts. If your child is inclined to tell you what he or she did that day, listen intently. Above all, make no demands. By spending this focused time with your child, you are communicating a beautiful message: *you are nice to be with.*

Enjoying Family Time

In addition to time alone with various family members, there is a need for family time, time to be together, time to be a clan. We once had a cocker spaniel who would express a sense of the joy about the pack being together. At night she would greet the family members as they came home at various times like any normal, friendly dog. But when the last person came home, she would go into ridiculous gyrations—leaping in the air, rolling across the floor, and wildly shimmying on her back. Most humans are not so brazenly uninhibited about their feelings, but it feels wonderful for the clan to be together in one room, to see one another's faces in the glow of evening lights.

Time to Be Alone

We must provide for alone time in our lives. Everyone needs time to think, to muddle through problems and tasks, to plan, and to dream. Mother needs to go to her room and close the door from time to time, and if she believes that her family will wilt if she is not constantly sprinkling them with love and concern, everyone is being deprived of experiencing self-reliance. Everyone's character will be weak—including mother's.

Everyone in a home needs a space of his or her very own. Often children have their own rooms. Dad enjoys a den or the basement and even the garage as his own. Shared space includes living rooms, family rooms, and the kitchen. Mother and Dad usually share a bedroom. So what about a personal space for mother to enjoy as a separate person? I think that most of our homes need such a space if they are to help a woman feel sustained and important. If you do not have your own room, you should be able to spend time in the bedroom alone when you need to and know that you are off duty.

What It's All About

Life seems to be busier these days. There is less time for the home arts, but this does not need to mean that there is any less love. Mother may not be filling the house with the cinnamon aroma of an apple pie, but she can exchange love in less time than it takes to bake a pie. Love is better, not only because it has fewer calories but because it will not make a mother as tired. The direct expression of love is better than one hidden in an apple pie—no one has to interpret it. The task of the female ego in motherhood is to overcome female masochism. If her home truly supports her life, she will be free of the inner conflicts that lead to martyrdom.

ᔥ 6 ᔥ

The Female Ego
in Love

Let there be spaces in your togetherness.
Kahlil Gibran

Why Do People Fall in Love?

We usually let ourselves love deeply before we know ourselves very well. According to Freud, an unconscious approach to such matters is best. He felt that the conscious mind is very good at deciding such questions as where to live, how to live, and how to spend money. But in making the most important decisions of one's life, particularly whom to marry, the unconscious mind possesses the deepest wisdom. I think that this theory works in practice only when a woman is flowing freely and is emotionally in touch with her basic, strong feelings. A woman who is primarily a people-pleaser is not likely to make a choice on behalf of her true self.

Waiting for a Strong Man

Many women feel that success in love is the true measure of their personal worth. A woman who has been conditioned to be a people-pleaser needs someone to want her helpfulness, to receive the gift of herself. Her very being constitutes a hope chest, filled with talents to be used by a man. She needs someone to whom

150

she can adapt. She lacks life and energy without a man to make demands on her.

The people-pleaser may find the controlling, macho man very appealing. He provides her with someone forceful, sure, and demanding to flutter over. Never mind that he might also be a bully or a narcissist or lack tenderness. A more reasonable, gentle man might rob her of the raison d'être that she seeks outside of herself. An adaptable woman needs to borrow an inflated ego to compensate for her own undeveloped one.

In examining yourself, it is important to ask, Am I most comfortable with a man whom I perceive to be stronger and more forceful than I am? A healthy female ego enjoys feeling strong, too. The healthiest contact for your ego is with someone who is a peer and an equal. Otherwise, you risk feeling diminished. You need to question the fantasy of romance based on domination and subordination. Love between two strong people is the most exciting and certainly the most healthy kind.

Women Are Changing

In addition to their traditional role of emotional caregivers, women are becoming breadwinners. Earning power means psychological power. Money is strength and leverage not only in the world but also within the family. A woman can choose not to claim this power on her own behalf, and many working women continue their self-sacrificing and people-pleasing habits. Changes are taking place, however. Eventually a woman gets tired of being assertive on the job and then becoming sweet and slavish when she is with a man. I observe this change occurring across many generations of women as they develop ego strength.

Love Can Overwhelm the Ego

Falling in love is an experience that most women think they want more than anything else. At the same time, falling in love can be the easiest and most devastating way for a woman to lose her sense of herself. The main issue for the female ego in love is to deal with the threatened loss of self. (I am discussing primarily issues of heterosexual relationships, but the general discussion of the skills of loving and the ego problems in falling in love apply to women of all sexual preferences.) A woman must have a strong ego if she is to have deep love in her life and not lose herself.

Yet the need to love and to be loved is profound and human. If we try to escape our love needs, they increase. Attempts at self-sufficiency can make us more needy and lead us to cynicism and despair. Even a painful heartbreak usually does not inoculate a person from trying for love once again.

We are born into a family system which is essentially a love unit and in which children are the products of a love relationship. Even though we may sometimes do it badly, loving is a primary human activity around which we structure our lives. Love involves deep feelings with which we should become comfortable, and love embodies skills at which a woman should become proficient.

Born for Love

The instinct to love and to form a mating bond takes the form of intense sexual and emotional desire for another person. The numerous cultural traditions and familial expectations surrounding marriage are essentially a formalization of the human desire to mate. A woman may be too adaptable in the role she plays in marriage, but her desire for a mate is not an adaptation. The desire for a mate comes from within, and it is natural for a woman to want to fulfill that desire.

I have worked with women who strongly want to get married and yet criticize themselves for having this desire. If a woman has the strong urge to marry, she should not consider that desire a weakness or an aberration. She might better spend her energy solving the problems of her ambivalence or lack of skill in loving or the problem of actually finding a mate. Our lives do not have to be ordered entirely according to our instincts, but we are more at peace when we accept the instinct to mate as natural, not as a sign of negative dependency.

Love Makes a Difference

A committed love relationship is not the only source of fulfillment, but love is certainly one of the major ways to find meaning in life. Shared joys can be greater than solitary ones. Generosity is more rewarding than selfishness. Differences cause us to grow. Strokes help us to blossom.

Sam came to therapy originally to deal with his grief over the loss of a child by an early marriage that ended in divorce. Eventually, he brought his girl friend, Faye, for couple counseling. He complained that she was pressuring him. She was discontented because she saw him only two nights a week. They were in a holding pattern, and she wanted more. Through increased communication they realized that their relationship was at a dead end if they did not intend it to grow. Gradually Sam let Faye become closer to him, and he shared with her the pain of losing a son with whom he had spent very little time. They decided to marry, and a beautiful change has occurred in both of them. It could best be described as a relief from loneliness. They have long and deep conversations, and they find that needs are being met that they did not realize they had.

My client Melanie married for the first time at the age of thirty-seven. Once very controlling and obsessional about details, she has become much more open and fun-loving as the result of a marriage in which she has embraced many new experiences that have taught her the pleasure of being occasionally impulsive. "It used to take me a week to pack for my vacation, and now I will throw together a suitcase on the spur of the moment and go away with Peter for the weekend," she once told me.

Committing oneself to someone else often adds an emotionally charged quality to a previously humdrum life. I have found the relationships that have offered healing, such as the cases of Sam and Faye and Melanie, the most inspiring. None of us had a perfect childhood, and for many people marriage provides a profound corrective experience. In becoming dependent on a mate, many self-sufficient people claim their emotional health and their humanity.

Dating, Not Mating

Some women hold onto their identities by not taking the risk of forming a truly intimate or committed relationship. Dating, instead of being the pathway to mating, is the permanent structure of such a woman's love life. She values the superficial aspects of courtship more than commitment.

The woman who is dating often wants proof of love in the form of treats and presents because she has not tapped into a deeper level of knowing that she is loved. When people mate, there is a deep and unspoken commitment, along with the spoken ones, on which they rely and trust. In dating one is trying to make an impression, whereas in a mating relationship one focuses more on trying to help. Dating is being seen at a party with the most eligible guy. Mating is staying at home with a guy who is no longer eligible because he belongs to you. The daters ask, "Who pays?" The maters say, "Who cares?" Dating focuses on the now; mating focuses on the now plus the forever after.

A woman who fears mating will find blemishes in her dating partner when the contact with him becomes truly intimate. Dating is a means of having contact without commitment. Her negative scrutinizing can be a compulsive mechanism to ensure that real closeness does not occur. A woman without solid confidence in herself feels that she has a great deal to lose in relinquishing a part of her ego in mating, even if it appears to promise a state of happily ever after. To separate herself from this threat, she will find fault with a man in her mind to make herself detach from him.

It is normal for a young woman to go through a period of heightened narcissism. For the adolescent woman, narcissism is a preparation for leaving home, going to work, and mating. She enjoys her own assets and takes pleasure in being appreciated and courted. Narcissism becomes pathological when self-love is substituted for the love of other people. The healthy psychological growth pattern is from narcissism to mutuality, in which one responds generously to the needs of another person.

A person without a strong sense of self will remain arrested in narcissism. She is more excited by her image and her social contacts than by loving contact. She requires entertainment and stimulation to buttress a shaky identity and to substitute for the love she is not allowing herself to experience.

Dreams to Nowhere

A healthy female ego lives and loves according to the *reality principle* and is not sentimental or eternally wishful. If your ego is not attuned to the realities of what is happening, you will make the wrong decisions for yourself. A woman is much better off knowing and forgiving the shortcomings of a man than not knowing what his shortcomings are. If you live in a dream world, you put life on hold. No ordinary man is good enough for a woman who is too sentimental and out of touch with reality. As a result, she either will be without a mate or will be disappointed in the one she chooses when she discovers his imperfections. She will be deprived of the joys the real world has to offer.

A Loveless Life Script

Many women with whom I have worked have experienced no deep and loving commitments in their lives. Upon examining the reasons why, we have often found that love was not in their life scripts. They had been conditioned to live without love.

When a woman has been well loved by her family, she usually seeks the same attention in the world. When my daughter Angela was three, I enrolled her in a morning nursery school. I was apprehensive about leaving her at the school on the first day. She had probably picked up some of my anxiety because she began to complain about going. Together, my husband Steve and I escorted her to the school, and as we drove home Steve comforted me with these words, "We have been very loving to Angela. She will expect to find love wherever she goes. If there is a warm person at nursery school, she will reach out to that person." His words were uncanny in their truth. When we arrived to pick her up, she was sitting on the lap of the most motherly of the teachers, looking at a book.

When I think about the loveless lives of some of the women with whom I have worked, I realize that there are many forms of script limitations leading to loveless living. Some women learned as they grew up that they were not supposed to love anyone but family members. Such exclusivity leads to lovelessness later on.

Certain loners with whom I have worked are disengaged from the process of loving. These women never received enough love to enable them to separate from their parents and become whole people. Lacking in both dependent and independent stroking, they function as incomplete beings. The resulting sense of personal inadequacy keeps a loner from seeking love.

Another group is the waifs, women who are waiting and longing for love. These women cling to relationships that never meet their inner needs. So hooked are they on longing that they do not stop clinging to an unsatisfying relationship even when opportunities for love come their way. They are afraid to give up the "bird in hand."

Sometimes a waif is someone who never had to work at love and had everything automatically given to her. A woman who has been overindulged will be helpless to initiate love in her life. She will wait and long for her prince to come, rather than making efforts to find him.

Some women exhibit a very subtle loveless life script. In therapy they pretend that their childhood was rich in love, when actually they lacked loving support. They do not recognize that the love they received was deficient because they have erected defenses to keep from feeling the pain of being neglected.

Louise was always worrying about the welfare of her parents and her brothers and sisters. She visited her parents as often as possible and overlooked the fact that they gave back very little affection and preferred one of her sisters. Her defense was a fantasy belief: My loving you means that you love me. Louise filled herself with her own caring for her parents and her siblings, exempting them from any responsibility to love her.

Such a generous and overcompensating woman unconsciously wishes that by her being a loving person, love will magically come her way. The truth is that only generous people will reciprocate love; stingy people will continue to take and never will give.

Coming to terms with the lack of love in your life is a very painful part of the psychotherapeutic process. But until a woman has a firm and clear grasp on the dynamics of a loveless script, she will continue to live it. Adapting to having absolved everyone of the responsibility to love her creates many problems in her life. If you have the problem of a loveless live script, get help.

People need to be taught how to love others. A woman who feels strongly about her right to have what she wants will be a good teacher. Displeased when he withholds and graciously loving when he treats her well, a confident woman will teach a novice husband or lover how to love her well.

Looking for Mr. Right

Several years ago I spent a week interviewing new clients at the counseling center where I practiced. Almost every woman I saw lamented that she did not have a serious relationship. Most of them seemed to be passive and bewildered about their situations. Something that was supposed to happen had not, and they did not have a clue as to how to make a relationship happen. Visiting singles bars and casual dating seemed to lead nowhere.

That weekend I began to give this subject serious thought. At first I exempted myself from being able to contribute any personal data because I had married ten years earlier. I thought that times might have been different then. But I soon realized that I had another reason for not wanting to tap into my own experience.

There was something about my courtship that had always disturbed me, and I did not want to unearth a painful memory. The minute I met Steve I was crazy about him, but he seemed a bit reluctant to get involved. It was I who engineered the relationship. I was not obviously aggressive, but I certainly did plenty of plotting and scheming behind the scenes. I had swallowed my secret hurt at not being pursued and promised the sun and the moon. I felt particularly bitter when I found out that he had once chased a former girl friend across the country and back. I believed that such urgency had not flowed in my direction because I had been so willing to say yes. In my heart of hearts, however, I am a realist, and I decided that not being dramatically courted was the trade-off that I was making in order to get the man I wanted. After all, he was mine, and we were deeply in love.

In resurrecting my buried hurt about not being courted according to my fantasies, I became curious and wondered whether my story was unusual. That Saturday night we were going to a dinner party with our closest friends. I took an informal poll. I asked each married couple, "Which of you did the choosing, you or he?" Some answered that they both did. But nearly every couple admitted that there was more energy on one side than on the other. The overwhelming majority of the men said, "She chose me." I have learned that women generally are in charge of the emotional aspects of life and that they have a lot of influence over their own courtships. As one man put it, "I chased her until she caught me."

When a woman undertakes the courting of a man she needs to be sure that she is looking for a real man, not for perfection. Being with a man is one of the answers to happiness, but he does not have to provide *all* the answers. Removing the pressure of great expectations can enable a woman to choose a man whom she understands as a mixture of strengths and weaknesses.

Promises to Keep

When a woman courts a man, she makes him promises. She does not usually promise to be a fabulous girl friend, but rather to be a best friend. Many a clever woman demonstrates the biblical notion of being a helpmate. She will type a man's papers, help him pick out his clothes, or cook him a wonderful dinner. A woman usually courts a man by promising nurturing in a form that is easy to take. This ability to nurture is often what a man wants in a wife who will be the mother of his children. The modern female helpmate often promises to be a wage earner, and many men want to marry women who will contribute to a two-paycheck household for a significant part of their married lives. Courtship is tricky because it involves making promises. A woman will discover that if she woos a man by promising everlasting maternal care, he will resent her if she does not provide it. This promise can translate into a lot of work. Your ego must decide what you are willing to give. The artful display of those gifts is the essence of courtship.

The Responsive Woman

There is something wonderful about an emotionally alive woman, so long as her responsiveness and caring do not lead to her being easily manipulated. Courtship is the proving ground on which a woman demonstrates her responsiveness. The man may bring her flowers, but her exquisite reception is the real prize. The worst thing that a man can say about a woman is "She leaves me cold." A frigid woman seems hardly a woman at all. With ego strength, you can avoid the extremes, expressing your warmth without being a people-pleaser.

Requiring Respect

As well as making promises to a man, your ego must decide what you expect to receive for yourself. A woman with a healthy ego usually expects both respect and commitment. It is impossible to sustain love without respect, and this is why it is difficult for a man to love a woman who makes herself into a doormat. One of the problems with compulsive people-pleasing is that it is a quality *that most men do not respect in themselves*. If a woman wants love, her ego must seek respect.

One of my clients complained about her uncommitted boy friend. She was particularly distraught when he did not invite her to dinner to celebrate her promotion at work. When she invited him, he could not decide which evening would be convenient. She solved her problem by giving him the following message: "I will be having dinner with Diane and John on Friday. If you want to come, let me know by tomorrow. Otherwise I am inviting another person." Several such maneuvers soon had him respecting her needs.

In another doormat relationship, a woman informed her neglectful beau that she was available for only two nights per week. She asked him to let her know one week in advance whether he wanted to spend those evenings with her. Bewildered and hurt he asked, "What will you be doing on the other nights?" "That is my business," she smartly told him.

Mr. Right is not a fantasy. He is a real person and probably an imperfect one. You can forgive his human weaknesses, but you cannot forgive his disrespecting you or withholding loving concern for your feelings. If he is unaware of such behavior, enlighten him. If he is stubborn, you may have to confront him. Your goal may be love, but that does not mean being soft. Real love embodies the hard virtues of respect and commitment.

Commitment Is Respect in Action

Commitment has a meaning that goes beyond a promise to stay for awhile or even forever. Commitment means that a person cares about the results of her or his behavior on the other person. It means that you can count on someone paying attention to how you are feeling and caring about your feelings. You get what you expect. Sometimes you need only to ask.

Muster the ego strength to confront a man if he is not treating you well. Be confident in the knowledge that you will both be happier if you treat each other well. The healthy female ego knows this and is not timid about doing whatever she needs to do to ensure mutual love based on respect and commitment.

The Politics of Courtship

The sexual revolution has changed the patterns and politics of courtship. Twenty-five years ago a woman was careful about saying yes to sex because she used sex as leverage to gain a man's commitment. Sex with a so-called good woman used to be a reward to a man for good behavior. Good behavior usually meant either marriage or a diamond ring and a promise. Those standards worked when women married in their late teens. But maintaining leverage in a relationship by withholding sex—particularly as women marry later in life—gives a woman the wrong messages about her sexual needs and puts her out of touch with her needs for intimacy and sex. If nice girls don't have sex, the message is loud and clear that her own sexuality is somehow not OK. And yet there are some reality issues surrounding sex that a woman must consider.

A woman needs to protect herself with the knowledge that sex often will lead her into a deep emotional attachment, even if the man would not be a good mate for her. Many women experience deep bonding with men when they become sexually involved. Many men, on the other hand, like to believe that they are immune to any attachments that mean so much that they might get hurt. They mentally practice distancing themselves and think that they have it made if they can feel close to a woman and detached at the same time.

A woman who is using her ego will be able to size up a man and not give him a deep emotional commitment if he is not offering the same to her. Be honest about your own love style, particularly deciding whether your emotional bonding is the result of sexual intimacy, as it is for many women. There is nothing wrong with this; in fact, it is an aspect of being emotionally integrated. Ask yourself the following questions about the man with whom you are involved. Remember that no one is perfect and that men are allowed to have immature qualities. The issue for the female ego is to understand what she is dealing with, plan strategies to change the situation, and have the courage to cut her losses if the situation is impossible.

- Is this a good person for me to become deeply attached to? Look carefully at his track record in relationships to discover his script in regard to women. Also look for serious problems, such as substance abuse or a basic lack of respect for women. You can save yourself a lot of pain by using your ego to check him out before you get in too deep.
- Is this man experimenting with his own sexual liberation? If so, it is not necessarily a problem, but the sexual revolution passed some men by, and they still believe in the "good girl," "bad girl" categories. He may not respect the women who get involved with him sexually.
- Do we want the same things from this relationship? Do not be afraid to communicate what you are looking for and encourage him to do the same. If one of you is secretly looking for a mate and the other wants a very casual dating relationship or a good friend, guilt and hurt feelings will be the ultimate result. Be forthright and honest, and your ego will protect you.

Finding Mr. Wrong

Their upbringing sets up many women for mistreatment. If your self-esteem is based on pleasing others, it is easy for someone to say to you, "I am not pleased," or "Jump through a few more hoops!" Men, with their self-seeking orientation, can unwittingly exploit a woman whose life is devoted to pleasing others rather than herself. The solution to this problem has a great deal to do with choosing a mate wisely, not with a view toward finding a perfect man with whom passively to merge oneself but toward finding a man who is willing to grow and struggle toward a mutuality and reciprocity that is possible when you are both committed to being truly loving.

There are four categories of men who will cause problems for a woman who seeks a fulfilling relationship. Each one has a deeply ingrained method of operating, which he does not question. He is difficult to change because he feels that he has no problems. You can learn to recognize a man who is not worth your investment. When you spot trouble, confront him, and see if he is willing to work toward change.

Mr. Playboy

Some women I have worked with have been deeply hurt by an attractive man who is compulsively on-again, off-again. Gayle told me about what she experienced when she went to a party alone because her boy friend, whom she had dated steadily for nine months, was out of town. She was shocked when she arrived at the party and saw him there. He acted embarrassed to see her and blatantly ignored her. She was so upset that she decided to leave and had the terrible experience of seeing him at the elevator with another woman.

Rachel, who is married, discovered by the grapevine that her attractive husband had a reputation of being a womanizer. She was shocked to discover that he had more than one ongoing relationship outside of their marriage. When confronted, he was sweet and charming and assured her of his devotion to her. But his behavior did not change. When she threatened to break up the marriage, he undertook therapy and was able to change his behavior in favor of genuine intimacy and commitment.

Mary came into her session with me one day in a state of euphoria. She had met a stunning man who indeed sounded like a prince. He said that he was very lonely, and she was thrilled to find such an attractive and available single man. As it turned out, although he was not a womanizer, he was a charming bundle of promises and retreats. He had an elusive quality and was never really there for Mary when she needed him. He often took her to wonderful places and bought her beautiful gifts, but he was inconsistent in the timing and frequency of his stroke-giving.

Often the man who is a playboy is very narcissistic. You are really competing with his love of himself, even though he might express this trait by womanizing. Narcissistic men can be enormously charming, and they create a magnetic field with intense energy flowing toward the self. They often possess the skills of a good actor. Sometimes a narcissistic man is a loner, who enjoys his loneliness and the attention from women that it inspires. But the tragedy is that this man is imprisoned in a system in which he can love only himself. As attractive as he is, he has little to give to other people, particularly intimacy and commitment.

What is so confusing about Mr. Playboy is that he will do things that approximate fairy-tale dreams of courtship. He will send you rare flowers, but the message is really "Admire my great taste." You might go to exciting places, but inside you feel like an exchangeable prop or a foil. For you to change the situation you must confront him with your feelings. The salvation for a narcissistic man is involvement with a real other person.

If you are concerned about an elusive Mr. Playboy, you need to be honest with yourself about the prospects that he will change. A narcissist is sometimes suffering unconsciously from having been wounded. In childhood, some highly important person let him down in a significant way. Such a blow to the ego was compensated by the attitude, Who needs them! I'll love me! Or the opposite might have occurred: someone overindulged the child in such a way that he did not learn to become caring toward other people. The problems are complex, but when such a man is faced with a relationship that is not working, he may be willing to work on himself. Professional help may be necessary.

You can protect yourself from Mr. Playboy by recognizing him and trusting your own reactions. If you get the impression that you don't count very much and your feelings are being ignored, you may want to get out before you invest too much in a one-way relationship. You must also speak up and let him know of the effects of his behavior and not let him charm you out of your own reactions.

Mr. Bully

A woman who is on her own side will want to avoid a relationship with a man who compulsively treats her badly. Bad treatment may take the form of mild put-downs. A man might question your logic, your memory, and your grammar to make himself feel powerful. He fools himself into believing that his criticism is helpful and well-meaning. A woman with an ego will let him know that negative criticism is not helpful because it undermines her ego.

In a relationship with Mr. Bully, people-pleasing can be pure masochism. I have observed women twisting themselves into emotional pretzels trying to believe that a man is loving them or helping them by his negative comments. The problem is that such a man often believes his own rationalizations for his behavior. The female ego needs to stay with her own truth and not believe the distorted thinking of a bully. *If what he says hurts, it is not helpful.* Loving confrontations can serve a purpose, but in general, a continual habit of criticism from an intimate is hurtful. A man might love a woman in his heart of hearts, but if he cannot take her responses to him seriously, his love is little more than a sentimental fantasy.

I have found in working with couples that they get in the habit of exchanging negative strokes because they do not know how to exchange positive ones. Often a man who acts like a bully is afraid to express tender feelings and to appear weak and vulnerable. He needs to know that kindness is not weakness and that being loving will actually make him feel stronger. A woman needs to believe this, too, and not go along with a man who is maintaining unnecessary defenses at her expense.

The worst bullying relationship that compulsive people-pleasing can invite is a sadistic one. Ignoring her own feelings, a woman attempts to please someone who has a reservoir of anger about past misfortunes. It is as though he harbors a monster, hidden away inside, who once persecuted him. Unable to untangle his troubled psyche, he seeks an object upon which to unleash his profound

frustration. He plays out a drama of abuse and remorseful rec-
onciliation which sets the stage for another round of abuse, echoing
themes from his disturbed childhood.

A woman cannot change this bullying behavior, and she should
be honest about admitting the truth if she is involved with a sadist.
The way out of such a relationship is to respect your own feelings.
You must not harbor guilt because you are not causing his behavior.
Respond appropriately to yourself; do whatever you need to do to
take care of yourself. The best idea is for a woman not to get
involved with a pathological bully in the first place.

Mr. Goodboy

This is a man who wants to have control over a woman, and
the problem is that life with him is extremely dull. When Kate
described her marriage to me, she had trouble explaining why she
was so unhappy. She mentioned that her husband never bought
her exciting presents because they were too expensive. He was
humorless and had no desire for adventure. Kate felt guilty about
criticizing him because he was a very good person—responsible,
hardworking, and serious. But their life was exceedingly dull.
Whenever Kate tried to explain to him what she wanted, she could
not get through to him. He seemed to be so smugly content with
himself that Kate's unhappiness did not matter to him. As long as
he felt in control, he was happy, and Kate had no emotional
leverage.

Kate's husband was more attached to rituals than he was to
people. He focused on keeping their life meticulously organized
and wanted Kate to follow along with no surprises please! Kate was
starving emotionally. She felt that she had become such a well-
ordered machine that all of her distinguishing characteristics were
dead. She was being stroked for being punctual instead of interesting, for being organized instead of creative, and the most precious parts of her were starving for love.

Kate made the change that many women need to make when
they are being overly controlled in a relationship. She became

involved in a more exciting world outside of the home. Kate came to terms with her passivity and realized that it was up to her to create a life that would work for her. She went back to school and studied art history, which had interested her many years before. She is now working at a gallery and has increased her circle of close friends. She and her husband are struggling with the fact that they have many differences. The issues of conflict between them have not been resolved, but Kate now feels like an honest person who is living her life as herself instead of living in an adapted mode.

Mr. Pygmalion

In the ancient Greek myth, Pygmalion, the king of Cyprus, was a sculptor who carved a statue of a beautiful woman, Galatea. His creation was so beautiful that he fell in love with it. In the play *My Fair Lady*, Henry Higgins works to carve a lady out of a rough cockney lass.

If Mr. Pygmalion comes into your life, you may feel flattered to have someone take so much interest in you. He might enjoy helping you fix your body, your wardrobe, your education, and your psyche. The problem with Mr. Pygmalion is his premise and his motivations. He believes that there is something wrong with you, which he must fix, and he might require you to be dumb as a piece of stone so that he can control you. There is no greater attempt to control than actually "creating" another person. Mr. Pygmalion has a problem with narcissism and can love only that which he has created himself. He sees women as objects to be fixed.

A woman is in trouble if she presents herself to a man as raw material for him to work on. Perhaps one of the most ridiculous forms of people-pleasing is for a woman to present herself as if she has no ideas, no experience, and no history. If you take this approach as a way of enhancing a man's ego, you will appeal to a man who wants to control. He will not want you to have assets of your own or possess independent self-confidence. Allowing a man's ego to rule your life imprisons you in stone, where he can chip away at your self-confidence in his attempts to fix you.

A woman with an ego belongs to herself and looks for a man who loves her as she is and will support her growth. When I think of the unhappy women I have worked with, I remember many of them telling me that they wished they had taken a more critical look *before* they got involved.

When Love Becomes War

This subject deserves a book of its own. You may find out that for one reason or another, Mr. Right was really Mr. Wrong. In many cases there is extreme incompatibility, and the divorcing spouses feel that they have no choice but to split.

To deal with incompatibility, you can try to learn the skills of loving, which are discussed at the end of this chapter. Many people learn to tolerate differences that originally seemed impossible. If your differences are irreconcilable, however, you do not have to go to war.

When couples make war instead of love, they are involved in a desperate psychological game in which the ammunition consists of negative strokes. She criticizes his paunch, and he denigrates her friends. Each is trying to maintain a sense of being OK at the expense of the other. Receiving a barb from her husband stimulates her to send one his way in an attempt to recover her equilibrium. But he throws her off again with another barb that is just a little bit more nasty. Such couples are reminiscent of two-year-olds banging each other on the head simultaneously and crying in pain. They don't know how to stop. When both people are playing an "I'm OK; You're Not OK" game, escalation is inevitable. This is the stuff that many divorces are made of, just as this is the existential system that leads to war. Even the suggestion of divorce is received as a part of the war game. Separation is such a threat that people will go to war with each other to save face.

I have known divorce lawyers who have left the business because they became so jaded by seeing what people do to each other in the throes of a warlike divorce. Divorce is a time to mourn, to deal with losses and carry on. You can no more be a winner in a divorce than at a funeral. War will only increase losses. If a woman is involved in a relationship that is not working, she must use her ego to seek a reasonable and peaceful solution to differences. Learning pacifism (not to be confused with passivity) instead of retaliation will help her to keep her ego intact.

Building Ego Boundaries

It is natural to experience apprehensions and fears about making an intimate commitment. When a woman falls in love she asks herself many questions. Do I want to adjust to this person? How many compromises will I have to make? Do I want to spend the rest of my life with him? Might there be someone better? It is natural to ask these questions, to want to be certain about making the right decisions.

Realistic Fears

Making a commitment raises another set of concerns, based on fears. These are not just rational questions about the wisdom of a commitment. They are somewhat irrational fears, and they can cause a woman some suffering when she prepares herself for marriage. A woman might fear relinquishing her privacy, which she has enjoyed up to this point. She likes space of her own and the freedom to come and go, unaccountable to anyone but herself. A woman might fear being taken over, particularly if her man has a dominating personality or a large and forceful family. The man with whom you are involved is bound to be different from you. You may fear betraying your value system, whether it be religious, a sense of economy, or a philosophy of life that emphasizes particular values. Women also experience a fear of somehow getting lost. A woman often fears that marriage will mean that she will drop out of the world and forget her old friends, her old interests, and even her familiar personality. These fears all point to an identity

crisis in which a woman thinks that she might be losing valued
parts of herself on behalf of a relationship.

I believe in trusting your feelings—all of them. Your emotions
send profound messages about yourself, expressing your concerns
about losing your identity. If you listen to your fears you will find
that *basic issues of safety are being raised*. Closeness seems threatening to you. When the ego is unsafe a fear message is released.

The solution to this identity crisis is for the female ego to make
her boundaries clear. Only by maintaining ego boundaries can a
woman have closeness and intimacy in her life without giving up
her identity. A woman does not need to feel helpless or overwhelmed just because she is in love. No part of herself should ever
be betrayed in order for her to be close to another person. She can
keep her religion, her values, her friends, her work, and her personal views.

You Are Your Own Protector

If you are fearful of losing your identity in a relationship, it is
important that you not look to a man to be your protector. He
might lovingly say, "Trust me." But you cannot expect to have any
protector except yourself because only you know what is best for
you. You must hold fast to yourself because if you unnecessarily
give up too many of the meaningful parts of yourself you will feel
hopelessly lost. You might find yourself looking to your mate to
give you back to yourself and feeling betrayed by him when he
cannot.

Fear should make a woman feisty. Fear should make her stubborn. Fear means that she needs protection. But for the woman
who is conditioned to please others, fear can mean surrender.
Unfortunately, romantic fantasies are often based on surrender,
but what makes good fiction does not necessarily make good living.
The best and most significant intimacy takes place when you trust
your lover enough to risk setting up boundaries for yourself.

A widow in her fifties was contemplating marriage to a man in
his sixties. She had always loved homemaking and had created a

beautiful little home for herself. His house was larger, and they agreed that she should move in with him. The house would require extensive redecoration to please her, particularly because nothing had been done to it for many years. The widow was haunted by a nightmare fantasy of moving from her warm, colorful little house into his large, bleak one. Wise woman that she was, she did not trust his promises to redecorate. To relieve her anxieties about possible future battles, she made certain that all of the work was done before they married: carpets, painting, furniture, and a new kitchen. Love does not have to mean human sacrifice.

The Problem with Merging

For a relationship to work well, there must be a meeting of two different people. When the people begin to merge with each other and give up their uniqueness, the relationship becomes boring. Boredom indicates lack of life, disengagement, and depression. For a relationship to be healthy there must be excitement, and excitement comes from two people being different. When there are differences, there is a promise of adventure. Early in a relationship that intense feeling we call falling in love stems to some degree from the excitement of a new and different world being opened to us by another person.

There is something missing in a new relationship, however. That is the peace and comfort that comes from having known and trusted each other for a long time. Human beings need peace of mind as well as excitement. I am not suggesting that our relationships should be dull. My point is that they should be rich. There is no place like home, and a homey, familiar love relationship is rich in shared memories, inside jokes, easy traditions, and the intensity of familiar sensuality. In its own way this is exciting, too: it offers the excitement of relief and refreshment. There is great joy in knowing that one's needs for strokes will be abundantly met by the warm smile and hug, the familiar shirt, and the natural closeness that comforts the soul.

The problem in many long-term relationships is that boredom

sets in because the partners merge and no longer relate as two separate people. They stop making contact altogether. A husband becomes primarily a body facing a television. A wife retreats into obsessive housekeeping or in becoming a talking machine rattling on about details that bore even herself. If you maintain your individual identities, the boredom of merging will not happen, and your relationship will intensify in richness as it matures.

Territorial Rights

Developmentally the birth of the ego takes place at about the age of two. There is one favorite and powerful word that every two-year-old uses to excess: no. The powerful word no is what ego boundaries are made of. The two-year-old rejects her food, rejects all suggestions, and wants to do everything herself without interference. When her negativity is not respected, she resorts to a vicious temper tantrum to make her point. With every vehement no, the terrible two mortars another brick into the fortress surrounding her ego. No is the word of assertion. It makes other people shrink back and lets you take charge and do things your own way. It tells people to let you grow. At any age, to protect your ego, you must be free to say no whenever you need to.

As a woman learns the courage to say no, she gains respect, claims power, and feels strong. The people around her respond even though they might not like her assertions. Those respectful responses aid the growth of her ego.

Often when a woman is not pleasing to other people, she panics. She fears that she is turning into a monster. At times, she might act like one. This choice is crucial to her life, and it is a choice between symbiotic love with its accompanying lack of identity and self-respect with one's separate identity intact. A woman must have the courage to risk survival without love. Like the two-year-old climbing down from a comfortable lap for the excitement of independence and exploration, the self must be chosen over loving attachment. Independence and self-respect might feel a bit colder, but they are more exciting. The mature woman is independent and capable of self-support when necessary. Moreover, she sets up a life in which she can get TLC when she needs it.

This is the cornerstone of a foundation in which a woman can have both love and identity. A woman with an ego says, "I love you, but I love myself first." In the long run, her love is more potent, for people learn that she gives because she chooses to give, not as a compulsion.

Learning to Love

A woman with an ego will have both love and identity if she views love as a skill instead of a warm blanket. The term "falling in love" can imply losing one's bearings and being out of control. I think that committed love occurs in two parts. Falling in love is the part that means intense desire. Learning to love means developing skill in loving. When a woman learns to love she learns the specific behaviors that will sustain both the love relationship and her own identity.

There are six basic skills that support and make possible the maintenance of a love relationship. All of these skills build your ego at the same time that you are building a relationship because they help your ego function in the service of your needs, rather than being overwhelmed in blind adaptation to another person.

• The first skill is *communicating*. This is the most important skill, and if you are good at it you will be doing all of the others as well. There are reams of literature telling you how to communicate. It is better to plunge in and do it. The principle here is to talk. Have long, good talks together that take up a great deal of time. There is no better way to structure your time than to explore every subject you both can think of. The more you talk, the more personal the conversation will become. As you talk, your trust will grow, and you will dig deeper into yourselves to share intimate information. It takes a long time to become close, and therefore it requires long conversations. This works only if there is one other ingredient: listening. When people don't talk, it is usually because neither is a sensitive listener.

Listening takes concentration and intelligence. No one wants to tell her secrets unless she has an eager listener, and no one wants to bare her soul to a dummy. In communicating, or talking and listening, nothing should be judged. You may want to explore a subject from many angles, or compare differences of opinions, but everyone has a right to his or her own thoughts and the right to change opinions. Talking is an intimate activity, and a person must feel that he or she is safe and accepted when talking. In spending time talking with your partner you will gradually get to know that person and how to treat her or him. That person will learn the same thing about you. At the same time you will become stronger as an individual person. We define our unique selves when we talk.

- The second skill is *asking*. This is the point at which people usually experience resistance in moving from falling in love to learning love as a skill. Without this skill, however, love will die from disappointment. It may not feel romantic to ask to be taken out to dinner, but the resentment of deprivation is even less romantic. Most people are not very good at mind-reading. You must become very good at articulating your needs. Ask for what you want. This cuts down on ulterior manipulating, disappointment, and anger. If you do not ask, you are to blame for not getting what you want from others. It actually is a relief to know that your fate is not in the hands of another person, particularly if that person lacks imagination or nurturing skills. It is possible to be romantic within this method. If you are asking for tenderness, it helps if you ask in a tender way. A responsive attitude toward the other person is required as well. Asking is not forcing someone to say yes. The other person has the right to say no, and you can have the ego strength to deal with that as well.

- The third love skill is *saying no*. Learn to maintain separateness and distance so as to keep your individual self intact. This allows real relating to take place. When you say no, it usually is because saying yes threatens you in some way. You can reject the strokes that do not feel good or that do not support your growth as a person. You can say no with a closed door or by taking a solitary walk when you need time alone. You can say no when you are asked to do something that you clearly do not want to do. You can say no whenever you need to protect your time, your talents, or your energy. Saying no is one of the main cures for people-pleasing.

- The fourth skill is *saying yes*. Yes does not just mean agreeing to do something for someone else. Yes also means receiving the positive. When we say a resounding yes, we are opening ourselves to an experience that feels good. We need to partake of the goodness that is around us if our relationships are to thrive and our egos are to keep strong. Appreciate the person you love simply because it feels good to do so. Enjoy your closeness. If you think something positive, say it. Get in the habit of discovering things to love whether in each other or in the world that you can love together. Say yes to love, and enjoy building good morale in your relationship.

- The fifth love skill is *solving problems*. You must have a mutual willingness to listen to what the other person does not like. You do not listen with an ear to adapting but in order to understand the needs of the other person. A genuine complaint has a need behind it. If a woman does not like her husband's table manners, what does she want instead? If a man hates the Saturday routine, how would he like to spend the day? By translating negative reactions into requests, the ego can solve the problems in a relationship. In my family we have two rules that govern such occasions. One is that everyone can and should express strong feelings. The second is that problems are to be solved. The first without the second would be an exercise in hysteria. We have found that there is a certain skill in getting all the feelings out so that the need is revealed. Then a person can move to a solution. This process keeps a relationship flowing on a positive course without being phony positive. Phony positive is when you smile and carry on in spite of resentment or hurt. If that happens, rule number one was not followed, and a person is holding onto a negative feeling instead of discharging the feeling in order to solve the problem. For this process to work, people have to be willing to change their behavior so they can find solutions. To solve problems, all those involved must agree to be shaped up from time to time. It takes a strong ego to admit to being wrong and to promise to change your ways.

• The last skill is *exchanging strokes*. I once heard a veteran marriage counselor who had practiced for forty years say that he thought the most important quality in a successful marriage was generosity. I would like to amend that term to mutual generosity. The greatest joy in life, in my opinion, is giving. But you can sustain true giving only if someone is giving to you freely and joyfully. A good marriage partner is one who is very good at meeting the needs of the other.

Love and Ego

When a woman learns how to communicate, her identity comes into sharp focus for herself. When her partner listens to her, she receives valuable affirmation. When she listens to her partner, she has the joy of intimacy, of being let into his emotional life. When a woman asks for what she wants, she takes charge of getting her needs met and frees herself from the tyranny of dependency and needy despair. When she says no, she maintains her dignity and conserves her energy. When she says yes, she receives the gifts of love and joy. When she solves problems, she rids herself of bitterness and makes necessary changes in others and in herself. When she exchanges strokes, she grows in self-esteem, and she feels the potency of being needed by someone else.

At its best, love helps the female ego. The best love supports our growth. If we are loved for our own unique selves, a relationship can help to give us ourselves. We do need love, not as a substitute for autonomy, but to support autonomy.

7

The Female Ego in Work

First say to yourself what you would be,
and then do what you have to do.
Epictetus

Playing the Game to Win

Very often the male ego is motivated by the desire to dominate. Domination in its refined expression means mastery. In the world of work a woman operates the way men do when she plays the game to win. I get a kick out of the women who run their ideas up flagpoles or say to me, "Will you run that by me again?" They speak the lingo of their business because they have joined the team and are giving it their best shot. The key to business success is in really becoming part of things and at the same time looking out for your best interest—and many women are learning from men how to do this.

There are others who feel lost. In the frame of mind of people-pleasing, they smile, make nice-nice, and wait for someone to tell them what is going on and what to do. Politics are beyond them or beneath them, and they are desperately looking for fair rules or a strong person to follow. A woman with such an imprisoned ego needs to be set free. She needs to learn how to be political and how to plan strategies on behalf of her own future.

Many of my clients are women in the working world, and the problems they bring to therapy have to do with the politics at work. I often hear myself saying to a woman client, "Why not plan a

177

strategy?" If a game is being played, *play*. Learn the moves; avoid the traps. *Win*. Make things go the way you want them to. This means having a *working ego*. If you refuse to play politics, it means you have lost. Not to maneuver is not to play. You have already taken your marbles and gone home.

A winner uses her marbles. Many women have much more power than they let themselves use. I encourage women to use all of their energy as forcefully and willfully as they can. The days of the passive woman are over. The world is a political place full of self-seeking people, some of whom are difficult to deal with. One must weave a skillful course to accomplish good things, whether it is in a family, an organization, or a corporation.

Is Manipulation a Bad Word?

For many, many years our forebears were furry creatures who walked on four legs. As humankind evolved, these creatures stood on their hind feet. This meant that their forefeet could be free to *manipulate* the environment. The freeing of the hands to manipulate was a key event in human history. A winner does not live with her hands tied behind her back. She manipulates with the best of them, using her ego.

To manipulate means to plan, to play, to learn, to process, to try, to learn from failures, to change, to try again, to succeed, to balance, to adjust, to change course, to prioritize, to avoid pitfalls, to negotiate, to mediate, to sublimate, to express, to argue, to be quiet, to steer, to steer clear, to dig deeper, to smooth over, to assert, to assent, to veto, to negate, to improve, to destroy, to build, to invent, to copyright, to adorn, to decorate, to plan, to expand, to divide, to subdivide, to assemble, to fix, to test, to manufacture, to sell, to buy, to invest, to profit, to multiply, to give, to receive, to venture, to speculate, to develop, to prove, to win. One way to keep your ego weak is to stay on the sidelines of life, allowing yourself only to stroke or to cling.

The word "manipulation" often has a negative meaning, suggesting that people are being used as objects or made to do things against their wishes. I am not suggesting that a woman learn to treat other people badly but that she treat herself well by learning the art of politics, which political scientists define as the art of the possible. In a positive sense, manipulation means knowing how to get things done.

What really holds a woman back from maneuvering and planning strategies is that *she is not sure that she really deserves to get her own way.* In the heart of hearts of every winner is the concept of entitlement. This is not the same as greed, excessive narcissism, or exploitiveness. This simply means *I deserve.*

The Winner's Credo

Work on developing your sense of entitlement. Think about the specific things that you want from life. Then ask yourself if you really believe that you deserve to have what you want. Work to *give yourself permission* to make your life go the way you want it to. Here are some guidelines for claiming entitlement:

• I deserve to structure my time the way I want to. All I have in my lifetime is my time. My lifetime is my time.
• I deserve to make the world as I want it to be. I am entitled to create an environment that reflects my values.
• I deserve to develop whatever parts of myself I want to develop. I don't need to be adaptive or rebellious. I am the decider. I have an ego. I make my life work.
• I deserve to give my caring to whomever I want to. I do my own prioritizing.
• I deserve to have physical space of my own to share or not to share.

A sense of entitlement lets you dream your own dreams. A sense of entitlement allows you to set your sights high and make the political affiliations that will facilitate your getting the opportunities you most want for yourself. If you believe that you deserve a lot, you will intensely pursue success in your work, pouring on the energy that is needed to get where you want to be.

Becoming a Strategist

A woman who is successful in business has an ego that works for her. If she wants something for herself, she finds a way to get it.

Getting Your Act Together

You must be honest about your talents and aspirations. If you are chronically angry at work, you must not be doing work that satisfies you. Don't wait for things to get better. Know yourself and decide what you really want.

Invest in your development. If you need to take courses or get professional guidance, do it. Investing in the mastery of salable skills is the best insurance policy you can give yourself.

Be prepared for the large opportunities. If you need a graduate degree, the struggle of a few short years will be worthwhile. Plan for the future in terms of the bottom line. If you are studying art history, think about being an art dealer and add a few business courses to your curriculum. Translate your deepest interests into something that will earn you real and sustaining strokes: money, prestige, and a lifestyle you want.

Focus on creating the future. Know where today's activities are leading you tomorrow. Too many women have said to me, "If only I had thought ahead." Use your ego and think ahead, and spend your energies on projects that really will get you somewhere.

Persevere in getting what you want. No one is seeking you out; you must seek others. Your ego must be out there on the line, asking for what you want and displaying what you have to offer. Fight discouragement when someone refuses you, and go somewhere else.

Be ruthless in your focus. You must decide to get your act together no matter what. Each day, do something toward your long-term goals, and don't let anything or anybody get in the way of your most important project: *your life.*

Doing It Right

Memo the world. When you are at work, be sure that as many people as possible know who you are and what you are doing. Get as much mileage as possible out of your accomplishments. A woman with an ego keeps herself in the foreground of people's minds instead of being some else's backup.

Go for top billing. If it was your idea or your project, your name should be at the top. Don't let others steal or co-opt your ideas or take the credit for your work. The closer your name is to the title of a piece of work, the better.

Expect a lot for yourself, because you get what you expect. Know what the top people in your field are paid and make sure that you play in that league. This means that you must also expect a lot *from* yourself. The successful women are the ones everyone knows can be counted on to deliver.

Don't get hung up on criticism. There are very few people in the world of work who are deeply gifted in the art of developing human relationships. Let your friends stroke your ego when it falters. But at work hang in there and take the criticism and nit-picking evaluations with the best of them—and learn from the experiences. If you spend your energy suffering from or avoiding criticism, you will miss the learning to be gained from that criticism.

Be a specialist, and you will gain respect. A woman with her own finely developed expertise is starting from a strong position. She may want to go on to more general administration in the future, but special skills will give her a chance to stand out and shine. Your ego feels strong when you know that there is one thing that you are really good at.

Enjoy your work. Women have the reputation for being more interested in the relationships at work or in what is happening after hours than in the work itself. Demonstrate your interest in what is going on *at work*, and live it as wholeheartedly as you can while you are there.

A *Piece of the Action*

When you play honest politics, you simply position yourself well and maneuver within your situation in order to get things done. There are several principles to keep in mind in working to have a piece of the action.

- Information is power. Everyone wants to know what is going on, and you must keep your eyes open and ears tuned to know what is happening. The best position is one in which you are a conduit of information and have a reputation for being in the know. Know where information is traded, and be sure you are there.

- More is better. You cannot put too much time or effort into your work. We know that a woman usually has to be better than her male peers, so you must stretch to the limits in offering your very best work product.

- Tradition counts. As a woman you are likely to be perceived as an outsider, so don't do things that will be threatening—especially to people's harmless traditions. Figure out exactly how things are done, and then do them that way, distinguishing yourself by doing them well. By giving support to traditions, you will have the best chance of being let into the club and of putting yourself in a position to change the traditions you don't like.

- Be part of the action. When important things are happening, be there. There are some days when it is essential to stay late because there is an important deadline, or a deal in the works, or a crisis in the office. Even if it does not directly affect you, you will want to be part of the in-group that later reminisces about "Remember when. . . ." There will be many such opportunities for you to position yourself as either an insider or an outsider.

- Prepare to call in your chips. In work, helpfulness to others is not a given but is a system of trade-offs. You cultivate relationships and support others with a plan one day to call in your chips. If you establish relationships well and deliver on your commitments, you will at some time call upon your contacts to help you out. These reciprocal networks are worked out over a long period of time, and you must be willing to pay your dues before you can cash in.

- Learn about trading perquisites. The art of lunching is just the beginning. Clever political strategists play "I can get it for you wholesale" and "Can you use my cabin in the woods?" A reputation for having goodies to offer goes a long way in the materialistic world of business.
- Always deliver the goods. You can have all of the personality skills in the world, but you will eventually do yourself in if you are discovered to be all promise and no delivery. In the political arena what counts is the woman who can be counted on. A long track record of reliability is where it's at.

Female Issues

Men are often your role models at work, but this does not mean that you want to be an imitation man. This will not make you successful because by contrast women who dress like men and try to act like men often seem weaker or cuter than they are. The way out of the gender problem is to be serious and *task-oriented*. Men understand task orientation because that is the way most of them live. At work, task comes before gender.

Sex appeal does not help you to get ahead in business, but attractiveness does. Your aim at work is to be respected for your competence and your power. You must fight your own resistance to being authoritative. You sabotage yourself when you rely on being sexy, being weak in any area, or in looking to a man for the answers. Do not let yourself be tempted to play the game as an insecure female. If you do not have full confidence, fake it as a man would.

Helpfulness is not a given or a must, but a great work product should be. Be ready to give aid, but watch for signs that your willingness to take on others' problems is eclipsing the excellence of your own work.

Men are not really your enemies. They are victims of a culture that may cause them to play an adversary role toward women. Use your observing ego to see this, and you will rise above some of the petty dynamics between men and women.

A male superior may sometimes seem to be an enemy to you because he has the power that you want to have. Men do play macho games, which they have learned to play in order to make it, and they are usually more fully on their own sides than women are. See these games as givens, so as not to be immobilized by anger at men.

Resist becoming fragmented. You will find that men are not as fragmented by juggling home and career as are women. A man lets his company own him while he is at work, and therefore he is free to focus on what he is doing. This focus leads him truly to master his work. If you allow yourself to be fragmented, you may become demoralized, and your work will suffer. Consider the possibility that you may be carrying around guilt about your split roles and that this guilt is unnecessary. Women are expected to feel guilty when they are not slaves to their families, and it is up to your ego to guide you out of this unproductive pattern.

Don't underestimate the importance of money. Materialism alone leads to a miserable life, but for a woman with good values, money can provide opportunity, pleasure, and security.

Sometimes you need to work to find out how great it is to have a family. Learn to appreciate the contrasts in your life and that you have the power to choose your priorities at various times in your life.

The Feminine Solution

Women have their own special talents and perspectives to offer in the world of work. Knowing this can help to bolster your ego and can show you some of the options open to a creative female ego.

Women have had to work very hard on developing their egos in order to function in the world of work. The result is that many women have the capacity to express *real power*. A woman does not achieve power by putting someone else down, by puffing herself up, or through intimidation. A woman who has worked on herself and struggled with her inhibitions and with a culture that has opposed her development has laid the groundwork for self-esteem based on her relationship to herself. This is not unlike a common occurrence in therapy, in which clients after a period of work on themselves discover that they have increased their earning capacity. Free of inner conflict, they are much freer to apply themselves. Women who have conquered adverse circumstances develop a reservoir of special strengths.

Women in general have much better skills in dealing with people than men have, and because businesses are people places, women have an advantage. Women will surely become the leaders in the sales forces in the future. They are very good at understanding where other people are coming from and tailoring what they say in a way that is appropriate to a specific customer.

When women are relating to others, there is a rich exchange of strokes. Men can be terribly guarded and reduce everything they have to say to the realm of the rational and the colorless. Women, on the other hand, generally offer a part of themselves when they communicate, and listeners know they are really getting something.

Women are not afraid to cooperate in the interest of getting a job done. Obsession with grabbing credit and power plays can slow things down, and women do not need to go through macho power rituals in order to communicate with others. They can therefore be much more efficient because they are less likely to create unnecessary standoffs and instead focus on the task. When a woman becomes confident in a business situation she may discover that she is better than her male associates at getting to the point and moving forward. Women who run their own small businesses often work on the basis of a cooperative model as well as a competitive one and find that an obsession with competition can reduce their productivity.

More than one corporate officer has told me that he has discovered that if he has a really tough job to be done he finds a woman to do it. Women are becoming extremely ambitious and have been willing to work twice as hard as a man when necessary. As women earn a reputation for being hard workers, they will increasingly gain their share of top jobs. Because the Equal Rights Amendment has not passed, there is little momentum and no mandate for promoting women, and many women find themselves in businesses where the highest they can go is the bottom of the top. But that situation is changing and will continue to do so. The answer for us all is to keep our egos out there doing the best job we can and pressing for the best opportunities for ourselves.

Polishing Your Persona

When a woman is beginning her career, one project that she needs to tackle is her external image or persona, as Carl Jung called it. Many women think that simply being a good person or being competent is all that they can do to get ahead. The fact is that there is an important psychological mechanism known as tranference from which a woman can get a lot of mileage. Positive transference is a process by which other people imbue you with great expectations simply because of how you appear to be. After seeing so many women go from nowhere to somewhere in this area, my aim is to help others do the same.

Tara was a successful office assistant in an art museum. Her creative style of dress was appropriate to that environment. She looked distinctive wearing pants, tunics, and chunky jewelry. It was interesting to watch her change her image after she entered law school. By the final year she was wearing elegant dark suits and a silk blouse with contrasting bow or a string of pearls. This change was less a matter of self-expression as it was of looking like a winner in her chosen profession. She noticed that people had a different reaction to her when she was in her lawyer's costume— they took her more seriously.

Of course, it is absurd to think that the criterion for competence is what suit you are wearing or whether your blouse is made of silk or polyester. But your clothes and general demeanor are an indication of what you think of yourself and where you place yourself in the hierarchical scheme of things.

It is helpful psychologically if your persona accurately corresponds with your true and inner nature. Yet the persona is different from the true self. Most people do business with us, judge us, and evaluate us on the basis of our outer selves. Our intimates know what is within, but others may not care, be perceptive enough, or have the time to look deeper. It is therefore the task of your ego to make sure that you represent yourself as well as you can.

A very bright woman sat weeping in my office behind a disheveled mane of auburn hair. She was wearing a tight, provocatively cut sweater and a pleated skirt. She was a natural beauty who had never achieved a polished look. She was crying because she had been denied her title at the bank once again, and it seemed that less capable people were being promoted. As gently as I could, I told her my basic, truthful reaction. "Courtney, you don't *look* at all like a banker."

Women who are successful on the job have an aggressive, healthy attitude. They have set their egos to the task of making a good impression by being tastefully and strongly visible. As I have worked with women and observed them in the process of developing strong egos, I have developed some guidelines about how to put together a set of ego skills that make a solid impression.

- **Take a Good Look at Yourself**

    We all have a psychological capacity which is known as an observing ego. This is a part of you which is somewhat detached and can therefore observe you even while you are engaged with others. You can monitor how you are doing and what impression you are making. If you feel insecure or highly invested in a new situation, however, you may not allow yourself enough detachment to monitor yourself or the reactions of other people. You may also remain blind to the impression you make because you are *afraid* to know. Your worst fear is to see that you are doing badly. But take heart. Have courage. When you get an accurate reading of the image you project, you will discover that you, like all the other people in the world, have both strengths and weaknesses. You are a mixed bag. And the women who have more assets than liabilities are those who have worked on projecting their best selves.

• Get an Accurate Picture

If you want to get an accurate picture of yourself, you need to go beyond your own observing ego and ask for feedback. The best feedback comes from trusted friends. If it is to be helpful, this feedback must be as objective as possible and include your good points as well as the areas that need work. Much of the current self-help material advises us to fix a multitude of things that are wrong with us. It is very easy to draw the conclusion that we are primarily a bundle of problems. This is why it is imperative that you first focus your main efforts on knowing what your *assets* are and highlighting them.

Carla is the manager of a showroom for an industrial design firm. In seeking feedback about her image she discovered to her surprise that she was most admired for her height and her bold, statuesque build. She always had tried to downplay her size, but the positive feedback made her take another look at herself. She began to wear flowing, beltless dresses, which emphasized her height and strong bones, and high-heeled pumps, which she had always avoided. Carla became comfortable with the sense of power that she was projecting.

Phyllis is a former housewife who returned to the advertising world. Her suburban best dresses seemed to her suitable enough for the office. In a woman's workshop she received the feedback that despite her basic good looks she appeared a little square and out of date. With encouragement, she began to project a more tailored, serious look. Not only did her feelings about herself change, but she emanated new energy and more personal strength.

You need the input of others in order to highlight all of your best qualities. A good way to begin is to write down your own observations of yourself. Make lists under the categories of personality, character, talents, and appearance. Then get feedback from the person in your life whom you trust the most. It could be a woman friend, your boy friend or husband, or a relative. Find out if that person agrees with your list. What would she or he add or subtract? It helps to know that you have a dazzling smile or that your dry wit is very amusing. Get an accurate picture of how you come across and then, like an artist, decide how to project your best self.

• **Make a Plan**

In addition to understanding how you come across and which assets you want to highlight, you need to make a good plan for yourself. Over the years, I have learned about successful image building from working with clients in the glamour professions of entertainment and fashion. We can all learn to communicate powerful messages through our image, whatever our field. Since you inevitably send out messages about yourself, you might as well deliver the one you choose.

The professionals in image careers give a great deal of thought to defining exactly what image they want to express. Consider some of the possibilities: intelligence, refinement, business skill, power, nostalgia, romance, ruggedness, youth, classic values, avant garde, wealth. Also consider that you might inadvertently be communicating an image of being disorganized, belonging to a low socioeconomic group, being out of date or faddish, having limited growth potential, being a little girl, a sex object, insecure, or flaky. You need to raise your visual consciousness and realize that you can communicate many different messages. The most important question to answer is: How would I really like to come across? Look at pictures of women, scrutinize the women you admire, and read the literature on image building. Then formulate in your mind a clear image of how you want yourself to appear. The very act of forming this clear and focused picture in your mind's eye will get you going in the right direction.

Once you have decided how you want to project yourself, begin by assembling one perfect outfit that embodies your best look. Then you can slowly build a high-quality, efficient wardrobe that represents you well.

• **Get the Help You Need**

A woman with ego strength knows when she needs help. Many successful women have their own personal backup team of experts. A trusted and skillful hairdresser is a must. Find a clothing shop with a salesperson who has a great eye and a sense of your taste. You can have clothes made for you if your figure is not suitable for off-the-rack clothes. Get advice from skillful friends or experts about your best colors and the best style of clothing for your work and get tips on makeup from a professional. The professionals in media fields who must make a great impression get help from many sources. Don't you deserve the same?

• **Learn to Project**

You may need to become more expressive. You must send your signals into the vibrating field of social exchange. You must impress the eye, send out brain waves in the form of your ideas, make sound waves with your voice, and vibrate with movement and intensity. Do not wait for the perfect way to participate. Begin to project yourself. You will get better at it just by doing it and observing your performance objectively.

Ask yourself the following questions to see if you have a problem with shyness and are holding yourself back from projecting yourself adequately. These are tough questions designed to uncover the psychological problems that some shy women have.

How do you feel when someone is looking at a piece of work that you have completed? If you feel like crawling into a hole and are uncomfortable about being evaluated, consider the possibility that you have a problem with shyness. Underlying a shy withdrawal is a combination of anger and fear. The shy person, untrusting of others, tends to express power through withdrawal instead of healthy self-assertion. A woman with a healthy ego will actually enjoy the attention of being visible and will welcome feedback from others.

When there is a crisis at work, do you tend to pull back and wait for the trouble to blow over? You may be aware of the fearful part of your shy response but not of the hostility you are covertly expressing. To disengage when there are problems to be solved and quietly watch other people struggle will not win you friends.

Do you dig in your heels and bite your tongue when an aggressive boss pours on the pressure? A shy person will shut down in the face of work pressure and often will feel that her boss is a terrible monster. If you do this, examine whether you are setting others up to be negatively aggressive as a foil to your own passivity. Some women are so used to playing the game of victim that they fail to see that their harassing boss is harassed himself. In that case if you express energy and concern, he will relax and act like a human being.

Do you harbor private resentments such as wanting to see your boss have a hard time? Such vengeful thinking leads to passive-aggressive power maneuvers that can only work against you. Not trusting yourself or the other person to work things out, you will frustrate others by your failure to be straightforward.

Everyone has power. It is the job of the female ego to express her power in a healthy and productive way. The person who is open and forthright inspires trust. A worker is expected to engage wholeheartedly in her work, and if she disengages she will be a loser. The woman who watches the clock and is more interested in what she is going to do after work is not projecting herself in the workplace. Sometimes you may feel bored or weary, but you must still project a self that is *turned on.* If I were to name one quality that every winning woman I know possesses, it would be her *energetic engagement* in her work.

- **Avoid Coming On Too Strong**

Some people are the opposite of wallflowers: they overproject. Yet like the wallflower, they also are ignored. The most important thing to realize about image is that image is in the mind of the beholder. Your job is to give clues to other people. If you leave nothing to the imagination, or leave no silent spaces for the other person to think and "process" you, you will not be perceived. A woman who comes on too strong is sometimes confused about why she is often the victim of rejection

In a women's workshop, our group was dominated by Elaine, who was bright and bursting with ideas. She seemed so confident and successful that other members wondered why she had sought a therapeutic experience. Elaine admitted to us that she was often ignored. One member of the group suggested that maybe she intimidated other people. This remark broke the ice, and other group members admitted that they shared the same reaction. They did not exactly dislike her, but they found themselves being more quiet than usual in her presence because they could not match her intense energy. Elaine was coming on so strong that she caused other people to raise their defenses. When they withdrew, her pattern was to become even more outspoken.

Coming on too strong is essentially a defense against a bad sense of self. Such a woman is hiding behind a persona that is larger than life in order to cover her feelings of insignificance. The tragic result is that her behavior makes others withdraw and contributes to her feelings of insignificance.

It is possible to change this pattern. Women like Elaine must realize that they are pushing other people away. They must become aware of the feelings of others and give others space to relax and express themselves. Her goal must be to feel happier and more in harmony with others. Some telltale signs of this problem are being overdressed for the occasion, talking too much, and having more energy and hype than other people.

Sensitivity to the reactions of others, learning to be part of a group rather than a constant star, and behaving and dressing in harmony with the group will enhance relationships and therefore promote more secure inner feelings.

In an age of increased assertiveness for women this is a tricky issue for a woman to handle. The female ego must sort out the complexity of what behavior is neurotic people-pleasing, what is healthy self-assertion, and what is going too far. A male therapist friend of mine was perplexed. He took a woman to dinner and found that he was offended by her behavior. "I am trying not to be uptight about strong women, but I had a miserable evening," he told me. "At first, I admired her assertiveness," he said, "but by the time the evening was over the restaurant had made her a dinner that was not on the menu, changed our table and the heating in the room, and left things on the table that they normally remove. Not only that but she was so flamboyantly dressed and animated that we were the object of the attention of other people."

• **Put Your Best Foot Forward**

Making a good impression has to do with caring about ourselves and the other person. We care enough to give each encounter our best shot. When you devote yourself to this process, your caring will communicate powerful positive energy.

You must have the humility to know that the best you can project will not be perfect. Do it anyway. Some women fear the risk involved in giving a situation their best effort. Be humble enough to put yourself on the line, and learn from your mistakes. If you fail to get the job after the interview or fail to make the deal, there will be other opportunities that you will win. At least you did not let yourself down. And remember, an impression is not the whole ball game, nor does it express your total self.

Your ego will grow in strength if you maintain a positive approach to projecting yourself and *do not expect perfection*. A focus on being perfect will ultimately make you obsessed with your flaws. As a result, you will feel negative and be more rigid than spontaneous. For the female ego the task is simply to give it your best!

• **Engage in Self-Evaluation**

A healthy female ego can deal with negative criticism and still stay on a positive track. Use criticism as a basis to improve so that you grow in competence. My client Beth is a producer of Broadway plays. She told me about working with a famous veteran playwright who directed his own plays. They opened out of town, which gave them a chance to try out the play on an audience and fix the inevitable flaws that show only when a play is actually running. During those weeks, they intently studied the reviews. Beth was excited about the positive comments they received. But the more experienced playwright was uninterested. "Those will not give us what we need right now," he said to her. "We need to study the negative comments and discover what they are telling us. We need to fix everything we possibly can before the play hits Broadway—and *those* critics."

A real professional welcomes criticism, not the kind that is intended to demoralize but that which will enable her to correct her blind spots and make her projects work. If you are to be an effective communicator, your audience needs to understand your message. Work is a process, and there is great joy in improving. Even if you did a poor job, better to know it so that you won't do it again.

When you are evaluating yourself, don't forget to notice a job well done. Beth told me that she and the playwright basked in glory once the work was over and they had achieved a New York success. One of the problems with workaholics is that they do not handle successes well because they do not know how to assimilate positive feedback. The healthy ego is fueled by successes and learns how to build on what works. Your ego needs to enjoy success in order to have emotional energy to continue in your growth.

It's a Macho World

It is very important to become proficient at your job and to play to win. Scores of women are doing this, and their egos are alive and well in the area of self-development. But in spite of women's gains, there is a dark cloud over the horizon. The major issue for the female ego in the world of work is that it is still a macho world, and from one perspective we could say that men have better egos than women. This gives them an edge we should know more about. To understand the fundamentals of how the male ego operates, let us take a look at a man's childhood conditioning.

The Male Advantage

Men are given better lessons than women are in the art of self-development. We may wonder why. Perhaps it's because men have more aggressions and physical prowess. Have they bullied their way to superior positions? Or could they be smarter? I don't think so. I believe the answer lies in powerful cultural scripting that is becoming outdated but has fostered exaggerated differences between two groups of people who have more in common than not.

But let's forget the why's and look at the how's. How have men been trained to develop superior ego strength in many areas of accomplishment and leadership? First, boys are often more desired and favored by their families than girls because they are believed to be the true heirs. The male is the standard-bearer, the totem, the symbol of the family. He carries the family name. A family with only daughters experiences the death of its name in verbal and social usage. On a primitive level (and we are primitive underneath) this is the death of a family, the death of a clan. So most of us look for a male heir, and the male derives from this a fundamental sense of self-importance.

So now we have our little son. How is he going to be educated to fulfill his special role? First, he is probably paid more attention as a small infant than are his sisters. Studies have demonstrated that mothers are often more comfortable giving physical stroking to boys and are more likely to hold baby boys than baby girls. This form of nurturing provides an essential basis for self-esteem.

In the rearing of a boy, there is usually an expectation that he will be involved in the world, accomplishing great things in the society of men. Boys begin learning about this role in the play yard, discovering how to be a leader, how to be a team player, and, above all, how not to be a sissy. Aggression counts in sports, and when he makes a winning thrust, he receives powerful reinforcement in the cheers of buddies, who as team members have benefited from the young prince's prowess. Passivity and waiting on the sidelines identifies him as a wimp.

Domestic chores are delegated to girls. Young boys already are part of a class system in which they have the backup of female servants who do the functional work. (It has to be done, and almost anyone can do it.) It's OK for a boy to be messy (unconcerned with trivia) and slow to get started in school (not adapting too soon and thereby being his own person). Boys can swear (be verbally aggressive), be gross (desensitize themselves), and get very angry (not be internally blocked). By not having to make nice-nice and be a goody-good, a little boy prepares to have a man's ego.

Boys know that they have muscles, and that is another reason why they have strong egos. The foundation of ego development is in what is called the body ego. Long before we can think or talk, we experience ourselves and the world through physical sensations alone. We may then go on to higher planes of experience, but it is a mistake to let go of being grounded in fundamental body experiences. It is well known to therapists that mentally ill people have terrible body tone and are physically lethargic. Body flab is related to psychological flab. Boys stay tuned in to their muscles, moving through space, engaging in solid physical contact, being tough, and delighting in physical surges and urges. They talk body language and laugh with glee. And in the process their egos grow stronger and stronger.

A major distinction in the education of a male is that he gets most of his strokes for things that he *does*. His worshipful parents are thrilled when he walks, talks, scribbles, hits a home run, catches a fish, looks at a star, or builds a fort. In contrast, he is somewhat deprived of strokes that relate simply to being a pleasant person: having a sweet face or curly hair, being good company, or being kind, cheerful, sincere, or helpful. For a boy these qualities are not enough. He has to get out there and prove himself.

So there you have it—a blueprint for filling in the gaps in the education of women. We belong to the human race and no longer need to participate in archaic scripting rituals. A female can lead the family line, play on the team, flex her muscles, and take action.

The Macho Seesaw

It is very difficult for the female ego to grasp the extent to which men play by very different rules from women in the workplace. Men often seem not to play by any rules at all. The slogan should be amended to read, "All's fair in love, war, and work." For a woman who has grown up believing that it is nice to be nice, the cutthroat tactics employed in the world of work are shocking. A woman's ego can be hurt at work when assumed trusts are betrayed, associates are discovered to be lying, and people conspire to make her look bad or steal her credit. The jungle is not a pleasant place in which to find yourself if you have not been trained in jungle warfare.

It is not exactly that men are not playing by a set of principles. It is just that the macho principle is very different from the rules that we learn at mother's knee. According to macho principles, it is perfectly acceptable to be not nice, even mean, cruel, and demeaning of others. Macho is the embodiment of what the transactional analysts call an "I'm OK, you're not OK life position." It is an artificial existential position because the deep truth about life is that everyone is OK and possesses unique gifts. Because of the artificiality of this view, a man must continue to put great energy into maintaining an attitude that overrides the truth of everyone's unique "OKness."

The macho guys want the world to be in two teams: the good guys and the bad guys. And when a man acts like a heavy, he does so to make sure that everyone knows which team he is on. In essence, the macho principle follows the code of Tarzan: me strong; you weak. This code is played out through an endless number of corollaries. Some of the better-known ones are I'm smart, you're dumb; I'm crude, you're genteel; I'm the boss, you're my slave; I'm a bully, you're nice; I'm in power, you're not; I've got guts, you're a wimp; I figured it out, you didn't; I'm a male, you're a female.

This is the game men have been playing with each other since

toddlerhood, when in the sand box they banged on each other's
heads with shovels and their mommies cooed, "Boys will be boys."
Such initiation rites continue through the traumas of college haz-
ing, army induction, hospital internships, and brutally unfair corporate carrot chasing.

The Seesaw Principle

The macho mentality is a seesaw mentality. Being on the up
side implies that someone else is on the down side. The macho
person can't afford to let someone think he's on the down side.
Being on the up side of the equation is what is known as power.
Macho power implies an object—power over someone else. In
order to function, the machos organize themselves into clubs and
pecking orders to let you know who's up and down in relation to
whom.

Then Little Mary Sunshine enters this scenario. Where does
the female fit into the macho world? If a woman stays at home
she does not risk being on the down side of the macho seesaw
because she had disqualified herself from playing. But if she decides
to play, she may be in for some ego bruising. Her childhood
initiation rites probably did not include being cracked over the
head in the sand box or on the football field. Unfortunately for
her, men will use the same tactics on her that they use on each
other to keep themselves on top and others on the bottom. Men
are good at these maneuvers because they have been playing this
game for a long time. The top layer of the corporate cake is small,
and it is considered to be the spoils of the few men who won every
match, beginning with the one in the sand box.

Because of her inexperience with the seesaw principle, a woman
is usually placed on the down side of the equation. Mature men
who have grown beyond the seesaw principle in the world of work
are unfortunately rare, and a woman needs to know that she will
be the victim of prejudice, even if it goes unspoken by those who
are savvy enough to keep their prejudice a secret.

The Authoritarian Personality

The manifestations of the authoritarian personality are so clear that you can take a test to find out if you are one. The authoritarian personality is a defensive mode in which a person likes to put other people into categories. My son Michael described a camp counselor who said of the boys in his tent, "John is the lazy type; Joe is the touchy type; and David is the type of guy who doesn't know how to act yet." Michael said, "The trouble was that he gave everyone a label for the wrong reasons." Michael got three cheers for his perceptiveness that night.

The authoritarian person likes to put people in categories, label them, and blemish them. This person is looking for everyone else's faults in order to aggrandize himself. He develops a set of behaviors into a high art, sometimes well-camouflaged as humor or a perverse love of people. The teller of ethnic jokes, mother-in-law jokes, or dumb women jokes is busy making himself feel superior. He is joining the "winning" team at the expense of someone else. This behavior is a compulsive mechanism in a person who is able only to tease instead of express warmth, blemish instead of compliment, and complain instead of appreciate. He intimidates others, partly because nobody has the nerve to speak up to him. He will be surprised when someone calls his bluff and tells him to monitor his effect on others. He is on a self-deluded fantasy trip in which he thinks that he is building himself up. People with authoritarian personalities actually are miserably unhappy in their inability to appreciate others.

Confrontation is needed, but how you go about it can be tricky in the world of work. You must use your ego and your brains to decide upon a skillful plan of action. Be aware that if you cannot get this person to change by direct confrontation, he is your enemy. I know from having worked with many people at top levels of corporate management that antisocial behavior is not appreciated. Many bosses have been let go because of the dreadful morale of

their staffs. Don't be afraid to complain to other people in authority
and do anything in your power to stop the person's intimidation
tactics. Above all, hold onto your own ego, knowing that such
authoritarian behavior is not worthy of respectful cowering.

Why is the authoritarian person so compulsive about making
other people not OK? Why is it so difficult for a chronic grouch
or complainer to say something nice? Why is a prejudiced person
so rigid in classifying humans by their perceived inferiorities or
shortcomings? It is because that person fears being on the down
side of the macho seesaw. Putting others down reassures the macho
man that he must be up. He must maintain a one-up, one-down
system at all costs. Lurking beneath the surface is tremendous fear.
He is running scared because in his heart of hearts he knows that
his position is untenable. He refuses to remember that at some
time in his life he felt terribly inadequate. This is why painful
initiation rites set the stage for struggle on the macho seesaw. By
experiencing excruciating humiliation, a person sets his sights on
never being there again. The familiar story of starting on the "bottom" and moving up to the "top" carries with it a horrific fear of
sliding back down again.

The Paranoid Puff-Up

Now we get to the reason why this bully's behavior is so intimidating and even frightening. Have you ever seen a psychotic person
walking down the street? Unfortunately, in any large city, there
are many mentally ill people walking in the streets. A paranoid
schizophrenic can be seen from time to time standing on a corner
or in the middle of traffic yelling and cursing, giving venomous
speeches that are frightening to witness. These people are very
frightened themselves, and they are enlisting a primitive ego defense in their own behalf. They are scaring everyone else as a way
to rampage against their own internal demons. This is known as
the paranoid puff-up. It is a grown man putting on a scary Hal-
loween mask. The threatening demeanor of men who are macho

in the extreme is a weapon to scare the enemy. Frightening the other person will allay such a man's own internal fears. This insight will not make you immune to all of their scare tactics or hurtfulness, but it helps to remind yourself that you are dealing with someone who is defending against his own insecurity and fear.

Never Show Your Flaws

Because macho is a game based on a phony idea that some people are superior to others, it offers a great opening for lying. The essence of the macho lie is not only that the other person is not OK but that the macho man is perfect. The "I'm the most OK guy in the world" persona is expressed in a form of macho optimism, which I call *aggressiveness with a smile*. This friendly aggressiveness has little to do with friendship and is employed as a power play against the other person. Feigning friendship in order to get what he wants from you, he almost believes his own act and thinks that he is being magnanimous. Do not be duped into becoming involved in a phony relationship. You will sense the putdown if this aggressive friendliness feels like a power play. The cheerful puff-up is the flip side of the paranoid puff-up.

I have found in working with men that it is very important to chip away at the layers of macho adaptations if I am to help a man claim an honest emotional life for himself and find satisfaction in his relationships. Such a man can live with a crippling blindness based on the assumption that everything is OK as long as he has come out on top. I see men thinking that they have won when they have demoralized their wives in arguments. I have seen a man maintain a rigid, cheerful facade, refusing to "give in" to a suicidal daughter's plea for help. I have seen the damage done to female egos by men being excessively critical and withholding positive affirmation. The macho principle that has baffled me the most is the notion that kindness is weakness, when there is so much nurturant power in kindness.

Armed with Awareness

The most important defensive weapon for the female ego in entering the jungle of the macho world is insight. To play the game to win in such a world a woman does not have to say, "I'm strong; you're weak," but she had better say, "I'm strong, too!" If she can do this without going to war, she will break up the macho dynamics and will be in the only real position for winning. In this position, everyone can win: "I'm OK; you're OK."

In her job with a computer firm, Page found herself in the company of overt machos with whom she was supposed to design educational software for children. Whenever she was with the four men who were on her team, they would refuse to discuss work and would immediately discuss sports, about which she knew nothing and cared less. They always made her feel that she was not part of the club. Her only recourse was to complain to their supervisor that they were making it impossible for her to have the materials and information that she needed to do her job. She remained strictly task-oriented, knowing that there was no way for her to change the men. Inside she was in pain and desperately wanted them to be nice to her. She made sure that she did an outstanding job and then finessed a transfer to a division in which there would be less personality conflict to impede her progress. During the time that she was in this ego-bruising situation, she had to act like the new kid on the block—which meant waiting for them to get used to her, not trying to change them, and not tempting their sadism by showing her hurt feelings. In such a situation, having a strong ego is the only way to survive. By remaining as analytical and strategic as possible Page was able to survive this situation and go on to a better one.

On the other end of the continuum is the macho gentleman. He is often so polished and dignified that he can easily maneuver a woman into taking a traditional role that she does not seek. He actually can make it attractive to a woman to relinquish her power. Hired as an administrative assistant, Sonya had her own secretary, but in various ways her boss indicated that he expected some traditional female nurturing. The beautiful paneled offices filled with English antiques almost made her feel as though she was in a nineteenth-century novel, and she found herself fighting her inclination to be a feminine accessory for her boss. Initially she was flattered when he would call her in as a sounding board for his ideas. Then she realized that not only was he picking her brains, but he was wasting her time. Sonya learned to refuse him—in the most elegant way she could muster—because she had too much work to do. Keeping her mind on her work and her goals kept her from serving her boss in a way that was not in her own best interest.

To deal effectively with a macho man, you must realize that he is expressing a cultural phenomenon. Everyone is to blame for its perpetuation. Individual men are merely fulfilling their conditioning when they play games, and women tacitly support these dynamics by playing a complementary role. To show you how the macho dynamic is perpetuated, let's look at a typical power tactic.

The Silent Treatment

A macho man sometimes uses silence and withdrawn behavior to make other people feel uncomfortable. When they are in a state of discomfort, others will rush to fill the silent vacuum and will give as much of themselves as possible. An investment banker once acknowledged to me that his favorite tactic in making deals was to say nothing until the other person started to squirm. This would give him a psychological advantage because the other person would often show his hand.

It is not the goal of a macho man to hurt others through using the silent treatment (although that can be a social consequence); rather, the goal is to serve his own ends in getting from others the information, the power, or the acquiescence that he needs to accomplish his work task. A good player of this game can sit in a meeting just looking at you. You will respond to your own discomfort and express your impulses to make things nice socially. It is an artful and highly manipulative device to withhold strokes so as to make other people scramble for you.

If a woman ever thinks that she can shame a good gamesman out of what he is doing because he is not being nice, she is wrong. She needs to catch on to a reality that might be outside of her own experience. Such a gamesman has no guilt feelings about what he is doing. He has no desire to empathize with other people, and if they are suffering it is not his problem—it is theirs. In such a situation, a people-pleasing woman is tempted to fill the silence with all her thoughts, give her warmth for his coldness, make nurturing allowances for his insensitivities, or give patience and understanding in exchange for his deliberate obtuseness. In each case, she is rewarding his behavior and perpetuating it.

Changing Your Game

When a woman discovers what men are doing to her, and what she is doing to support this behavior, she is tempted to deal with it by becoming a man-hater. At this point she must keep in mind that man-hating is just another trap. She must summon the ego strength to acknowledge what men do and be able to say, "This is the way it goes. Even though I don't like it, this is a part of reality that I must find a way to deal with." The macho man manipulates, but his object is not to hurt others. He is most likely blindly following the macho traditions of how to be a powerful man.

The best way for a woman to deal with this problem is by working on her own inner attitudes. She will be best able to defeat the macho games when she changes the way she supports this dynamic. The typical macho man presents a sentence with blanks in it. A woman needs to curb her compulsion to fill in the blanks, giving away everything she has to offer for free and supporting his with-holding tactics. She should ask herself, What can I get for myself? instead of What can I give? Don't be afraid of silences, but call the macho bluff and be silent yourself. Trade information and ideas, instead of giving them away. Remind yourself, I don't have to be helpful!

You will begin to relinquish your compulsive niceness when

you form strategies on your own behalf. Look for ways other people at work can help you or you can get around them. If you want to win in your dealings with a macho man, arm yourself with knowledge of his weaknesses, just as he is willing to take advantage of yours. You must know the areas in which you have the edge over him and those in which he tends to be out in left field. Conquer your fears of not being forever nice, and become a realist.

Armed with His Weaknesses

- Be aware that macho men are often terribly out of touch. They do not know how they affect other people because they are unaware of other people's feelings. By seeing this as a weakness, you will not be so intimidated by their gauche and insensitive behavior.
- A macho man can be vulnerable because he has many unmet needs. If he is a workaholic, he is ultimately playing a losing game in which life holds very few real joys or pleasures. When you see that he is out of his depth in any frame of reference other than his own world of work, he will not look so powerful to you—quite the opposite.
- A major downfall for the macho man is his lack of skill in human relationships. As a result, he does not possess the inside track on people, nor does he gain real trust and loyalty. When you see how he blunders, and how blind he is to the reactions of other people, you will perceive his insensitive treatment of you in a different light. You will see him as weak instead of powerful.
- Paranoia lurks under the surface of most macho men. That is why they have to play everything so close to the chest. Just the suggestion that something is going on that they do not know about can send them into emotional tailspins. They are living in the dark about how people really feel, and this lack of insight sets them up for trouble.

Claiming Inner Power

I have worked with women who complain intensely that they are mistreated but still see their boss as being powerful, almost godly. After having them analyze his weaknesses, I direct them in a Gestalt exercise to teach them to diffuse the power with which they have imbued him.

If you have a problem with a macho authority figure at work, sit in a chair facing an empty one. Picture the man you are dealing with vividly in your mind and pretend that he is sitting opposite you. If possible, have a friend help you with this exercise by witnessing it and cheering you on. Start by calling the authority figure by his first name. You are going to tell him exactly what you think of him, emphasizing the negative, especially everything that you would not dare to say to him in person. Use as many curse words as you would like, and get it all out. While you are doing this, *do not cry*. This is not an exercise in feeling like a victim, even though you might feel like one much of the time. You are working to diffuse his power over you by making clear what is wrong with *him*. Point out all of his blind spots, his errors, and his insensitivities.

In the second part of this exercise you are to get deeply in touch with your own power. Kneel in front of a couch on which there is a pillow. In a controlled manner you are going to clasp your fists and rhythmically pound the pillow so as to feel a physical release—but do not hurt your hands. Use one of the following phrases, or make up one: "I hate what you do." "Stop your power plays." "Cut that out." You are working on claiming your own power and self-confidence. Do not feel sad; express feelings of anger and outrage, even if the tears are flowing. Angry feelings contain your power. Claim the force of your anger, and you claim your dignity.

I once used this exercise in therapy with a woman who was suffering a form of sexual harassment from her boss. He asked her personal questions about her love life which she refused to answer, but she felt constantly on edge. Indeed, her boss was winning at this wicked little power play by making her squirm and feel uptight. In the session she yelled at him and pounded on the pillow. At the end of the hour she said, "I can't believe that after all this I now have to go back to the office and face him. I haven't figured out what I am going to do." I suggested that she not worry about a strategy because the important thing was that she was clear about her own feelings. The most amazing thing happened. Her boss never made offensive remarks again. He somehow sensed that she would no longer put up with his obnoxious behavior and that he no longer had a victim.

When you have reached the point that you will no longer tolerate being mistreated and you feel your dignity with all your might, you will scare away many of the people who would otherwise try to pull some numbers on you. The self-confident woman knows when she has been insulted and discounted, and she hates such treatment. It does not make her into a nice people-pleaser; it makes her cold and angry. She centers on that attitude. A bully knows who he can push around and who he can't. You must have an inner attitude that says, Don't step on my toes! The answer is to have heartfelt dignity and use your head in every situation.

The Sleepwalkers

The extremely macho man is not really alive in his unconscious and unaware state. Paranoia and prejudice give him tunnel vision. Realizing that her opponent is basically out of it, an aware woman might decide that instead of making an issue out of his behavior, she can simply ignore him and go on with her work. She does not always need to fight to win. Sometimes she needs only to duck or step aside when the sleepwalkers are walking toward her.

If you are dealing with a macho man in business who is not central to your purpose, learn sidestep techniques. Sometimes you may appear to be a people-pleaser, but you in reality are using niceness as a power play. *Strategic niceness is different from com-*

pulsive niceness. You must first know what you want, so as to avoid being sidetracked by human obstacles. You might observe that the man who is being withholding and difficult is under stress himself. You could then plan to treat him as he wants to be treated: be pleasant, give him a stroke, and do your job. He may already have problems dealing with people and will be devoted to you if you are not confrontational. Use this strategy on difficult people at work who are not central but must be gotten around.

Even if a central person is difficult and out of touch, you must plan how to use your power to prevail against this obstacle. You might want to vault over him to a higher division, duck him through a lateral move, or gang up against him by joining his enemies. Confrontation is needed for serious abuse but is not necessarily the best technique for political maneuvering in the macho world.

Men Are People, Too

If a woman wants to deal in the macho world, she has to bring a man down from the pedestal of power on which *she* has placed him. Learn to see men as *people* and refute the myths of our macho-based culture.

John Wayne is one of our mythological heroes. Even if you are not a fan of Western movies, you are not likely to see him as a weak man. During his terrible illness with lung cancer, he was still portrayed as a tough guy who was defeating the Big C. As vulnerable as he was to his disease, he died a hero. This is the way we like to see men, and many of them work to fulfill a charade of total strength and power.

With no malicious intent, however, you can also clearly see that many males are dependent on a woman or a job or both. All men were once vulnerable little boys, and many of them tolerated some abuse or neglect in childhood which was very painful to them. I am acutely aware that many men are vulnerable to addiction to cigarettes, alcohol, or their work. The task of the female ego is to see such a man as a human being and not as Hercules.

If you are to see a man as human, you must give up your desire, conscious or unconscious, for a man to be strong on your behalf and to have strength that you can borrow. Say these words to yourself: There is no such thing as a totally strong man. If that statement is true, how do you feel about it? Can you be happy without perceiving men as predominantly strong? Does this make you feel insecure or disoriented? Only when men are demythologized will we all be able to give up phony macho games.

To claim your independent self, you must separate emotionally not only from your mother but also from your father. This means giving up the fantasy of the perfect protector and source of inspiring strength. This dream is especially hard to give up, and you may require therapy if you are longing for a father-daughter relationship that you never had. Our images of strong men are largely myths. Men are whole humans with a mixture of strengths and weaknesses. Men themselves have trouble giving up the macho ideal, but they will claim health and wholeness when they admit their humanity and connect more deeply and fully with other people. Men have as much to gain as women do by giving up the macho mentality.

Sex in the Office

The workplace is becoming a mating arena. As more women enter the work force, male and female executives with the same socioeconomic backgrounds are working side by side. There have always been sexual vibrations between men and women in the workplace, as well as every other place, and with more women at work, there are more sexual vibes to deal with.

Work is a good place for men and women to meet. It is the place where people look their best and demonstrate their assets. Among my clients in the last two years, a female lawyer married a lawyer whom she met during a negotiation, an advertising account manager married a man from the creative writing end of the business, and a woman doctor married a colleague. All the words of caution in the world are not keeping men and women from mixing business with pleasure, and I predict that this trend will increase.

Work is not necessarily sexy, but people are, and the stimulation of work can do its part in arousing the libido. Many women are troubled by having to sort out issues of sexual harassment from normal games of friendly persuasion or sexual admiration. Some women are quick on the puritanical trigger when they sense a man's sexual vibrations.

Feeling Uptight

When a woman obsessively accuses men of having "only one thing on their minds" she is probably betraying her own sexual repression. Your ego strength has a great deal to do with body ego. Healthy body ego means that you are comfortable with your body and all of its various sensations and functions. If you lack a confident body ego, your sexuality will be low or repressed. As a result, you will feel especially insecure when you are with someone who is comfortable with and even expressive of his sexual feelings.

There is another reason why you might feel uptight about sexual vibrations coming from a man. Men often deal with their uptight feelings by coming on too strong. By being crude or blunt about sex, a man is protecting himself by trying to scare you off. He is also fooling himself by thinking that he has sexual confidence.

If you have problems with sexual repression, as a great many women do, you will be troubled either by a man who is enjoying a moment that has sexual overtones or a man who is crudely coming on too strong. In either case, whether the man's behavior is appropriate or inappropriate, you must take responsibility for your own feelings. If you are uncomfortable about sex, it is because you have strong sexual feelings that you have not learned to deal with. Your unconscious mind tends to rule your life because you project it onto the world and find it everywhere you go. In addition, your unconscious mind communicates to the unconscious minds of others.

Getting Comfortable

A woman needs to be in touch with her sexuality so she can deal effectively with the sexual situations in which she will find herself. Working near any human being gives an opportunity for intimacy and closeness, and you may encounter a very strong erotic attraction. You need to accept it, enjoy it, and decide how you will respond to it.

The male ego is generally based on a very healthy body ego. Many men are completely comfortable with their bodily sensations in relation to women. When a man feels erotic vibrations in his office situation, he is relaxed. He might, for example, see the outline of a beautiful breast through a silk blouse. He looks at it, imagines it undraped, fully enjoying the thoughts and images. He experiences a sensation in his pants and thanks the gods that he happened to be there at that moment. In response, some men will smile and go about their business. Some will encourage themselves in fantasy toward climax. Others might say something, make a move, or turn on heavy charm in pursuit of the stimulus.

A woman, being human also, has the privilege of allowing herself to enjoy her sexual feelings. Enjoying sex is an experience of power because it releases joy and positive feelings. The sensation in the pants requires a chain reaction of body chemistry—adrenaline, tightening of tissues, and secretion. In a basic way, this reaction is power, which a woman needs to understand. Enjoying her body will build her self-confidence and her ego.

Feeling comfortable with sex and enjoying sexual feelings will help a woman at work. She will not feel that men have power over her because they are comfortable about something that she is not, and she will not inflate a situation into something more that it really is. When you are comfortable with sex, it does not rule your life. You will feel freedom in choosing whether it is appropriate to act on your impulses, knowing that one sexual impulse is not a big deal—as pleasant as it might be.

Charlotte told me about sharing a business lunch with a male client. The French restaurant that she chose was quiet and inti-

mate, with the tables set far apart. She and her client felt disarm-
ingly alone. She asked him an important question about his firm,
and he responded by telling her how attractive she was. She was
stunned and nervous and told him that he was being sexist. He
asked her why, and she said, "Because you wouldn't say that to a
man with whom you were having a business lunch." That seemed
to stop him, and he looked a bit sheepish and hurt. Charlotte
swallowed hard and then said, "You know, Frank, if you had not
said something like that to me, I probably would have looked at
myself in the mirror in the ladies' room wondering if there was
something wrong. To tell you the truth, I think that you are quite
attractive." They both laughed and felt that the tension between
them had dissolved. Then they could transact business.

Acknowledging feelings allows them to dissipate. It is not always
appropriate to acknowledge sexual feelings directly, but if you don't
admit them to yourself, they are likely to intensify and make you
feel uncomfortable. When you know your own feelings and accept
them, you will be able to deal with them in whatever way seems
appropriate. You will also be less awkward in dealing with men
who make passes at you. Many women are caught in the bind that
Charlotte was, feeling insulted if he admires her and insulted if
he doesn't. Often the answer is simple: Enjoy!

Work Strengthens the Ego

To develop our egos we need two kinds of strokes. The first is
unconditional love, a sense that we are lovable no matter what.
But as we grow from that solid emotional base, we must learn to
earn love, to get strokes for what we do. Our worth can be expressed
concretely, whether it be net worth or the sense of accomplishment
for a job well done.

Applying yourself to a task or a set of problems to be solved
challenges and exercises your ego. The ego functions well in focused work: planning, prioritizing, researching, assimilating, and
creating. A working woman can feel strong and independent when

she is tenaciously applying herself to stimulating work.

My client Monica complained that her husband was too involved in his work, and she spent a lot of time focusing on the emotional nuances of their relationship. She often complained to him, "You don't love me enough." At times he was preoccupied, but he loved his wife and was a devoted husband. When their child entered school, Monica found an absorbing job. Her attitudes began to change as she became involved in the currency of work: work products, honors, and money. She discovered that her own actions could generate direct rewards, and she began to understand her husband's pleasure in his work. Looking back at the prework period of her life, she realized she had been naïve: "I really did not understand Lee or know where he was coming from." Her worries about not having enough love ceased.

As valuable as the homemaker's work is, it usually does not do as much for a women's self-esteem as work in a job or the community will do. I have often heard homemakers express the sense that they don't really do anything. The truth is usually that they are not counting what they do. Perhaps that is because, in our materialistic society, what they do does not count. Our society does not recognize housework and mothering as real accomplishments but *expects* women to do these jobs naturally and with ease. Even when we ourselves deeply value what we are doing as homemakers and mothers, our egos still need outside validation.

In the world of work, a woman finds that everything counts. The time clock counts her work hours, her productivity is quantified by the volume of work she turns in, how many contacts she makes, or how many houses she sells. Her worth to herself is measured in her own growth and in the dollars in her paycheck. Everyone is counting, and the ego is happy. A woman feels much stronger when she discovers that independent sources of strokes are available to her through her own efforts. Sigmund Freud defined mental health as the ability to love and the ability to work.

Volunteer Work

There is another arena of woman's work that deserves to be praised. Scores of women have found satisfaction as unpaid skilled workers who make contributions of social significance. These women are active members of school boards, library boards, support groups for local and state governments, the PTA, the hospitals, the scouts, or many other good causes. Possessing admirably strong egos, they structure lives that have meaning without being hitched to a paycheck.

These women are not unlike artists who work simply to fulfill their calling. Their primary reward is quantifiable on another level. Their egos are strengthened by fulfilling their human desires to make a worthwhile contribution to the world.

Some people think it is folly to work for no paycheck. I have learned from women, however, that there are forms of validation other than money which can be rich sources of ego support. Experience in the volunteer sector takes a person beyond materialism. A successful woman pediatrician I know donates her services to a lower-income clinic one day each week. This is a day of joy for her, offering full affirmation to the humanitarian part of herself. She claims the luxury of doing doctoring she really enjoys. Her pay is a psychic reward.

A writer I know, who is pressed for time, nevertheless spends time with an elderly person twice a week, an assignment arranged through a charitable organization. The bedridden woman, a former scholar, thrives on the stimulating companionship of the lively young writer. Another woman friend with young children took on the task of discovering hidden and hungry shut-ins in our New York City neighborhood several years ago. Through the sponsorship of a local church she developed a successful food program for these people, answering their silent cries for help.

The woman who has discovered satisfying work in the community has found the joy of generativity. Erik Erikson described generativity as a culminating phase in one's life in which a person embraces the satisfaction of giving for future generations. Many women spend their entire lives within this enriching process. Such giving is not adaptive but is responsive—not only to a woman's world but to a chord of human longing within herself to be a giver of worthy gifts. The enriched lives of such women contain a message for retired people, many of whom need to find meaning by being useful contributors.

A woman with a service orientation has a purpose that can liberate her from household drudgery. Her time is precious, and she doles it out as carefully as does a woman with a paycheck. Just as she has learned ego strength, she models for her children a concern for the larger world. Usually she needs their help at home to carry out her tasks, which strengthens their egos. This expression of the female ego can benefit the self-esteem of a woman or man, and it certainly benefits the needs of the world.

Claiming Self-Confidence

When a woman forgets herself and simply does the job at hand as well as she possibly can, she has found the key to self-confidence: losing self-consciousness. Even if others are conscious that you are a woman, you must remember that you are a person. Once you have prepared for your job and polished your persona, forget yourself. The authoritative person is focused on the task and is applying herself, not thinking about herself.

You discover your deepest talents when you let yourself be the person you really are. You have a unique development and background, and you possess talents and skills. You can offer a human perspective that is not founded on imitating men or being a self-conscious female. Think of yourself as a human being first and as a woman second, and claim your dignity on the job.

ᨆ 8 ᨆ

The Female Ego in Success

You gain strength, courage and confidence by every experience in which you
really stop to look fear in the face. . . . You
must do the thing you think you cannot
do.

Eleanor Roosevelt

Challenging Your Script

The female ego in success is the woman who has achieved
autonomy. She has broken free of whatever is holding her
back and has taken charge of making her life work. Often the
beginning of her path to this destiny was filled with obstacles. Past
conditioning keeps us locked into patterns that enslave us.

Barriers to Success

The most profound conflicts about success usually occur within
your unconscious mind and are waged between your own desires
and the internalized voices of parents, authority figures, or experiences that delivered powerful prohibitions. As children become
socialized, they can become conditioned not to follow the course
of their own talents. Your barriers to success are to be found in
your own incorporation of these prohibitions.

When a woman makes the development of herself her number
one priority, she is rejecting the script that centuries of culture
have written for her. She must deal with the issue of outdoing
parents and even peers. She may not receive permission to do this
from the person she loves, her family, or her friends. No one will

216

fully understand her lack of time and energy. Only her deepest friends will still realize that she loves them even though she no longer calls or sends Christmas cards. Making up for lost time in self-development taxes a woman's time and energy in the extreme.

A woman who is making space in her life for growth sometimes finds her family and friends escalating their crises as a bid for her attention. But just as powerful are her own inner attacks of guilt when she is preoccupied with herself. She struggles with her compulsions to serve and please others at her own expense. Some women find it impossible to pursue their own growth with so much external and internal resistance.

Finding a Guide

A woman might seek a counselor to help lend insight and support in her battle with the barriers to success. A relationship with a friend, a mentor, or a therapist can be the springboard from enslavement to selfhood, helping you to overcome a script that is not working for you and giving you backup support for what you want to do. The best guides are people who have done the same things themselves and can show you the new paths. Sources of guidance are conscious-raising groups, support groups, training programs, or educational situations.

A word of caution in your quest for a guide: Choose your counselor or mentor carefully with one question in mind. *Does this person want to keep me dependent?* Do not go from one form of bondage to another. Make alliances with people who are fulfilled in their own lives and will enjoy you as a free person. Use your ego to decide which people will support you to be your true and independent self.

At some critical point in her life almost every successful woman has turned to a wise person who gave her permission to break the old rules and embrace principles of growth. We cannot struggle and grow alone. Every woman must have someone else in her corner.

The Female Automaton

A woman was referred to me by her supervisor at a midtown bank. She made an appointment to see me during her lunch hour. At 1:00 I opened the door to the waiting room and saw a woman of about twenty-five sitting numbly, staring into space. I thought she was probably frightened, as are many people facing a therapy session for the first time. She sat down in my office and began to talk in a hushed voice. She explained to me that she had recently received a significant promotion at work and that her boy friend had asked her to marry him. These successes were, as she put it, "More than I could have dreamed of." Emotionally, however, she was feeling terrible. She was becoming withdrawn and suspicious of other people. She had felt extremely anxious when she received her promotion and her proposal of marriage within one week. After the anxiety, she had lapsed into a state of being spaced out. She was so out of touch that the intervention of others was required to get her into therapy.

As the young woman talked, I became aware that under the trancelike exterior was a very bright person. I was also struck by her unusual beauty. As her story was revealed to me over many sessions, a clear picture emerged. She described to me the life of her mother, a bitter and unfulfilled woman whose marriage had ended in divorce. She told me that her mother would punish her by not speaking to her for days and that these "punishments" often coincided with key events in her own life such as the day she was in a play or the night of her high school graduation. She was never sure what she had done to exacerbate her mother's unhappiness, but she nevertheless felt pain and guilt.

Under a Spell

We could describe this woman as being under a spell. Her story is not unlike that of Snow White, whose stepmother was extremely jealous of her physical and spiritual beauty. Jealous people are unfulfilled people who are very angry when someone else has what they want for themselves. Their attitude says, If I can't have it, I won't let you have it either. A mother who is jealous of her daughter has enormous power—even the power to put her daughter under a spell. The message Snow White received from her stepmother was, Don't be a beautiful woman. Drop dead, instead. Snow White made a decision and implemented it with a behavior: This is too much. I'll go to sleep, and Mom will think I'm dead. She was then under a spell.

My young and beautiful client's mother had given her this message: Don't outdo me or I will never speak to you. To a young child such a threat is frightening and powerful. When she began to outdo her mother, she was so scared that she withdrew from the world like Snow White.

If you are to possess your own ego, it is important to get in touch with any messages that you have received from a jealous or controlling parent or sibling. You may be surprised to find that you are being loyal to such a message and therefore are spellbound, entangled in a psychological trap that is keeping you from fully living your life.

Spellbreaking

Rooting out your obedience to a negative script message is a radical process. It requires a close assessment of the commands you heard as a child and what you did to implement or follow them. The seeker of success in life needs to see clearly the negative part of her parents that she still is faithfully obeying. When you no longer need a perfect, godlike parent you detach and grow. Two transactional analysts, Eric Berne and Claude Steiner, discovered that in therapy a person can become free of the past by discovering his or her own programming in the form of specific messages they call injunctions.

I have used this method for many years in my work with women. Each woman's programming is unique, but certain patterns have emerged. The following messages are the ones I often find in working with women. Thinking about these examples and deciding whether they apply to you may help you discover the hidden agenda from childhood that is keeping you from going where you deserve to be.

Messages from a Family Member:

- Take care of me (and don't give yourself attention).
- Don't be beautiful (because I will feel jealous).
- Be what I want (so I can live passively and vicariously).
- Don't outdo me (or I will feel threatened).

Here is how these four messages can put a woman under a spell and how the spells can be broken.

Take care of me (and don't give yourself attention).

Samantha's mother talked incessantly, complaining much of the time about her physical ailments and general malaise. Everyone focused on her. If any other family member raised a topic of conversation, mother would change the subject right back to herself.

Samantha's decision: My main concern in life is my mother.

Samantha's behavior: Samantha was obsessed with taking care of other people, including her mother. She was chronically exhausted because her giving to others gave her no joy. She had a vague personality and a lumpy body. She seldom indulged in activities for herself.

Breaking the spell: First, Samantha learned to receive from other people and limited her contact with her mother to a phone call once a week (instead of daily). She accomplished this detachment with the help of psychotherapy. She needed a transitional relationship with someone as she unhooked from her mother. She also needed to experience a relationship in which the focus was on herself. Samantha reached out to others who would help her do what was necessary. She joined a group that helped her lose weight and a gym where she learned how to enjoy exercising. She also learned what style of clothes suited her best. With this support behind her, she began to discover her own true interests. She took a series of courses in computer programming. Her creativity soared, and she now works for a company in which she is developing new computer languages. Samantha learned her personal lesson of not letting others distract her from doing the many things that she needed to do for herself.

Don't be beautiful (because I will feel jealous).

Ellen was raised in a family that was very rigid. She was forbidden to have much social life and made to feel that dancing and wearing makeup were immoral. Her mother, who was substantially overweight, encouraged all of her children to have a plump, "healthy" look. She sharply criticized Ellen's favorite (and glamorous) school chum for looking "cheap" and "fast."

Ellen's decision: It is immoral to be physically beautiful.

Ellen's behavior: Ellen allowed herself to look plain, fat, and dumpy. Fortunately, however, she was beautiful in other ways, and she became an accomplished singer. Unfortunately, she became incapacitated by anxiety attacks while putting on her costumes and stage makeup and gave up professional engagements.

Breaking the spell: Ellen needed therapy to give herself permission to be beautiful. The most effective treatment initially was short-term work with a hypnotherapist who used guided fantasy to desensitize her from a fear of wearing makeup on stage. Using biofeedback she was able to stop the anxiety attacks that began when she picked up a tube of lipstick. By specifically facing her fears, she freed herself from the stumbling block in her career. She later worked with a therapy group that gave her loving support to be as beautiful as she wanted to be. In the process she lost her "baby fat" and resumed a successful career as a singer.

Be what I want (so I can live passively and vicariously).

Betsy's father put enormous energy and money into his daughter's ice-skating lessons. During her evening practice sessions he sat in the freezing arena coaching her form the sidelines. Whenever Betsy complained of fatigue, her father would say, "Just one more time, Betsy. Make yourself do it." When Betsy, who was a gifted skater, approached the final tests that could have led to international competition, her father canceled all her lessons and said that it was time for her to give up skating. (Jealousy had replaced the father's vicarious thrills.)

Betsy's decision: I can never enjoy my talents for myself.

Betsy's behavior: Betsy became a compulsive achiever and show-off but did not enjoy any of her endeavors. She could not decide what she wanted to do with her life and dropped activities whenever she began to show promise. Abundantly gifted, she felt like a failure.

Breaking the spell: Betsy joined a women's support group that focused on giving women permission and support to live on their own behalf instead of for others. They lovingly confronted her about being a show-off for others without enjoying herself. With this awareness she was no longer able blindly to follow her conditioning. The discipline and determination that she had developed as a skater were great assets as she rooted out the failure mechanism through which she compulsively discounted everything she did as not being good enough or worthwhile enough. Finally, Betsy went back to skating and became a professional coach. Using her insight into the student's role, she works skillfully with both students and parents. During the skating club's annual ice show she performs to the delight of her students and for the purpose of pleasing herself.

Don't outdo me (or I will feel threatened).

Beverly had an older sister named Erin, who was the family princess. Erin was given beautiful clothes, and Beverly received hand-me-downs. Erin's popularity in high school was celebrated in the family, while Beverly worshiped from the sidelines and was largely ignored. Erin dropped out of college after her freshman year and married her high school boy friend.

Beverly's decision: I never can be wonderful like my sister.

Beverly's behavior: Beverly never pushed herself to excel and achieve. She felt depressed and cynical about life holding any possibilities for her. She had planned to go to college, but when Erin dropped out, she decided that she wasn't very smart. She put down her own accomplishments as insignificant.

Breaking the spell: Beverly's biology teacher reached out to her and convinced her that she was bright. He helped her get into college, refusing to let her disown her talents. He knew the score and told Beverly the shocking fact that she was much more intelligent than her sister. With this support, Beverly freed herself from a spell that forced her to accomplish less than her sister. She went on to a successful college career.

Choosing Independence over Nurturing

Having successfully done battle with the ghosts of one's family and with the inner child's fears at not being obedient to them, a woman must battle with the messages that her present family and culture give her. The main such message is that her role in life is to support and nurture other people. Even if she is not a mother, she is often expected to be supportive at work or in relationships. Not only is she given the messages *Take care of me* and *Please me*, but she makes a decision to fulfill these expectations.

I think that women do as much nurturing as they do to keep other people dependent on them. By infantilizing others, a woman can avoid growing up herself, and our culture encourages women to nurture excessively as a way to keep them infantile and victimized. I am not suggesting that there is anything wrong with the nurturing role per se, particularly inasmuch as my own identity as mother, wife, and therapist has a strong nurturing component. It is partly because I have gone from having a big sister (little mother) complex to finding creative channels for my nurturing skills that I can say that I have "been there" and that such preoccupations alone do not bring fulfillment or self-confidence. I know from experience that a woman who is a powerful force in the lives of others can live with a diminished sense of herself. I have also had to face the fact that keeping others dependent on you is a way to stay in a dependent relationship yourself. Cutting the nurturing cord requires a woman to become a full adult. We must realize that everyone is ambivalent about having women grow up. If women grow up, they might not take care of us anymore. Everyone will have to grow up.

Nurturing and Self-Esteem

When I look at my own growth, I find a distinct equation in which the balance of time and energy given to my career development is in direct proportion to the time and energy subtracted from nurturing activities. This shift in balance has created a change in attitude that has radically changed my personality. I look back at another life, recalling myself typing in an office when my husband Steve was in graduate school. I stopped at 11:00 one morning and meditated with all my might, hoping to send him psychic energy during his midterm Greek exam. Today I forget my family entirely when I am working. My husband and children have grown with me as I have relinquished compulsive nurturing, but some friends who knew me when I had my nurturing big sister complex still drain me because of their expectations. Even though I work in a helping profession, I have learned detachment. Objectivity can be more helpful than empathy, and it is much less draining. Acceptance of my clients is more helpful to their independent development than getting *my* needs met through *their* progress.

To the degree that I have relinquished my primary identity as a nurturer and supporter of others, I have grown in self-esteem. It has taken me some time to understand why. When a friend says to me, "Don't you feel good about all the people you have helped?" I wonder why I do not feel a strong "yes" inside. But when someone says, "Your analysis of my problem was right on the button," I glow with pride. I know the difference between my life and the lives of my clients, my kids, and my husband.

A Working Ego

A successful woman who possesses mental and emotional health is not someone who has arrived at a particular destination and is resting there but one who is in a continual process of growth and change.

The woman whose ego is whole and functioning possesses the inner constancy of drive to pursue a project through to completion. There is nothing mystical about the relationship between psychological success and worldly success. Neurosis takes up a lot of time, and repression robs you of energy. I have been especially fascinated by some of my clients who have come to therapy to gain insight at a time of stress but who are extremely successful in their lives. I have been impressed by the efficient way they deal with reality and the great joy they take in living their lives with emotional fullness, even when embroiled in a struggle. I have worked with women who have had rich careers in politics, in entertainment, in business, in homemaking, and in the volunteer sector. I have been impressed to see how their egos operate in tackling a temporary emotional hurdle.

There are six characteristics that describe how successful women operate whether they are approaching a major or minor change in their lives. These dynamic qualities give these women strong egos and successful lives.

A Successful Woman Knows What She Wants

Usually she wants the best for herself, and she is decisive and uncompromising about her standard of excellence. Her manner can be intimidating to an insecure person because she goes immediately to the point in describing her goals, large or small. In a restaurant she quickly knows what she wants to order or knowledgeably orders the perfect wine. Knowing what she wants gives her personality a critical edge because she also knows the opposite: what she does not want.

My client Deanne is a furniture designer who manufactures what she designs. She once told me that the key to her success in work is very simple: she works only with the best fabrics, the best woods, and the best craftsmen. Others find her very demanding; she knows exactly what she wants.

A woman who knows what she wants has the desire for certainty. The successful woman does not enjoy feeling vague and undifferentiated. She wants clarity, focus, and direction—and she makes sure that she has it.

A film actress whom I am now seeing is at a significant juncture in her career. She has successfully starred in several films in which she has become stereotyped. She is presently examining her goals and has formulated a precise picture of what she wants for herself. Uncomfortable with the vague question, What's next? she has decided that to change her image she must play in live theater before she does another role in film.

A Successful Woman Goes for It

She allows no boredom in her life; she wants to finish things and keep moving. Her life moves at a lively pace because she does not unnecessarily drag out any project. She might be perceived as excessively task-oriented and impatient because she does not dawdle once she has decided what she wants. Her attitude is Let's do it.

A friend and colleague of mine decided to get her Ph.D. She did. The next year she decided to publish a textbook in her field. She did. The following year, at age thirty-eight, she decided it was time to have her family. She did that, too. She is now at home raising her two little boys with the same gusto she has demonstrated in her professional life.

A simple but accurate way to define neurosis is as an *interruption in a process*. Neurotic people are always being interrupted in the pursuit of their goals. Healthy people show no hesitation. Self-affirming and positive, they do the job sooner rather than later and hate the endless doing of something and never completing it. The healthy person does not hold back but enjoys a wholehearted flow of energy. This process can be seen in behavior as specific as speech patterns. Some people interrupt themselves with hemming and hawing and with an excess of tangential thoughts or unnecessary niceties. A successful communicator gets right to the point and speaks efficiently and directly. The neurotic person takes the long way, and the healthy person takes the short way because she values energy and time.

It is interesting to notice the telephone habits of busy and successful women. They do not talk just for the sake of filling time. Conversations have a point, and when the mission has been accomplished, they get off the phone.

A Successful Woman Likes to Finish

Once something is done, it is done. Successful women don't second-guess themselves and wonder if they might add to or subtract from a task. They like to finish because they want to go on to a new project or adventure. It is particularly on this point that I see a clear difference between the women who are successful in their lives and those who are not.

In contrast is the woman who maintains confusion by continually bringing up new subjects. She asks too many questions and seems to enjoy not coming to completion. This lack of closure keeps her ego weak, maintaining a psychologically undefined position. The successful person wants to move on, cut the tie to what has been done, and avoid boredom. Good decision makers usually enjoy being decisive and saying, "Case closed."

I was fascinated by the reaction of a woman who had greatly enjoyed her participation in her husband's political career. When it was time for him to retire, she closed up their Washington home with dispatch and immersed herself in a new set of projects in New York City.

Successful Women Have Many Interests

Having many irons in the fire is the key to closure. A person enjoys finishing a project when there is a new project waiting in the wings. A successful woman does not go from excitement to boredom but from excitement to new excitement. Life is a series of cycles, each of which stimulates new enthusiasm.

One of the most exciting women I know was a traditional and happy wife and mother for thirty years. When her children were grown, she and her husband moved to New York. She became an actress on television commercials playing the part of a glamorous silver-haired woman who got in and out of limousines. Then she became active in a charity that led to a position on the board of trustees of a foundation. To know her is to experience her contagious zest for life. She is distinguished by her high degree of interest in many things in the world. When she fulfills one interest, she uses the momentum from that accomplishment to go on to the next. She wants to create as much as she can in her lifetime, and her life offers her many opportunities.

Personal Life Is Important to a Successful Woman

The women I know who are successful place great value on personal relationships. They generally have a small circle of very close friends, and their friendships have emotional richness and depth. Their families are important to them, and they talk about them openly and candidly.

The successful women whom I admire seem to have nothing to hide and will reveal problems, foibles, and concerns unselfconsciously. They are candid and personal and care deeply about other people. A successful woman glows with a special vitality. She is very positively connected to her experiences. In her presence you have the sense that life is fully available to her and that she puts great personal investment into her experiences.

Centering

Most women need to concern themselves with centering. The reason that this is not such an issue for men is because most of them already are centered. Men usually have support systems and permission to have tunnel vision, which keeps them on the track of whatever they are doing or thinking. Many professional men I know seem preoccupied, and not always attentive to others, but they are usually very much in touch with whatever project they are concerned with.

Successful centering is necessary if one is to do work of quality. The centered woman is a highly effective nurturer if she focuses her energy on one person at a time. By beaming her energy on a single task, she can find creative ways to solve problems in work; she can concentrate on a course of study; and she is able to do her best in any endeavor to which she applies herself.

One of the main problems with people-pleasing is that a woman responds to whatever beckons to her, giving attention to a number of tasks that are not of her own choosing. The successful woman learns wholeness instead of fragmentation and focus instead of general responsiveness.

If the main work that you do is by its nature fragmenting, it helps to have an avocation that focuses you. Reading or studying is a good exercise in focus. An absorbing physical activity can bring the sense of self into a whole entity. I know women who have found places that center them. One busy writer/mother has a serene breakfast in a coffee shop every morning after her gang has left for the day. Find places away from home such as the library or the Y or your health club to serve as the place where you mentally pull yourself together.

Avoiding the Hype

In learning the art of negotiation, women are learning how to stick to a point and avoid being sidetracked. Businesswomen learn to stay cool during other people's three-martini lunches and get the job done with a Perrier and a salad. Some of my clients who work in fields that give them media exposure have told me that there is great danger of getting sidetracked by the hype of the media. Glamor and glitter can drain energy if you are seduced into believing that the superficial fringe benefits are the main event. It takes special ego strength to stay centered and potent in the middle of the hype that sometimes accompanies success.

One of my clients described how she got the break aspiring

actresses dream of. She was given a part in a play in which several of the other performers were famous veteran actresses and actors. When she arrived in Washington, where the play was to have a two-week engagement, rehearsals began. Between rehearsals was a dazzling series of parties to welcome the cast into the Washington social scene. My client suddenly realized that the other members of the cast had done performances hundreds of times and that for her this was time for work. To perform on their level, she needed to spend all of her spare time going over her work in her hotel room and getting as much attention from the director as possible. Had she not stayed focused on the task at hand and missed a few glittering parties, she would have missed using the opportunity to advance in her work.

Potency and Body Ego for Women

To be successful, a woman must have will, energy, and commitment. These qualities mean potency. Potency is the energy a woman puts into achieving her goals. Women have been conditioned to avoid aggressive self-seeking to such an extent that they do not have a metaphor for their own libidos. A man "has balls." We know the meaning of that term on every level, and it is considered a quality worthy of respect. A ballsy woman is something else, maybe not as nice as a woman should be.

Commenting on Jimmy Connors, as he surged toward an important win over John McEnroe, the sportscaster gleefully shouted, "He's pumped! He's pumped!" Men can have their erections, their thrusts, their urges and surges for winning personal victory. Our heroes excite us with their erotic intensity, as their potency manifests itself, taking form in a sport, a sharp wit, an incisive mind, or an artist's conceptions. The highly charged man exploding with his powers excites us and leaves us satisfied and fulfilled by his gifts.

What about female potency? Sexual potency is but one aspect of the successful woman, but it is a good metaphor for the rest of that woman's life. Successful women often take for granted their adventuresome and satisfying sex lives.

The potent woman is a charged person, expressive and not holding back on her energies, whether they be sexual, emotional, physical, intellectual, or spiritual. A repressed person is usually repressed in many areas. Sexual repression in a woman is part of a pattern of repression in other aspects of her life. Because of the interconnectedness of all of our energies, it is important to free ourselves in our most basic area of energy, which is sexual potency.

The most potent women that I know are active sexually. I have found that women who are becoming more powerful experience an increase in their libidos and greater frustration if they are not satisfied sexually.

My favorite movie about female potency is Antonioni's *Wife-mistress*. In the beginning of the film the heroine is a picture of impotence. She is the captive of her husband, languishing in her bed surrounded by doctors, servants, and medicine bottles. When her husband goes into hiding to escape a false murder charge, she gets out of her phony sickbed and assumes his business, which is collecting rent from his diverse real estate holdings throughout the surrounding countryside. Driving to remote places in a carriage piloted by a horse that knows the familiar rounds, she discovers the many exciting and heretofore unknown lives her husband lived. From brothel to humble farm to splendid manor she meets his lovers and experiences his adventuresome life for herself. As only Antonioni could contrive it, her husband suffers as he watches her come and go from his hiding place across the street from their home. He sees the wife whom he had imprisoned dramatically springing free and changing.

My favorite scene is when she finds a lover. Obviously, she has never experienced sexual passion before. A tryst is arranged, and after dinner in a mysterious inn in the Italian countryside, she and her lover ascend the stairs to their bedroom. They kiss in the hallway, and there is a moment when, for the first time in her life, her body is gripped by a sense of sexual urgency. At this moment she becomes potent as a human being.

A woman who is overadapting will experience a sex life that is essentially impotent in its lack of true richness and passion and at best is vicarious. She will watch how much she excites a man, or she will react according to a fantasy of appropriate female responses. The sexually potent woman, on the other hand, rejects sexuality prescribed by men. She is grounded in her own responses, holds onto the current of her own pleasure, and feels the intensity of sexual arousal and urgency for contact.

This is a time of change, and women are experimenting with ways to modify their past adaptations. Some younger women have opted for a unisex approach, emphasizing the similarities in the sexes. There is even literal evidence of the evolving "strong woman," as women develop their bodies and particularly their muscles. I am, for better or worse, biased toward the romantic, and I enjoy a certain amount of fireworks between the sexes and the mutual admiration that glories in differences. The part of machismo that I enjoy is that of the Latin male who preens and struts for the admiration of the female. This is macho in a form that is honest and not a negative power play. My attraction to this proud male has its complement in the sensual and equally potent Latin fe-male—a Carmen—who laughs, loves, and tells fortunes with the passions of a gypsy. I like these images because they are sexually charged and romantic, and the male and female have exciting differences that are equally potent.

When I was in high school and blossoming sexually, I was not allowed to look or act like a sexy gypsy. I certainly wanted to, but I was tamed by my saddle shoes, plaid pleated skirts, and oxford cloth shirts. Who ever saw a sexy gypsy in a button-down shirt? But there were a few signs of sexiness among my friends: one bleached a blond edge of the wave that hung over her eye, another bought snug-fitting angora sweaters, and another teased her volu-minous mane of hair and cinched her waist in elastic belts. Of the two that I still know about, their sexiness did not impede their growth. The one with the bleached streak has a Ph.D., and the one with the large hairdo and small waist is a foreign correspondent for a newspaper. A successful woman cannot be categorized as sexy, and thereby discounted, because she expresses a whole and complex personality which includes sexuality.

The Impostor Complex

Even the women who have achieved what most of us would consider stunning and glamorous successes in life fight private battles with the impostor complex. One set of skills is needed to operate successfully in the world and another to assimilate what you have done and to live as the new person you have become. Sometimes a woman comes to therapy because she is depressed following a personal victory. The spoils of her victory were earned in vain because she cannot *enjoy* them. *The female ego in success must learn to love what she has and not discount what she has earned.*

Many women have told me that they experience disengagement in moments of personal triumph. A woman who listened to a citation given to her at a banquet said, "It was not really me they were talking about." Another woman who received an award in journalism said, "I felt as though I was not even there." A strange lack of joy drains the joyful moment of its meaning; a disembodied zombie accepts the prize on behalf of the victorious woman. She forgets the work she did to earn what she achieved, fidgets self-consciously, and wants to leave. It is in reaping the honors of success that a woman most often battles with the impostor complex.

The I-Am-Only-Lucky Syndrome

Women are still influenced by the image of a woman who has it all. We somehow believe that there is a way to have everything without working for it. Even when a woman does work for and earn what she has, she may receive it in a vacuous way, discounting her hard work. A woman needs to feel comfortable about creating her luck and then take credit for it.

A *Sign of Growth*

Everyone struggles with the impostor complex at times of change of status because it is part of the growth process. We must become comfortable with being grownups, relinquishing immature dependencies and wearing new positions of authority with dignity. The impostor complex is bound to be an issue for a woman whose professional success or accomplishment gives her more validation from the world than other women in her family have achieved. This is not an impossible problem, but rather one more challenge to the female ego. It is sometimes necessary to work on oneself to become comfortable with a change in status.

Sometimes a woman believes that she does not deserve what she has earned. Conditioned to put others first, she refuses to give herself first-class status. When she achieves success, this woman will give herself regular, negative strokes in the form of discounts. When she does something well, she tells herself that her accomplishment is not very important. Thinking she is being serious and mature, she becomes disinterested, detached, and impersonal. The truth is that she does not know how to feel personal pride. She does not give her ego the strokes needed for accomplishment, but in a sophisticated, breezy manner she takes praise lightly. She views the celebration of herself as embarrassing and unimportant. Meanwhile, her ego suffers.

The habit of discounting can be a subtle obsession. Feeding on little negative brushoffs, the woman is starving for strokes but does not know how to partake of them. To deny your achievements is not modesty, it is foolishness. You need positive strokes to fuel your energy so you can achieve more. Failure to gratify your ego will ultimately limit your achievements. If you know who you are, claim your honors, and accept your authority, you remove the disguise of the impostor and express the strong woman that you really are.

Countering Discounts

Stop the inner habit of discounting your achievements, so that your ego is able to block the discounts that are bound to come your way in the world. Discounts to a woman can be very subtle and often come in the form of "friendly jokes." When a man says, "Our office looks more beautiful now that you are around," he may be attempting to minimize the important cutting edge of your professional significance. Do not laugh at yourself or even smile unless you want to give positive recognition to a put-down! The discounter will note the way you ignore his remark, look, move on, glare, or change the subject. By ignoring put-downs you effectively express your own inner attitude of self-respect and refusal to be discounted.

Elizabeth walked into the office of one of the partners in her law firm. "That is delicious perfume," said Howard. Elizabeth ignored his remark, took the agendas out of her briefcase, and passed them out to the participants at the meeting. She refused to relinquish her power in running the meeting, and Howard looked foolish by getting a zero response.

Women can be made to feel like impostors in many ways. They are ignored, denied rewards, and passed over for important assignments. The macho silent treatment can elicit the impostor reaction in you if you are not aware of the game. The important thing is your own inner attitude about your importance and competence. When a man in business gives you a blank stare, implying that you have said nothing worthwhile after you have given a full presentation, don't squirm. And don't talk anymore. Stop and quietly stare back. This takes ego strength, and it feels great to be self-affirming even when others do not give you affirmation.

Personal Pride

Personal pride is the answer to the impostor complex and the underlying second-class syndrome. We can take a lesson from the men who wear their badges proudly, frame their honors and hang them on the wall, and enjoy whatever bears their name. A woman with ego strength can feel good and proud when she reflects upon her own good work. She gives herself permission to count and value her accomplishments. Recognition strokes incite further accomplishments. I have suggested to women who have a problem with chronic discounting that they list what they accomplish each day and work to feel good about every item on the list.

One such woman was Jennifer, who was raising two young children and whose homemaking included being a hostess at business dinners for her husband and his clients and going on business trips with him. She told me about the terrible sense of inadequacy that came over her at a dinner party when a man next to her asked her what she *did*. "I suddenly felt that nothing I did was important," she said. "He had a look on his face that seemed to indicate that everyone at this particular gathering should be distinguished in the world of work." We practiced playing the evening over again, with Jennifer proudly saying, "I am a homemaker and mother." She let herself know all of the work that her homemaking and motherhood entailed and how proud and fulfilled she feels in what she is doing. The key to feeling at home in the world is having pride and self-confidence. Eleanor Roosevelt had the right idea when she said, "Nobody can make you feel inferior unless you agree with them." A woman must fight the impostor complex within herself and be ready to stay on her own side when someone tries to minimize or discount her worth.

Self-Made Woman

We are all impressed by success stories and have fantasies about what creates success. We often are tempted to believe that if our caregivers had been different or if our life circumstances had been less oppressive, we would have had a better opportunity for success. And yet, the people we consider outstanding successes have usually overcome major hurdles. Successful people usually won their success through a combination of contributing factors. Some significant relationship has given a successful person a *sense of entitlement*, and a difficult challenge has taught that person to *experience personal power*.

A *Sense of Entitlement*

Sometimes a woman seems to have been born to be a winner. Not only do the important people in her life want her to be successful, but they create an environment that makes developing a healthy ego a natural process for her. Her caregivers believe that she is entitled to have whatever she needs to facilitate her growth and her happiness, and she grows up believing this herself. Her family generously gives whatever she needs, whether it is driving her to a friend's house, arranging for dancing lessons, or going out for a quiet cup of tea to talk over her feelings. Because they spend time with her, she grows up knowing that her life is a source of joy to others as well as herself.

If you were not born into such an emotionally resourceful family, you still can develop a sense of entitlement. There are many fulfilled women who have had difficulties in childhood ranging from poverty or emotional or cultural deprivation to psychological or physical abuse. Such a woman can find herself longing intensely for better circumstances. My life has got to be better than this, she says to herself. A powerful sense of longing leads her to seek her own entitlement.

Using skills of observation, she looks around to see what is happening in other worlds. She might see that a confident classmate is always beautifully dressed. She notices how other children's parents behave. She searches out behaviors and values that are appealing to her. Her inner loyalty may be to worlds other than her family's, and in minute ways she begins to model herself after people other than her family members. When her privileged schoolmate goes off to tennis camp, she practices on the garage wall or school backboard every day. She learns to sew and wears Pendleton plaids like the other girls. Her lucrative baby-sitting business keeps her in sweaters and knee socks. She learns early that she has little support and must invest in herself.

Experiencing Personal Power

Children who develop skills, whether they are in the form of academic success, work, or artistic achievement, experience power. In this area the child who has been raised with material privileges sometimes is at a disadvantage. One can become demoralized by receiving rewards that are not a result of her own work. Many of the women I know who are successful as adults had the experience of being important to the running of their families as children. Resentful as they might have been at the housework and baby-sitting they were expected to do, they felt powerful and resourceful because they were needed.

Every woman needs a challenge so she can grow. That challenge can be to live up to the expectations of a family in which there is a tradition of professional or academic success, or it can be the challenge to overcome adverse circumstances. The finest therapists that I know have become wise through experiencing and overcoming emotional pain. A sense of entitlement can make you feel worthy, but meeting a challenge is the only way that a woman really develops herself. No matter where we start out in life, fulfillment essentially means being a self-made woman.

Avoiding the Pitfalls

Becoming a self-made woman is an odyssey, a journey filled with pitfalls and temptations. One pitfall is that of longing. Although longing for something is the emotional fuel for a journey toward something you want, it can be an unhealthy emotion if you cling to it rather than act on it. Healthy growth occurs through active and positive pursuit of what you want. Why is longing a pitfall, even a temptation? If you are not used to having your needs met, longing can become a habit, even an addiction. Sometimes getting what you want is a letdown because you find out that the goal is not as good as it was reputed to be. Often, the *process* proves to be the greatest pleasure.

The truth is that dreams and longing alone cannot meet a woman's needs. A dream is the rainbow, not the pot of gold. The experience of having is much different from longing. It is devoid of angst, and can be likened to a simple sigh of relief. To get what you want is to neutralize your strivings and to savor many small pleasures. There is rarely one huge, fulfilling moment that approximates in pleasure one's depths of longing. A self-made woman is committed to leaving the have-nots and joining the club of the haves. And when she experiences the boredom of having, she looks for meaning on a higher level: the realm of giving.

Getting the Right Support

Once a woman is on her own in the world, she needs to develop relationships that support her sense of entitlement and challenge her to grow. The self-made woman has a remarkable character, which combines openness, humility, and perseverance that does not alienate others. She channels her aggressiveness into working on herself. Instead of falling into the trap of jealousy, she develops charm. She inspires other people to love her, not reject her. Even if she once lacked solid familial support, she finds ways to be emotionally fed by friends and mentors. The self-made woman who had solid family backing as a child learned that she must make it on her own when she joined the adult world.

Your Own Heroine

Self-made women are voyagers who use their egos to choose goals wisely and create their destinies. They view success as emotional fulfillment, pleasure, and self-respect as females, as well as in work of their choice. They believe that they are good people who deserve to have what they want.

Don't we all love a story about a person born in a slum who rises to great heights? Isn't it fun to see pictures of women before and after they have applied makeup or changed their hair styles? Even more exciting are pictures before and after weight loss. I take great pleasure in the effects of a good therapeutic experience—

thinking about how people I know have gone from despair to joy or have changed a losing course to a winning one. The drama of people who change and better themselves is inspiring. We identify with these heroines and hope that we too can change and become our best selves.

Once a woman has become her own heroine, has claimed her sense of entitlement, and faced the challenges life has brought to her, she enters a new phase of her life in which she lets herself feel strong and proud, enjoying what she has accomplished. A strong trait I have observed in self-made women is that most of them are not bitter about their adverse experiences in life. They are women who conquer limitations, and their joy is in the challenge. Such a woman once said to me, "I am no longer angry at my parents for not sending me to college. I am, instead, very proud of myself for finding my own way in life."

9

The Female Ego in Maturity

Life shrinks or expands in proportion to one's courage.

Anaïs Nin

We all face a major identity crisis called aging. Even as our bodies age, we must work not to lose our egos. A mature woman can deal with passing time in the same way that she deals with all the other challenges in her life. She must hold fast to her ego, make decisions, and make her life work.

The Myths of Maturity

There are many myths about maturity that keep us from attaining real maturity. These myths also cause us to relegate the older people among us to a strange, inhuman planet which we all unwillingly may inhabit at some point. Examine these myths and see if they are limiting your prospects.

• Old People Are Blessed with Maturity

There is a myth that what you give to life is harvested in old age and that old people possess philosophical wisdom that sustains them. In working with all age groups, I have observed that middle-aged people usually have more to sustain their lives than old people do. We have romanticized the disengagement process of the de-

241

pressed elderly so as to justify our unwillingness to confront the idea of aging and the issues raised by the aged. There are mature and immature members of all age groups. According to my definition of psychological maturity, mature people are vitally engaged with life, and immature ones are passively or helplessly waiting on the sidelines. The women who experience a fulfilling old age are the ones who continue the pursuits that have always given them pleasure.

• Maturity Means Being Square

When I was a child many of my relatives said that I was mature for my age. To me that meant that I was square—a large lump of child who did not know how to play. I was frozen in a pseudo-serious guise of profound politeness. That was an unpleasant place to be. Mature in that context meant boring. Today when I speak of maturity, I have almost reversed that early meaning. The mature woman is a whole person with many facets. She is an expressive person who wants to be where the good times are happening.

There are many women who hide behind a pseudo-maturity that embraces the myths of ageism. An immature woman of twenty-five or seventy-five lets herself become dowdy and functional; her human spirit is lost under layers of adaptations. For her, aging is an excuse for a grand climax in the play of people-pleasing and avoidance of risk. She is sexless, humorless, fearful, and dependent. This is not maturity; it is the fulfillment of immaturity.

• You Must Start New Ventures When You Are Young

The main excuse I hear immature women give for not doing what they need to do is, "It's too late." They use age as an excuse for not growing up. Our increased life expectancy has given us decades in which to practice the new skills we learn in middle age. The story of Grandma Moses not only illustrates the principle of developing a new career at age seventy-five but also that she had time in her favor. Grandma Moses was an artist for twenty-six years.

It is out of date to use late timing as an excuse. I have a client who began her career as an actress and model in her sixties and another who is a professional musician and began in her thirties.

- **There Is Joy in Idleness**

  This myth can cause us to seek situations that lead to a sense of uselessness and despair. Some of the most unhappy women I know structure their lives around manicures and shopping excursions. The tragic assault to the egos of retired workers who are stripped of the schedules and responsibilities by which they previously defined themselves is well documented. Idleness may work for those who always have been disengaged, but they may have become accustomed to living with depression.

  Idleness is disengagement from life, and it lowers ego strength, eventually undermining confidence. *Satisfaction comes from the experience of contrast.* A lazy vacation is glorious for someone who has completed important work. Hard work makes idleness worthwhile and restorative. But then one needs to be back to work again. When one is older, it becomes important to define work activities outside of the structures that force retirement. If you have rejected the myth of idleness, you will explore artistic pursuits, study, helping professions, or entrepreneurial activities that have no age limits and are fulfilling.

- **People Should Retire Gracefully**

  The message to retire gracefully is as misguided as the lifetime message to a woman that she must live gracefully on the sidelines of life. The mature woman knows that her ego must stay alive and vital. Self-expression is the meaning of fulfillment for women of all ages. A woman should never retreat gracefully from life but should forthrightly find a way to combat the forces that would keep her quiet and insignificant. You must not buy into any system that would keep you shut down, half alive, and depressed. *Never retire from your life.*

Maturity and Playfulness

There is a paradox about maturity. The mature and actualized person is like a child in some ways. My clients who are outstanding successes in their careers are unconventional in the way they approach their work because work and play have become part of the same process. The spirit with which they work can be unusually playful because the natural, spontaneous, and creative child within is given free play.

Being responsible does not mean being rigid, and being mature does not mean being too conventional or serious. One of my best examples of maturity is my own grandfather, who was a rancher, surgeon, and legendary country doctor who started his own hospital and trained his staff. He played his many roles with courage and style, but underneath seemed to me to be a playful kid, as if he saw the world through the eyes of a child. He always had a teasing joke or a crazy adventure in mind. I adored him as both friend and grandparent. But sometimes I wanted him to be more "grown-up." Kid to kid, he met me on my own level and would not let me retire him to the realm of the old fogies. I now see him as a stunning example of ego strength—a man who never stopped playing the game of living. You must stay with your spontaneous self and always know that your spirit is much younger than your age.

Losing Your Ego

An expression used in regard to maintaining sexual potency is Use it or lose it. The same is true with ego strength. You must use your ego in order to retain its power. There are times throughout our lives when we sense that we are getting older, and we feel that we are losing part of ourselves. When this happens, our life begins to lack meaning and our self-esteem is low. The inner question during such an identity crisis is Am I still me?

Here are some of the symptoms of losing your ego. These are often attributed to the aging process, but they really are symptoms of the disengagement of the ego and can occur at any age.

- **Inertia**

    You might feel that you have nothing to do or that you do not want to do what you usually do. Your hunger for meaningful activity is not being satisfied, and the result is that you shut down to avoid boredom.

- **Anger at Other People**

    You might feel that other people are the problem. You can feel anger in the form of paranoia (their anger at you) or because they have let you down. Your suspicions and jealousy isolate and impair your ego's reality-testing mechanism. In a stroke vacuum, you distort the significance of being let down. Your subsequent disengagement from relationships is a vicious cycle in which lack of strokes breeds lack of trust.

- **Depressing Rituals**

    If you lack satisfying contact with stimulating activities and relationships, you may become caught up in depressing rituals. Boring but habitual ways of doing things can become important fetishes—substitutes for the real thing. You can have so much investment in the arrangement of your drawers, the routines of your household, or the dull mechanics of your job that you are consumed by trivia. Depressing rituals are ones that do not involve much negotiating with people and weigh upon you as empty but very necessary. They do a poor job of meeting your need for challenging routines.

- **No Stimulation**

    You can have such rigid control over your life that nothing unexpected ever happens; you take no risks and entertain no unusual ideas or urges because you magnify fear of failure.

These four symptoms could describe an overworked housewife, a career woman in a dead-end job, a burned-out entertainer, or a retired person who has found nothing to do. When you are losing your ego, the world seems to have nothing to offer. This negativity is a challenge for you to make important changes in the shape of your life. If you do not, and instead give in to negativity and depression, you will disengage from life—which means letting go of your ego.

Maintaining Your Ego

We can never protect ourselves by separating from life, and we do not "find ourselves" in a vacuum. *We find ourselves through what we do.* The experience of identity is in engagement and contact. Here are four ways for you to maintain your ego:

• **Accomplishment of Projects**

Men know how to strengthen their egos by doing projects. We all find ourselves through concrete expressions of ourselves. Without projects we feel useless and can even begin to doubt that we exist. A completed task provides a mirror in which you can see yourself and let other people know who you are. Everyone has talents, and when you use your best talents on the most challenging projects you can find, your ego expands to its fullest expression. Mastery is your base of self-confidence.

• **Relationships**

Maintaining your ego means that you have relationships in your life that give you love, support, encouragement, and challenges. But just as important is staying interested in other people. Self-absorption is terribly boring. Share the lives of others not as a people-pleaser but as a truly interested friend. Relishing the diverse qualities of other people keeps us from becoming narrow, and our egos from becoming introverted and rigid.

• **Joyful Pastimes**

We need routines in our lives that are a source of joy. They could be traditional dinners with family or evenings of bridge or conversation with friends or weekly excursions. These are routine pastimes that are easy to enjoy. There is nothing wrong with rituals if they add richness to life. Such habits of living give continuity to life, reminding us of childhood and promising always to be there for us.

• **Adventures**

We need to have experiences that are utterly new. With the world changing quickly, it is easy to feel that your era suddenly died and left you behind. Keep yourself current, explore new ideas, embark on adventures. Your ego needs challenges and stimulation. You can travel or take trips in books. Courses, group experiences, meditation, physical activities, learning a skill—all can be resources to open new worlds for you. Curiosity about new things outside the self keeps the ego refreshed and alive.

Maturity is a passionate connectedness with life. The mature women among us live with whole hearts and minds that are vitally connected with currents of life. They love their friends, they love their work, and they love their play. That elusive word *happiness* is one of the fruits of maturity.

Capitalizing on Yourself

Capital means investment. Investing in your ego also means making sure that you have enough money to sustain you through life. Financial assets are the best insurance policy you can get; they liberate you from ever being demoralized and dependent because you do not have enough money to live well. Too many women make the mistake of investing in love alone and neglecting the economic mastery of their lives.

Even a married woman with an affluent lifestyle often is not rich—her husband is rich. A woman with an ego makes sure she and her mate have equal control of the family finances. Women need to be interested in money and know about their assets, insurance policies, income, and expenses. Not knowing creates basic insecurity in the present and threatens tragic consequences in the future.

Money determines the quality of life for an older person, and a woman with an ego realizes this and plans in advance. Somerset Maugham once wrote, "Money is a sixth sense, without which you cannot make a complete use of the other five." It is difficult to engage in projects, joyful pastimes, and adventures as an older person without money. A healthy income supports a healthy ego. Men know this, and as they get older they take increasing pride in their net worth as an ego enhancement and a source of security.

A Relationship with Yourself

A mature woman has given up people-pleasing and measures herself by her own standards rather than by how helpful or appealing she is to others. Perfectionism holds many women back because it keeps them from loving themselves. In the arrogance of thinking that you can do anything perfectly you fall on your face. Your task as a mature person is to keep your sights high without becoming a self-rejecting perfectionist. One of my favorite therapeutic exercises for the building of self-esteem is for a woman to make a list of the qualities she likes in herself. Her resistance to this process tells a lot about the internal critic who must be conquered. The critic usually begins by saying, "It's not nice to like yourself." Perfect modesty is the first commandment of perfectionism. Becoming comfortable with genuine self-love, which is not grandiose, is an exercise in both humility and self-expansion. A woman who can do this with ease can lovingly receive the gift of life. She is saying yes to pleasure and thank you for joy.

Self-love also removes a woman from the fear of exposure. There is an openness, a beautiful transparency, and a simplicity to the self-accepting woman. She has nothing to hide and everything to express. The philosophy of self-love says, I am an ordinary human being, and that's pretty special. The woman who relinquishes perfectionism and embraces self-love has the freedom to achieve genuine self-development.

Retreat from Adaptations

A mature woman has such a good relationship with herself that she senses when she is getting off her track and decides how to correct the situation. Usually a woman needs to find ways to strip away her multitudinous adaptations to others and achieve her integrity by seeking time to be alone.

There was a time in my life when I was caught up in the superwoman syndrome of running my practice and then rushing home to kitchen and station wagon duty. I was neglecting myself and was plagued with a chronic stiff neck as a result of fatigue. Inspired by a colleague, I decided to take a vacation alone. This was a radical idea to me and my family, and it was one of the most restorative experiences I have ever had.

I chose an old mountain hotel in the Catskills, which was a three-hour bus ride from my home. I took long walks alone amid beautiful scenery, had a daily massage, and had room service bring my breakfast in the morning. I put fresh flowers in my room and spent hours doing absolutely nothing but lying on my bed and savoring time and space that were mine alone. For the first two days I did not enjoy myself because I allowed all of my negative feelings to surface. I felt the exhaustion that I had tried to suppress (and thought I had conquered) by continuing to rise above my fatigue. I learned that in a retreat one feels worse before one feels better. Gradually I regained a sense of well-being. The last morning I got up at 4:30 A.M. to climb a mountain and see the sun rise. In five days I went from feeling lost to feeling solid and whole. It was a matter of finding my center again.

You need time alone to establish a good and mature relationship with yourself. This time gives you a chance to know yourself as a real and complete person, and it is the only way fully to explore your plans, dreams, and perceptions. By establishing regular times to be alone, you will get very good at using the experience productively for yourself. Women in therapy often share with me the results of an evening of productive focusing on themselves. They use their time alone to determine how to lead a full life, to let reality make impressions on them. It is a time to receive—to have what you have and to experience where you are in your development as a person. This inner relationship with yourself maintains your power because you are taking time to make your own informed decisions about your life.

The emotional result of having a good relationship with yourself is self-confidence. You claim your life as being separate and independent of everyone else's. Self-confidence does not result from getting applause from strangers. It is not something another person can give you by building you up or by arranging your life for you. Confidence is seized by a woman who is aggressively doing her work, seeking love, and making her own decisions.

Dare to Win

Don't be afraid to compete and to stay in the ball game. Whenever you feel jealous or envious of someone else, treasure that feeling. Your ego is saying to you, I deserve to be there too. Then convert your jealousy to the positive energy of pursuing that goal. When a woman client experiences the painful urgency of rivalry, I think to myself, Good. She really wants to be in the game herself. Women who *never* feel the appetites of ambition, jealousy, or even greed expect very little for themselves. In the guise of being mature and above it all, they drop out of the game. *Dare to want more for yourself.*

You may be called selfish, but remind yourself that it is *selfness* that you seek. You may be tempted to become indispensable to others. Know that giving away all of yourself will not earn you security or love. Treasure your talents as you would those of your mate, your friends, or your children. Decide how to spend your time and your energies. *Dare to belong to yourself.*

What if you get something in your life that someone else wants? Don't believe that the pie of life is so small that your win is another's loss. You may inspire envy and jealousy, but you also may be raising the consciousness of family, friends, and colleagues, showing them that more is possible for a woman. The female ego breaks the mold, develops herself more fully, embraces a selfness that is new in women, and chooses pleasure over sacrifice. *Dare to win!*

Renaissance Woman

This expression aptly captures the character of a vital female ego. During the fourteenth and fifteenth centuries—the period in European history that we call the Renaissance—there was a magnificent flowering of culture. There were amazing achievements in painting, literature, sculpture, and architecture. New truths about the natural world and the nature of man expanded the human consciousness, and people developed themselves more fully in a greater variety of ways. To be a Renaissance woman today is to be aware of every facet of yourself, to develop your various interests, and to live as a whole person.

A Renaissance women today knows that many of the best human experiences are within her reach. She no longer needs to be impoverished but can exercise her vital powers in ever-widening arenas. This is a wonderful time in history to be alive and to be a woman. We have many good models. We are fellow adventurers and risk-takers. We are creatively integrating roles that we once learned were oppositional. It is true that woman have many battles yet to win, particularly in the chambers of high corporate power and government. But there also are many chances now to live a life that is richly balanced!

A contemporary Renaissance woman is not spellbound by authorities but is grounded in her own human spirit and her desire to grow. She gravitates to the places where she will find life, movement, and excitement. She is interested in the affairs of this world, rather than the cult of people-pleasing. Joy in learning and working replaces the ascetic life of being an obedient and good girl.

In Favor of Herself

As the female ego experiences her Renaissance, she is breaking the links of the chains that have imprisoned her: inadequate strokes, dependency, and fear. She embraces instead pleasure, power, and self-confidence—the hallmark qualities of the female ego. Her new power comes from knowing that it is neither selfish nor unfeminine to know what she wants and to be active in pursuing her goals. No longer a vague dream girl, today's woman has physical and intellectual power based on living as a whole person. She no longer overprotects her children, which means that their egos are stronger, and she has more time for the other facets of her life.

No More Fear

A Renaissance woman's self-confidence is largely based on her conquering of fear. Her fear of selfishness—which is really a fear of loss of love if she fails to please the other people in her life—is being overcome. She knows that she must trust in what her ego is telling her about the truth of her own life and that self-confidence is more important than dancing to the tune of others.

In conquering fear, the Renaissance woman gains wisdom and influence. By breaking with stifling and rigid traditions about her place on this planet, she liberates other institutions: the family, the home, and the workplace. Her newly found courage enables her to see things as they are, ask probing questions, and criticize rigid systems that don't work. In making her challenges, she is finding out that the rigidity of most systems is based on fear. Because she has conquered her own personal fears, she leads and facilitates change. Her courage has given her power as well as wisdom.

A Renaissance woman is mature in that she is vitally engaged in living and growing. By meeting the challenges for women at this time, her ego makes a vital and much needed contribution to human development and fulfillment. Through pleasing herself, she gives her greatest gift to others.

Bibliography and Suggested Reading

Beauvoir, Simone de. *The Second Sex*. New York: Alfred A. Knopf, 1953.

Berne, Eric, M.D. *Games People Play*. New York: Grove Press, 1964.

———.*What Do You Say After You Say Hello?* New York: Bantam, 1975.

Friedan, Betty. *The Feminine Mystique*. New York: Norton, 1963.

Harris, Thomas. *I'm OK, You're OK*. New York: Harper & Row, 1967.

James, Muriel, and Dorothy Jongeward. *Born to Win: Transactional Analysis with Gestalt Experiments*. Reading, Mass.: Addison Wesley, 1971.

Kaplan, Louise J. *Oneness and Separateness*. Franklin Park, Ill.: La Leche, 1983.

Molloy, John T. *The Woman's Dress for Success Book*. New York: Warner Books, 1978.

Perls, Fritz. *Ego, Hunger, and Aggression*. New York: Vintage Press, 1968.

———.*Gestalt Therapy Verbatim*. Moab, Utah: Real People Press, 1959.

Satir, Virginia. *Peoplemaking*. Palo Alto, Calif.: Science and Behavior Books, 1972.

Steiner, Claude. *Scripts People Live*. New York: Grove Press, 1974.

✿ Index ✿